THE ROYAL FLYING CORPS IN FRANCE

From Bloody April 1917 to Final Victory

By the same author:

Down in the Drink (1955)
The Ship-Busters (1957)
The Last Blue Mountain (1959)
Strike Hard, Strike Sure (1963)
The Thousand Plan (1965)
Great Mysteries of the Air (1966)
Aviator Extraordinary (1969)
Verdict on a Lost Flyer (1969)
The Schneider Trophy Races (1971)
Against the Sea (1972)
One Man's Jungle (1975)
The Blockade Busters (1976)
Survival in the Sky (1976)
The Hurricats (1978)
Not Here, But in Another Place (1980)
The RAF at War (1981)
Good Night, Sorry for Sinking You (1984)
Children of the Benares (1988)
That Eternal Summer (1990)
The Royal Flying Corps in France:
From Mons to the Somme (1994)

THE
ROYAL FLYING CORPS
IN FRANCE

From Bloody April 1917 to Final Victory

RALPH BARKER

Constable · London

First published in Great Britain 1995
by Constable and Company Limited
3 The Lanchesters, 162 Fulham Palace Road
London W6 9ER
Copyright © 1995 by Ralph Barker
The right of Ralph Barker to be
identified as the author of this work
has been asserted by him in accordance
with the Copyright, Designs and Patents Act 1988
ISBN 0 09 475170 6

Set in Linotron Sabon 11 on 14 pt by
Rowland Phototypesetting Limited
Bury St Edmunds, Suffolk
Printed in Great Britain by
St Edmundsbury Press Limited
Bury St Edmunds, Suffolk

A CIP catalogue record for this book
is available from the British Library

CONTENTS

1918

ILLUSTRATIONS

Sopwith Pups of 46 Squadron (*Jack Bruce and Stuart Leslie*)

An Armstrong-Whitworth FK8 'Big Ack' (*Jack Bruce and Stuart Leslie*)

P. N. M. 'Puggy' Shone (*Imperial War Museum*)

S. J. 'Squibs' Sibley (*Barry Gray*)

DH4 Bombers (*Jack Bruce and Stuart Leslie*)

A Sopwith Camel (*Jack Bruce and Stuart Leslie*)

The F2B Bristol Fighter (*Jack Bruce and Stuart Leslie*)

J. A. 'Jimmy' Slater (*Bruce and Leslie via Franks*)

C. M. 'Billy' Crowe (*via Franks*)

Arthur Gould Lee (*Alex Revell*)

Clive Collett (*via Franks*)

Alan McLeod in hospital (*Public Archives of Canada*)

Arthur Hammond (*Chaz Bowyer*)

John A. Todd (*Norman Franks*)

Oscar Heron (*Norman Franks*)

Todd's perforated Camel (*Marvyn Paice*)

Alexander Paice (*Marvyn Paice*)

Ewart Stock (*E. J. Stock*)

Ewart Garland (*Patrick Garland*)

ACKNOWLEDGEMENTS

As with the first volume of this anecdotal impression of the years of
the Royal Flying Corps, I have had unstinting help with my researches
from everyone I have approached over many months. My contacts
have included next of kin and copyright holders of diaries, letters and
memoirs; various museums, libraries and institutions; and correspondence with many distinguished air historians who, as before, have been
more than generous in making their own work and researches available to me. In expressing my gratitude, I must again absolve them from
any responsibility for the resultant narrative.

Contact and correspondence with RFC veterans sadly diminished
with time, but they included, especially, Maxwell Coote, Gerald
Dixon, Cecil Lewis, T. G. Mapplebeck, and Harold Tambling; all
but Gerald Dixon and Cecil Lewis since deceased.

Material extracted from Public Record Office Files includes: Personal Memoirs and Recollections of individual RFC personnel from
files in the Class Air 1 series. Among those quoted from this series
are D. L. Allen, J. O. Andrews, R. M. Bailey, L. E. O. Charlton,
W. S. Douglas, P. F. Fullard, R. M. Hill, A. C. Maund, C. F. A.
Portal, J. C. Slessor, R. Smith-Barry and D. F. Stevenson.

Other files in Class Air 1 from which material has been extracted
include Situation Statements, Squadron Record Books, Combat
Reports, Notes on Air Fighting, Notes on Running a Squadron, General Methods of Teaching Scout Pilots, and the sequence of meetings
of the Parachute Committee. The Air Board Meetings and Memor-
anda covering May–June, July–September, and October–
December 1916 are in Class Air 6, Nos 1–3.

Extracts and condensations from material viewed at the Department of Documents, Imperial War Museum are gratefully acknowledged, with thanks for Staff help, to next-of-kin and copyright
holders as follows: D. L. Allen, G. W. Armstrong, S. Attwater,

O. L. Beater, H. A. Blundell, N. A. Birks, L. S. Bowman, W. Sefton Brancker, A. W. Brown, C. Callender, F. Carr, J. G. H. Chrispin, W. Cobb (R. W. Cobb), W. S. Douglas, H. G. Downing (Carol Sherwood), L. F. Field, E. J. Garland (Patrick Garland), S. V. Gorringe (R. S. Gorringe), D. R. Goudie, O. Greig, P. R. C. Groves, T. E. Guttery (D. R. Guttery), P. Haarer, W. F. J. Harvey, J. L. Horridge, R. S. S. Ingram (Professor G. I. C. Ingram), Ronald Ivelaw-Chapman (John Ivelaw-Chapman), J. P. T. Jeyes (Anthony Jeyes), A. D. Light, N. Macmillan, J. H. Morris, E. R. Pennell (Rene Duperly), F. C. Penny (James and Joan Seakins), H. R. Puncher, J. C. Quinnell (John Craig), F. C. Ransley (Joanna Wrathall), W. R. Read (G. R. E. Brooke), E. J. D. Routh, H. B. R. Rowell (Elizabeth Rowell), J. G. Selby, R. F. W. Sheraton (Barbara D. Sheraton), J. C. Slessor, E. E. Stock (E. J. Stock), H. G. Taylor, H. S. Ward (T. C. Le Grice), R. L. Wightman, J. W. Woodhouse, H. Wyllie (John Wyllie). Also A Short History of No. 6 Squadron (Anon); and an Anonymous Diary of a Pilot.

Similarly, at the Department of Sound Records, Imperial War Museum: E. Bolt, C. J. Chabot, J. V. Gascoyne, A. T. Harris, J. C. F. Hopkins, A. W. H. James, A. A. N. D. 'Jerry' Pentland, F. J. Powell, H. J. Sanders, J. C. Slessor, A. B. Yuille.

At the Royal Air Force Museum, again with grateful thanks to next of kin, copyright holders, and Staff: E. Brewerton, A. S. W. Dore (Bingham Dore), T. Farquhar, The Henderson Papers, G. P. Jamieson, M. A. Kay, M. M. Kaye, W. R. Read (G. R. E. Brooke), H. J. Sanders, J. G. Selby, C. D. Smart (see also Museum of Army Flying), R. Smith, J. Worstenholme. Also Tape and Video recordings: J. O. Andrews, E. D. G. Galley, M. M. Kaye, C. B. Lefroy, Mrs Morley (Remembering Albert Ball), J. Oliver, P. N. M. Shone.

At the Museum of Army Flying: Major J. R. Cross, and H. W. Foot, Archivist. Also Wing Commander F. Prince, and Anthony Rosen, for help with the tracing and preserving of the Diary of C. D. Smart.

Friends of the Canadian War Museum, Ottawa, and particularly Philip Markham, for advice and for resolving many queries. The Canadian War Museum itself, the Stonewall Branch of the Royal Canadian Legion, and the Winnipeg Free Press, for background on Alan Arnett McLeod, VC.

The Royal Aeronautical Society Library, and particularly Arnold Nayler, Librarian, and Assistant Librarian Brian Riddell.

The Liddle Collection, The Library, Leeds University, with grateful acknowledgements to Peter Liddle for sight of documents in his Archive: V. Brown, P. F. Fullard, A. T. Harris, A. Perry-Keane, H. W. L. Saunders, B. Sharwood-Smith, J. C. Slessor, T. C. Traill, S. F. Vincent, H. P. Walmsley.

The London Library and Staff, for invaluable assistance.

For help with researches: Eton College Collections, through Mrs P. Hatfield, Archivist; Oundle School, through D. H. Ford, Archivist, for J. P. T. Jeyes and M. L. Hatch; Hertford College, Oxford, through Dr T. C. Barnard, Keeper of the Archives, and Roger Deayton, author of a History of the Old Caterhamians Association (for E. E. Stock); and Roger Lubbock, for extracts from letters written by his uncle, Tom Tillard, killed in December 1916. Also the Ministry of Defence RAF Personnel Management Centre, Innsworth, Gloucester.

I have also drawn on my previous work on the operational careers of some of the best known pilots of this era, British and German, on which several series of articles for the *Sunday Express* were based.

For help with finding and producing photographs I am especially grateful to: Chaz Bowyer, Jack Bruce, Bingham Dore, Wing Commander Freddie Prince, Norman Franks, Patrick Garland, Barry Gray, Peter Hearn, Anthony Jeyes, Stuart Leslie, Alex Revell, Carol Sherwood, E. J. Stock; also Imperial War Museum and RAF Museum.

Among Air Historians and Researchers who have helped me I must especially thank David J. Barnes, who produced a wealth of biographical material for me on a wide range of RFC personnel. I am also indebted to Jack Bruce, Chaz Bowyer, Norman Franks, Kevin Kelly, Paul S. Leaman (of Cross and Cockade (GB)), Alex Revell, and many others from whose historical work I have benefited.

The published sources I have used in my researches are listed on Pages 253–255. In all instances, whether of unpublished memoirs, diaries, letters, tapes, cassettes and videos, or of published works, every effort has been made to trace copyright holders where any substantial extract is quoted. The author craves the indulgence of literary executors or copyright holders where these efforts have so far failed.

NORTH SEA

BELGIUM

BRUSSELS ■

Dunkerque

Calais

St Omer

Ypres

Lys

Lille

Mons

❷ 4 April: RFC begin air offensive
to free (subordinate) British battle
area of hostile aircarft. Artillery
bombardment begins. 9 April on:
British and Canadian infantry take
Vimy Ridge.

Vimy Ridge

Loos

Douai

Maubeuge

Vimy

Arras

Bapaume

Cambrai

Le Cateau

Doullens

❶ Shaded area shows ground
given up by the enemy to consoli-
date defences and hamper British
communications and supply lines,
meanwhile distancing RFC from
its objectives.

Abbeville

Somme

Albert

Péronne

Amiens

St Quentin

Roye

❸ 16 April: main attack by French
meets immediate and disastrous
opposition, breakthrough fails, French
morale shattered, mutinies follow.
Pétain replaces Nivelle.

Noyon

Chemin des Dames

Aisne

Compiègne

Soissons

Rheims

F   R   A   N   C   E

Marne

Oise

❹ In April as a whole, newly designed RFC machines
fail to materialise, or are mishandled, losses escalate.
RFC suffer worst setback of the war. Haig obliged to
maintain pressure on enemy to protect French army.

Seine

PARIS

Disaster on the Hindenburg Line
March/April 1917

– – – Frontiers of 1914
▬▬▬ Limit of German Advance

0   10   20   30   miles   50

↑ Hazebrouck
20 miles

Lens

Scarpe

Douai

1st

Arras

Sensée

Cambrai

Doullens

Gommecourt

2nd

Bapaume

3rd

Pozières

18th

Albert

Bertangles

Ancre

Bray-sur-Somme

Mericourt

Clery

Péronne

Amiens

Corbie

Cerisy-Gailly

Mons-en-Chausée

Hamel

Athies

Estrées-en-Chausée

St Quentin

Villiers-Bretonnaux

Foucaucourt

Flez

Luce

Somme

Matigny

Moreuil

Ignaucourt

Mezières

5th

Ham

Nesle

Crozat Canal

Avre

Roye

Champien

Montdidier

Oise

Noyon

7th

6th

German Offensive
March 1918

| 0 | 5 | 10 | 15 | miles | 25 |

Original line on 21st March
Line on evening 5th April
Armies – British

French

German

[xiii]

1917

A NEW GERMAN WAR-WINNING STRATEGY: THE RFC OUTFOUGHT AND OUTCLASSED

THE hectic war of movement in the late summer of 1914, when the German dash for Paris and a quick victory was so narrowly frustrated, was followed by two years of largely attritional warfare. At the end of 1916, the combatants confronted each other across an unbroken front 350 miles long, stretching from the Channel ports to the Swiss border. It was a line that had altered little in the intervening years, despite costly attempts by the Allies to push the invading German armies back whence they came. And it was the Allies, still territorially deprived, who were planning yet another massive frontal assault, with all that this meant in human suffering and slaughter. To the Allied Command there was no other practical means of inflicting on the enemy the final and overwhelming defeat from which a just and lasting peace might be dictated.

The Germans were equally committed to a war of attrition. But they no longer believed in outright victory, not anyway by military means. Unrestricted submarine warfare, a strategy which they openly declared on 1 February 1917, was to be the route to victory: all shipping in the Atlantic war zone was to be sunk on sight. Meanwhile, as a direct result of their losses on the Somme, they were preparing to give ground, pulling back substantially but secretly, and constructing a new defensive line, devised by Ludendorff (but designated the Hindenburg Line by the British), well behind their existing defences. In justifying this withdrawal, Ludendorff wrote:

'The Army had been fought to a standstill and was utterly worn out.' Frightful as the cost had been, this was the achievement of the Somme battle. It had forced the Germans to change their strategic plan in a way which risked direct American involvement in the war.

The new barrier, stiffened by man-made strongpoints, would take all possible advantage of existing natural obstacles. The Germans would be fighting on ground of their own choosing, with a network of communications that would give greater economy in logistics and manpower, incidentally freeing fifteen divisions for the reserve. The whole edifice would constitute a fortress of such impregnability as to repel, with decimating losses, all attempts to invest it. Deadlock in the land battle, and a Britain starved out by the U-boats, would produce a compromise peace in which Germany would be permitted to hold on to her conquests. Such was the new strategy, and it seemed a reasonable gamble that any American reaction would come too late to affect the outcome.

Evidence that such a defensive line might be in preparation was first elicited by air observation in October and November 1916, but it was not until 25 February 1917 that six Sopwith Pup pilots of 54 Squadron brought back irrefutable evidence that German troops were withdrawing in stages to a new line from Lille to Metz. Captured documents, and the interrogation of prisoners, gave confirmation, enabling an unopposed British advance to begin on 17 March over ground deliberately devastated by the enemy to provide an obstacle in itself.

The plan for the 1917 Allied offensive was the brain-child of a new French commander-in-chief, General Robert Nivelle, who had earned a big reputation for his 'creeping barrage' tactics – the separate but simultaneous progression of infantry and artillery – during the second phase of the Battle of Verdun. He succeeded Joffre, who had been relieved of his command after the blood-letting on the Somme. Joffre's plan for a cautious, step-by-step advance with limited objectives was anathema to Nivelle, who favoured a single decisive blow at maximum strength. Lloyd George, who had succeeded to the British premiership that December, was also calling for a more energetic prosecution of the war. Despite the mis-

givings of the French High Command and the objections and apprehensions of the British C.-in-C., Douglas Haig, Nivelle's persuasive
advocacy of his plans enthused the newly-formed British War Cabinet. They agreed to place him in overall command, over the aggrieved
Haig's head, on the grounds that France, as the country that had
borne the brunt of the fighting so far and was still suffering occupa-
tion, should have the final say.

Haig would have preferred to attack farther north, in Flanders,
where one of his objectives would have been to clear the Flemish
ports and deny their use to the U-boats, and this was his ultimate
intention. The Admiralty were warning that with the U-boats in
control it might become impossible to hold the Channel crossing and
therefore to continue the land war. But any major offensive clearly
had to be an Allied venture, and Haig, after considering resignation,
gave way.

By this time Britain had five armies in France, holding the line
from Lille south to Peronne. The First and Third Armies were on
the Arras front in the centre, the Second was to the north, and the
Fifth and Fourth to the south and extreme south in that order.

A serious obstacle, of which Haig was well aware – and on which,
in November, he had expressed himself trenchantly – was the ascendancy over RFC hardware of the new German *Jastas*, which were
increasing in strength. Haig was no student of air strategy but he
believed in the air. Briefed by Trenchard, who had been warning of
the expected inferiority for many months, he expressed the opinion
that the RFC could not be ready to support a major offensive as
early as April, the projected date. 'Our fighting machines', he wrote,
'will almost certainly be inferior in number and quite certainly in
performance to those of the enemy.' Supremacy in the air, he pro-
tested, could not be looked for in April, and might even pass to the
enemy. Trenchard had stressed that new types of machine – namely
the Bristol Fighter, the SE5, and the Camel – which it was expected
would prove superior to the German, were not yet available. Meanwhile, however, his policy of maintaining the offensive, even in
adversity – indeed, especially in adversity – would be pursued. Trenchard would argue the RFC's case vehemently and persistently at

[5]

the highest level, so much so that in December the Army Council formally approved expansion of the RFC to 106 active squadrons and 95 reserve, plus two night-flying squadrons. But this was only the projection, and meanwhile, whatever the odds against, Trenchard – rightly or wrongly – would not plead the RFC's shortcomings as an excuse for delaying the land campaign.

Haig was right about quality; but in fact the RFC, with twenty-five squadrons on the Arras front alone totalling 365 aircraft, nearly twice as many as their adversary, had the advantage in quantity, and Trenchard was relying on this – and on the resilience of his crews – to offset the quality gap. He was well aware, though, that half the German aircraft were scouts, vastly superior to his own in speed, climb and armament, and that this was going to mean heavy casualties for the RFC.

Forecasts of three to four months as the average active service life of two-seater crews, and two and a half months for single-seater scout pilots, were soon to prove over optimistic, greatly underestimating the numbers of newly-trained pilots and observers likely to be needed in the next twelve months. Just when the training organisation at home under Jack Salmond was laying down new minima of flying experience before exposure to active service in France, inability to cope with the manpower demands of the squadrons was to lead to these minima being drastically curtailed. Casualty replacements, as hitherto, could only come from the drafting-in of inadequately-trained beginners.

Air operations, hampered by the weather, continued in a desultory fashion through the worst of the 1916–17 winter, though with a disproportionate increase in the activity of the German Air Force, which was seeking to reassert itself and to cover the withdrawal to the Hindenburg Line. The size and scope of this move took the Allies by surprise. German superiority was soon to be increased by a new and faster Albatros with an improved ceiling, the DIII, and the new *Jastas*. (Richthofen, who was awarded the *Pour le Merité* or Blue Max, Germany's highest award, in January, was now commanding his own unit, *Jasta 11*.) The principal change, first marked in December, was the more venturesome behaviour of German pilots, who no longer restricted their depredations to their own side of the line. In December alone, of twenty-seven British machines shot down, seventeen fell on the British side, a hitherto unheard-of proportion. The only RFC aircraft now capable of meeting the enemy on equal terms or better were the newly-delivered Sopwith Pups of 54 Squadron, complementing the Pups of Naval 8, which had been on loan to Trenchard since September. One captured enemy flying man, who had good reason to regret their introduction, threw a revealing light on Hun attitudes. 'We don't like Pups,' he said, 'but we don't worry about BEs unless they get in our way, and that's the end of them.'

The Pup, a light-weight tractor biplane, was nimble and sturdy but, although it had the advantage of being able to turn inside the Albatros, it was inferior to it in all other respects – speed, armament, rate of climb. The forerunner of the Triplane and the Camel, its delay in production, caused by a lack of official enthusiasm, meant that it was obsolescent by the time it arrived. A second Pup squadron, No. 66, arrived in March 1917, but pilots soon found that to live with the Albatros they had to use all the cunning and expertise at their command. The Tripe, although flown exclusively by the RNAS, reached the front in February, but the Camel, produced as an antidote to the Albatros, did not come into operation until June. There was some prospect, though, that a squadron each of Bristol Fighters and SE5's might be operational some time in April.

Assigned the subordinate role of creating a distraction in the north to divert German reserves while Nivelle broke through on the Aisne, the BEF was given no specific long-term objective. Its primary task was to capture the high ground at Vimy Ridge, three miles north of Arras and inconveniently on the wrong side of the line. This was an enemy stronghold, with well-embedded guns strategically placed. There was also a vast programme of air registration of enemy batteries and defensive positions to be accomplished beforehand. Most vulnerable, as always, were the photographic sorties, when pilot and observer tended to become engrossed in scanning the ground. One who was engaged in this task was 19-year-old Oscar Greig, flying an FE2b (Farman Experimental 2b) 'pusher'. Greig had matured from the callow youth who, fourteen months earlier in a Vickers

Gunbus, had lost his nerve temporarily after a horrific spin, just when he had been in line for a decoration that, as he noted in his diary, 'would please Mummy so'.

His new appointment as a captain and flight commander on 25 Squadron began badly when he sensed that his squadron commander, Major R.G. Cherry, resented him as an intruder: he had wanted to promote one of his own men. When Greig had to report that that individual, on posting home, had absconded with squadron equipment, he was even more unpopular. Another contentious point was Cherry's refusal to allow his crews to wear safety-belts, on the grounds that in a crash they would be thrown clear of their cockpits, instead of being crushed by the rear-mounted engine when it plunged forward, as it was wont to do. Greig had always worn a belt in the Gunbus and he didn't fancy being thrown out. He was aware, too, that Cherry was trying to get rid of him, and the final snub came when Cherry went on leave just before Christmas and left a lieutenant, not Greig, his senior flight commander, in charge.

Greig had been flying FE2b's in England and had grown to like them. He was disappointed on his first flight with 25 Squadron to find that under active service loading they just wallowed along, without the sense of liveliness and buoyancy to which he'd been accustomed. He wondered what Major Cherry's experience was, and he enquired of his senior lieutenant: 'Does Major Cherry ever fly these things?' 'No,' was the reply. In this Cherry, who held the Military Cross, may have been inhibited by Trenchard's policy at that time of conserving experience.

There were certainly squadrons where the avuncular commanding officer, running the squadron from a desk, was highly successful, and other squadrons where a commander who led his men in the air was seriously overburdened; but Greig didn't see Cherry as the avuncular type. Nor was he a disciplinarian – not, anyway, where flying discipline was concerned. Greig had been away from the front for fourteen months, much had changed in the meantime, and he was anxious to learn, but there was no practice flying, no ground instruction, and no rehearsal of communications systems. Especially important, but in Greig's view neglected, was communication between pilot and pilot in formation. Greig himself, as a newly-appointed flight commander, might well have sought to change this, but he was inhibited by Cherry's attitude towards him.

The task on 24 January was to photograph important rail communications in preparation for the attempt to capture Vimy Ridge. In the FE2b the observer operated the camera, which was fixed to the outside of the cockpit. Behind him, slightly elevated on the petrol tank, with engine and radiator immediately at his back, sat the pilot. He had a magnificent view forward, but could see nothing behind or below. The observer – in this case Second-Lieutenant J.E. MacLennan – had a front Lewis gun and another, mounted between him and the pilot, which, by standing up somewhat precariously, he could fire upwards and rearwards over the top wing. The FE was slow and not easy to manoeuvre, and although it had proved a match in the previous year for the Fokker monoplane, it was totally outclassed by the new German scouts. Thus, when Greig set off that morning for the Vimy Ridge area, he was leading – with streamers on his struts and tail to identify him – a formation of two groups of three. In each group, the leading machine carried a camera and the other two, for all their inadequacy, would attempt to provide close escort. There would also, more or less simultaneously – so they were told – be offensive patrols around and above them, and several other scouts patrolling the area. As it happened Greig was not worried: he had been lulled into a false sense of security. The New Year had begun quietly, he had crossed the lines eight times in the previous few days, and he had not seen an enemy plane. But these things could change overnight. What he didn't know was that Richthofen had made his first flight in the latest German fighter, the Albatros DIII, the previous day, had shot down an FE8, and would be looking for custom.

After climbing to 10,000 feet approaching the lines, Greig asked MacLennan in sign language – made necessary by the noise of the Beardmore engine, recently boosted to 160 hp – if his escort was in place, and MacLennan shook his head. This was disturbing. Greig was flying his usual machine, deliberately selected as one of the slowest, yet he had outpaced them all. He fired a green Very light

[9]

7

as the signal to close up and waited until MacLennan nodded the OK before setting course. MacLennan, too, was apprehensive: he was due to go on leave next day.

From his high seat Greig studied the terrain ahead, looking from the map to the ground, pointing the machine directly up the line of the area they were to photograph, noting landmarks ahead and keeping the machine on an even keel. MacLennan was leaning over the starboard side of the cockpit, looking through the camera sights and just starting to take the exposures. Neither man noticed that their escort had again dropped back. They were not being bothered by Archie, which was often a warning of fighter attack, but Greig thought the gunners were probably holding their fire until he had penetrated more deeply. In the next moment he heard machine-gun fire and saw a rash of bullet-holes appear in his left lower wing like the first raindrops in an April shower. So absorbed had they been in their task that they were taken completely by surprise.

Turning steeply towards the attack, nearly jettisoning the unsecured MacLennan, Greig tried to get the enemy plane in front of him, at the same time looking in vain for his escort. Another burst of fire, this time from the starboard side, silenced his engine and pierced his right ankle, knocking his foot off the rudder bar. Continuing to circle, trying to catch sight of his attacker, he was saved again and again by the bulk of the engine behind him as bullets poured in.

He was below 2,000 feet when the firing stopped and he headed at once for the lines, which were only three miles away. He was half-way there when MacLennan pointed dramatically upwards. A very fast scarlet biplane, after a murderous burst of fire, skidded over the top of them, so quickly that there was no time to use the back gun, and the front gun had jammed. Greig tried everything to restart the engine but it only spluttered and he had no choice but to land straight ahead, somewhere between Vimy and Fresnoy, avoiding the innumerable shell-holes by chance. Both men had bullet-holes in their leather coats, and MacLennan, like Greig, had been wounded. Germans were running towards them from all directions but they just had time to ignite the incendiary torch they carried and set the

[10]

machine on fire. There was no hope of escape and, when they raised their hands in surrender, bayonets were sheathed. A German officer who arrived shortly afterwards was pleasant and courteous and returned Greig's salute.

Greig was afterwards to rate his thirty-seven days on 25 Squadron as the most unpleasant of his war service, but at least he was remembered kindly by one new sergeant observer, H.G. Taylor, a Machine-Gun Corps veteran of the Somme whose first attempt at a reconnaissance sketch Greig had described as 'bloody marvellous'. And at least the final day was a memorable one, especially in retrospect when he learned that the man in the speedy scarlet scout had been von Richthofen himself. But for that he might have escaped.

It was the lack of on-the-spot squadron training, he believed, which caused his downfall. But in being shot down by the Red Baron he was in good company, and unlike all too many of his fellow victims he had escaped with his life. He may well have reflected that, despite the mischance of captivity, Mummy would not be displeased.

The tribulations of 21-year-old Eric Routh, begun after he had been appointed a flight commander on the rump of the massacred 16 Squadron (BE's), were exacerbated in the New Year. His flight was taking shape, but the quality of the intake exasperated him. Why was it that the hamfisted and the irresponsible all seemed to come to him? He assessed one of them as moderately good, another as having potential – supposing he survived those fateful first few shows – a third as altogether too nervous, a fourth as a good talker but a poor listener. Even when they were sent up merely to fly round the aerodrome for familiarisation they were apt to get lost. One who did not return was seen to collect an obliging Hun escort; seeing that he was flying solo, with no one to man the gun, the Hun pilot headed him off every time he tried to turn for home, finally motioned him to land on the German side, and alighted beside him to claim him as his own. Another newcomer, sent up with an observer, disappeared altogether. All had been warned not to cross the lines, but no one had seen a machine brought down, so after forty-eight hours Routh was writing to their next of kin, hoping they too were prisoners.

Born in Malta of a naval family, Routh was more worldly-wise than most young men of his time. Typical was the incident when the adjutant, a man of middle age, took him on in a drinking bout to cheer him up and had to be put to bed after eleven shorts to Routh's twelve. Next morning Routh was the one with the clear head. 'Sergeant Dangerfield has gone up with Lance Corporal Webb and has not returned. I told him to be careful not to lose himself. God knows how these people were brought up.' But his judgement of Dangerfield, for all his faults, was sound: he was a survivor. 'I expect he's sleeping the night at some comfortable chateau.' And so it proved.

Routh went on leave on 2 March, returning on the 17th to find that 'several pilots have been done down by Huns'. 16 Squadron was attached to the Canadian Corps, and the main work of cooperating with the First Army in preparation for the Vimy push had fallen to them. Of one of the missing men Routh wrote: 'I specially told him to practise sharp turns, but he would never do it. And I specially warned him never to dive straight away from a Hun – which he was seen to do. He would have been perfectly all right if he'd kept his head.' The observer, whom Routh had liked 'very much indeed', was a married man. 'He was a very stout fellow. I am sorry for both of them.'

He badly needed a pick-me-up. 'I went to Bethune this afternoon and had more champagne than I ought to have had. It did me a lot of good.' Certainly it seems to have done him no harm: next morning he did three hours 20 minutes' observing for the guns in the Vimy area, bringing back valuable information, and another hour in the afternoon. His spirits were restored, and when his former commanding officer on his previous squadron, No. 34, John Chamier, wrote and offered him a job as an instructor at Brooklands, he decided against it. 'It would become boring after a time.'

With formations of enemy scouts, six or eight strong, continually patrolling the lines ready to pounce, there was no chance of boredom for the corps squadrons or anyone else. One of the most desperate clashes occurred on 9 March during an offensive patrol by nine FE8's of 40 Squadron. Old Etonian Laurence Tilney, aged twenty-two, had just taken over the squadron from the forty-year-old actor Bobbie

Loraine. The FE8 was the latest and last – already obsolescent – pusher-type fighter of Royal Aircraft Factory design, similar to the DH2. Only two squadrons were equipped with it. Its top speed was 94 m.p.h. and it mounted a single forward-firing Lewis. On this sortie, one machine was forced to turn back with engine trouble (100 hp Monosoupape), but the remaining eight were swooped on by five Albatros DIII's led by Richthofen. Four were shot down and the other four forced to land in a damaged state, a catastrophe which persuaded the authorities to re-equip the squadron with Nieuports. A few DH2's which tried to help lost one of their number.

Outclassed though they were, the squadron had fought to the death, very nearly achieving the impossible by shooting down the Red Baron himself. With petrol pouring into his cockpit from a pierced fuel tank and his engine riddled, he looked a certainty for a 'flamer', but, mercifully for him and tragically for his future victims, he force-landed safely.

Something of what the half-tutored men of Routh's squadron were facing was recorded by another newcomer, Second-Lieutenant Gerald Jamieson. Jamieson crossed by sea to Boulogne on 7 March, joined the squadron next day, flew that afternoon on reconnaissance, and got 'Archied like the deuce'. On the 10th he did his first counter-battery shoot, and 'did it rather well so was sent up in the afternoon to do another'. The men who proved useful always got the bulk of the work. On the 11th, 12th and 13th he was taking photos, sometimes twice a day. On the 14th he was attacked by two Albatri and only escaped by stalling and spinning, from 9,000 feet down to 500 – but not before his aileron control had been shot away, his observer had been wounded, and he himself had had a narrow escape. 'My pipe in my pocket was shot clean through by three bullets.' Then on the 15th: 'My observer died overnight. My nerves in a terrible state.'

On the 16th he was up with a new observer to show him the lines, then in the afternoon on a shoot. 'It proved quite successful.' On the 17th they were attacked by two of the new Halberstadts and 'managed to bring one of them down on his side'. He was up twice on the 18th taking photos and patrolling, and during a shoot on the 19th he got eight OK's (the code for a hit) from the gunners and got

[13]

the credit for the destruction of a Hun battery. On the 20th he was taking photos seven miles into Hunland and only just got back after his engine was hit. On the 21st, after helping to install a new engine in the morning, he did an air test and a patrol in the afternoon, when 'nerves started to be groggy'. Yet on the 22nd: 'Tried flying again, nerves all right. Took some photos in the afternoon, quite successful.'

Jamieson had been up for two-and-a-half hours doing a shoot on the 23rd when he met an Albatros. 'My observer got an explosive bullet in his leg. Unconscious all the way home. Poor old Gay got shot down.'[1] But they were claiming two Huns between them. On the 24th, with his third observer, he was up for two-and-a-half hours registering targets. 'Plane had nine holes from Archie, one right through the strut.' He had to fly back low over the Hun trenches, 'could see them firing at me, let them have it too'. He was patrolling for another two hours in the afternoon. 'We lost one machine. My wounded observer getting well in hospital.'

During a three-and-a-half-hour shoot on the morning of the 25th on two Hun batteries he had a scrap with another Halberstadt. 'He beetled off to his lines afterwards at low altitude. Got a few shots into him.' Only the caution and inexperience of the average German pilot saved Jamieson and countless others in this period. Then on Monday the 26th: 'It rained all day. Went into Bethune.'

It was the first day since he arrived on 7 March that he hadn't flown, mostly twice. Clearly he had performed rather better than the average beginner, but his contribution, although immense, was not untypical. He was only remarkable in that he had been lucky enough to survive. Yet the ground offensive, and the air offensive proper that was to precede it, was still to come.

One man who was actually enjoying it all, if his letters to his family back in Gomshall, Surrey were to be believed, was observer George Downing, of 57 Squadron (FE2d's, with the new 250 hp Rolls-Royce engine). Norman McNaughton, Downing's pilot, was

---

1. Second-Lieutenant F.H. Gay. He died of his wounds.

of the fearless, daredevil type and they made a good team. With three others of their squadron they ran into five Hun machines and chased them off. Five minutes later they met another batch. 'My pilot dived straight at one of the beggars, and when I was quite close I fired 60 rounds right into him and had the tremendous satisfaction of seeing it depart in flames to Mother Earth. After that it was glorious sport, we fought four different Hun formations for 1½ hours.' Of another perilous incident he wrote: 'What a thing it is to have a man like that for a pilot, because he simply laughed! Guess I'd go anywhere with him.'

Items about colleagues who'd been killed or had had limbs amputated were mixed, in his letters, with typically boyish family jokes and facetious comments. No doubt, in a later idiom, he 'shot a line', though he and McNaughton were clearly in the thick of the fighting. On one patrol they were about ten miles over Hunland when Downing spotted through the glasses a formation of six Huns about 1,000 feet below them. 'Of course that was good enough, so Mac and I dived right into the middle of them, shooting right and left, followed by the rest of the formation. Our machine swung right on top of a Hun and I pumped about 50 shots into him. It was rather a rotten sight, the machine turned upside down and the unfortunate Hun fell out from his bus about 5,000 feet up, so I rather expect he hurt himself . . . We did not have much time for sympathy, as there were several Huns which required attention, and I managed to hook down another in the course of the fight. So altogether it was rather a good day for this child.' To this he added, surely tongue in cheek: 'I hope you won't think this job is risky but it is quite the reverse really, only one must make it sound a little exciting sometimes.' It didn't need much literary skill.

Men like McNaughton and Downing, working as a team, kept the German airmen from too arrogant an assertion of their superiority, and both were awarded the MC. Then, in June, Downing was sent home on a pilot's course. One could almost have wished they had stayed together. He had scarcely arrived at Castle Bromwich when he heard that McNaughton, with a new observer, had been shot down in combat; both men had been killed. Soon afterwards he noted: 'I see poor old Erlebach is killed. That just about finishes poor old 57 of the original lot.'

A job as an instructor, which his family favoured, was mooted when he qualified, but he decided it was 'quite time I interviewed Brother Bosch again', although 'I expect the mater will not be so pleased'. Here was another mother, like so many, torn between pride and apprehension. 'By the time you get this I shall have started strafing Brother Bosch again. Don't worry about this child. He's going to look after himself. I expect my luck will carry me through.'

George Downing had gone to France with 57 Squadron in December 1916, and on 6 November 1917, after a year as full of incident as any young man could wish for, or perhaps wish to avoid, his luck ran out, and he was posted missing, believed killed. His death was later confirmed.

Teamwork was equally important in the corps squadrons, more than doubling the chances of survival. One of the No. 5 Squadron pilots working with the First Army, flying a BE2e, was Second-Lieutenant Charles D. Smart; he was partnered as observer by a Lieutenant Hendry. On 1 March Smart noted in his diary: 'Things getting very hot round here, we had a machine shot down on each fine day during the last fortnight – I do wish my leave would come along.' He had hoped that his younger brother George, who had preceded him into the RFC and was now flying Nieuports on 60 Squadron from an adjacent aerodrome, might have got leave at the same time, but it hadn't worked out. Both were well-built six-footers in their early thirties and had been directors of their father's cotton mill firm in Manchester before volunteering for flying. George had begun as a sergeant pilot but had been commissioned in the field for gallantry.

One day when Hendry was not available, Smart was given an air mechanic named Tyndal as observer: it was Tyndal's first show. There was often a shortage of observers, but rarely of air mechanic volunteers: their reward, when they flew, was the princely sum of an extra two shillings a day. The trip was a testing one, 800 yards beyond the Hun front line. 'Did not fancy the trip with an inexperi-

enced man as gunner . . . I made Tyndal kneel at his gun the whole
time.' Tyndal seems to have taken it well, and fortunately they were
not molested. Fiercely Archied three days later on a photo recce,
showered with wood splinters, with his rudder jammed, and with a
large hole in his aft fuel tank, Smart was 'all the time in fear and
trembling in case the machine should catch fire'. But he got back
safely, and on the 9th he took Tyndal again, a sure sign that the
young air mechanic had made the grade. Next day, 10 March, Smart
went on his much-desired leave. But not for long. 'March 11/1917.
Arrived home 6am, telegram arrived 5pm recalling me. Do feel
pleased.' He had not been vouchsafed a single day.

The losses No. 5 Squadron were sustaining in preparation for
the Canadian assault had clearly inspired Smart's recall, but Ewart
Garland, a young Australian on 10 Squadron, also working for the
First Army, went on leave two days earlier and escaped the recall.
Garland had well-heeled friends in London, in particular a business
associate of his father, Sir Arthur du Cros, chairman of the Dunlop
Rubber Company in the UK: Garland's father was head of the Australian company in Melbourne. With the du Cros family, who treated
him like a son, he lunched at the Ritz with Bonar Law, Lady Curzon
and Mrs [sic] Astor, enjoyed the river at Maidenhead and the sea at
Brighton, and met, in their company, actresses Fay Compton, Binnie
Hale and Vesta Tilley. He had been born in Canada of an Irish father
and an English mother and was no prude, but he was shocked by the
squalor of the London streets, which he found degraded by hordes of
prostitutes who openly solicited servicemen of all nationalities and
ranks. Much the same, he supposed, as in Paris, which a friend had
described as 'one vast brothel'.

Unspoiled and highly literate, Garland made few friends in wartime London, outside the du Cros family. 'I don't smoke, I don't
gamble, don't play cards, don't go with "bad women"! These things
seem to be necessary to be in the swim.' His best companion was
his vest-pocket Shakespeare, which went everywhere with him –
especially over the lines, in case he was captured.

Charles Smart, after his hasty return, was back with his original
partner, Lieutenant Hendry, and they were soon in action. On 21

[17]

March a Hun got behind them threateningly, and Hendry took off his gloves and goggles and manned the gun. 'The Hun got right above us and then put his nose down and I thought to myself "Now for it"', wrote Smart, but seeing Hendry's reaction the German pilot wavered, pulled his nose up, and streaked off home. 'Some of these Huns are poor chaps . . . Hendry is a good chap and I like flying with him. He was worth watching with his steady Scotch eyes glued to the sights of his gun . . . I think he was a bit disappointed when the Hun turned away. I'm afraid I can't say that I was.'

On the 22nd Smart went, by tender, up to the old lines which the Hun had recently vacated, giving him a reminder of the gulf between his recent experience and that of the infantry, of which he had once been a part. 'Our shell-fire is truly terrible.' There was not a piece of flat ground anywhere, the trees were mere stumps, and worst of all, the dead, German and British, were still lying about in their hundreds from the previous July. 'I wonder what the mothers of these poor chaps would feel like if they could see their sons thrown about in heaps like so much garden rubbish. One can see from each man's attitude that he was carrying on his job when killed . . . Here and there a superior pair of boots show where an officer has fallen . . . I was glad to get away from this place.'

The RFC had 120 machines shot down in March, half of them on the British side of the lines, a sure reflection of the way the air battle was going. The hesitancy of many of the German scout pilots was disappearing as they gained in experience and confidence. In addition, many machines and a number of pilots and observers were lost in accidents. It had been impossible for Trenchard to husband his resources for the offensive, as he would have liked, and a recurring problem was that the RFC, unlike the Army, had no reserves to call upon.

When Garland returned from leave he found he had been transferred, with several others of his squadron, to help reinforce the overworked and undermanned 16 Squadron; it was one of the first squadrons to be increased to three flights of eight, twenty-four machines in all; yet they were still flying the outdated BE. The base at Bruay was very much a front-line aerodrome – a contrast to Garland's chateau billet and surroundings at 10 Squadron. The quarters were rough and ready, the Mess was like a canteen, and the casualties were so frequent there was hardly time to get to know anyone. The occasional loss at No. 10, always of an acquaintance and often of a friend, had made a greater impact. Curiously enough he was joined shortly afterwards by three pilots from 5 Squadron, among them his fellow diarist Charles Smart.

For the first time Smart found himself taking photographs, and he thought it 'a poor game, it is highly dangerous and it doesn't give one a chance of telling any tales ... The route you have taken is recorded on the photographic plates with the same clearness as the track of a snail is marked upon the wall up which it has climbed.' He was not altogether surprised that morale in 16 Squadron was not all it should be. 'The people in this squadron have fairly "got wind up" about crossing the lines, not without reason perhaps for a great number of machines have been shot down.' He found a wry amusement in a sort of anachronistic Catch 22: they were told not to cross the lines without an escort – yet no escort was provided for numerous jobs which could not be accomplished without crossing the lines. In his diary he quoted a stanza that seemed apt:

> Mother may I go to swim?
> Yes my darling daughter.
> Hang your clothes on a hickory limb –
> But don't go near the water.

THE BEGINNINGS OF 'BLOODY APRIL': BAPTISM OF THE BRISFIT

WITH the attack on Vimy Ridge scheduled for 9 April, Major-General Sir David Henderson, Director-General of Military Aeronautics at the War Office, felt constrained, at the beginning of the month, to justify the heavy and disproportionate RFC losses of February and March. The German retirement to the Hindenburg Line, he declared, had greatly extended the penetration necessary for all forms of reconnaissance and artillery cooperation. Types of machine in which great hopes had been vested, the Martinsyde 'Elephant', the FE2d and the Sopwith 1½-strutter, had not fulfilled expectations, the DH2 was outclassed by the new German scouts, and the arrival of the next generation of fighting machines, the Bristol Fighter, the SE5, and the Camel, had been subject to various setbacks, not least in engine production (partly owing to industrial disputes and wildcat strikes). Nevertheless a squadron of Bristol Fighters, No. 48, reached France on 8 March and was acclimatising, and a squadron of SE5's, No. 56, was about to leave for the front. Meanwhile the RFC, as an army corps, was obliged to meet army requests whenever feasible, thwarting any notion of conservation before the battle.

Henderson added one vital point that he rightly proffered in Trenchard's support: the work of the RFC was not to be measured in statistics alone. Against the record of positive and productive work

– of reconnaissance, artillery cooperation, contact patrols, and the bombing of enemy communications, strongpoints, and troop concentrations – the German Air Force was primarily engaged in the negative and defensive task of trying to shoot down British machines. Disproportionate as the RFC losses might seem, they should be measured against the losses amongst the German ground forces to which the RFC decisively contributed.

Scandalmongering at home, in the House of Commons, and in the Press, while adding not a single new machine to the order of battle, threatened instead to undermine in advance the morale of pilots and observers bound for the front. But one young Australian, Francis Penny, volunteering, after starting his pilot training, to help fill dead observers' shoes, got his discouragement *en route*. Crossing the path at Boulogne of a pilot on his way home, he mentioned that he was on his way to No. 12 Squadron. 'I've just come from there', he was told, 'and in the last month we've lost 20 pilots and observers, either killed or taken prisoner. I reckon you'll last about six weeks.'

No one had warned more vehemently of the likely inadequacies of the RFC for the planned spring offensive than Trenchard himself. And no one could have been more brutally frank with his crews about the odds they would have to face in the coming weeks. He continued his familiar 'gather round' invitations when visiting squadrons and at the same time he would ask what was most needed, Maurice Baring would 'make a note', and action would be taken. But at the beginning of April, on a visit to 25 Squadron (FE2b's and d's), he told the assembled crews that if they refused to fly the FE2b's any more it would be hard for him to take any action: he thought that every time they went up in them they were virtually committing suicide. The machines were obsolete, and he regretted he couldn't supply them with new ones. The best he had been able to do was to get them a few FE2d's (with the Rolls-Royce engine); but until new types were available he would rely on them to do their best.

The plea worked: when volunteers were requested for a photo reconnaissance of Vimy Ridge, everyone stepped forward, and Major Cherry chose three. Despite forming their customary 'ring o' roses' when attacked, two were lost, one to Richthofen.

The air offensive that was due to start on 4 April was no more than a progression from the costly preparatory work of previous weeks. And there was plenty of action from 1 April. Already, as observed by another diarist, Major A.S.W. Dore of 43 Squadron, Vimy Ridge was almost invisible under a blanket of shrapnel from British guns. Ignoring the Archie, and dodging a cloudbank, 34-year-old Alan Dore looked down on an area already pitted with water-filled shellholes. But when he led a formation of six 1½-strutters in the afternoon, they were driven back by snowstorms. Bad weather was the one obstruction that Trenchard's crews could not surmount.

Very much the old man of the squadron, Alan Dore had been a major in the Worcesters but had learnt to fly, started at the bottom on BE's with 13 Squadron, and joined Sholto Douglas's 43 Squadron as one of his flock. Working his way up, he had recently replaced a man of similar age, A.J.L. Scott, as flight leader. Jack Scott, a successful barrister before the war, and a friend of Winston Churchill, was 'rather a ham-fisted pilot', according to Douglas, and after breaking both legs in a crash he limped on sticks much as Smith-Barry had done. He had to be lifted in and out of his machine, but after serving with 43 Squadron as a flight commander he had graduated on merit and by sheer force of character to command 60 Squadron on Nieuports.

For air crews within reach of a town it was still possible to enjoy a night out, and the austerity that was emerging in England had not yet dulled the cuisine – or the cellars – in France. Farmers were still working their land almost up to the front line, spasmodically under shell fire. That evening another of Douglas's flight leaders, Captain D.C. Rutter, gave a dinner at Auchel for a twin celebration: his birthday and the award of an MC. 'A jolly evening,' noted Alan Dore. At ten o'clock next morning six of the party, led by Dore, set out to photograph a section of the Hindenburg Line. 'At 5,000 feet, with clouds above and below us,' recorded Dore, 'we saw some Huns.'

Presently Dore noticed a flight of what he took to be Nieuports apparently coming to join them, and when he heard his observer start firing he shouted at him to stop. But the red belly and fish-tail of an Albatros scout diving on another of the Sopwiths convinced him his observer was right. The attacker, as he afterwards discovered, was Richthofen. The Sopwith under attack, piloted by Lieutenant Peter Warren, disappeared into the clouds, apparently under control, but later Dore heard that a Sopwith had been seen to land east of Vimy. 'Hope they are prisoners and unwounded,' he wrote. He learned later that Warren had indeed survived as a prisoner but that his observer, Sergeant Renel Dunn, a 19-year-old former Oxford University student, had died of his wounds. This was Richthofen's thirty-third victory, and Dunn was the fifth fatality in what was to become infamous in the annals of the RFC as Bloody April.

Jack Scott had despatched three Nieuports from 60 Squadron to patrol the lines and help any reconnaissance machines in trouble, and these must have been the Nieuports seen in the distance by Dore. Outstanding among the Nieuport pilots was a comparative newcomer named Billy Bishop, one of a stream of Canadians who were to prove themselves unsurpassed as air fighters. (Ewart Garland, who had had the task of training some of them while he was 'on rest', wrote of one of them: 'Like all the Canadians he is very quick and seems adapted to the air.') A week earlier Bishop had chalked up his first moral victories: now he was the only one of the three Nieuport pilots to survive the subsequent clash with Richthofen's *Jasta*.

That same day Charles Smart was over the lines early to observe for a battery that he cursed for wasting the best part of an hour – and the best of the weather – through not reaching its agreed position and putting out ground strips and erecting its wireless mast until eight o'clock. Nevertheless he managed to observe 24 shots for them, 'and did quite well although no OK's were registered'. When his air mechanic observer passed him a note saying 'I feel kind of seasick,' a malady from which many observers suffered in silence, Smart scrawled back 'afraid you'll just have to stick it.' The delayed start meant that the airsick mechanic's ordeal lasted three hours 10 minutes.

There was no respite for Gerald Jamieson, the young man who had flown daily from 7 March to the 25th, often twice, lost two observers, and somehow recovered, for the moment anyway, from

[23]

severe attacks of 'nerves'. How long, at this pace, could he last? On 1 April, starting at 6 a.m., he flew twice in the morning, a counter-battery shoot and a photographic mission, and then did a patrol in the afternoon. On 2 April he suffered engine failure and only just limped back over the lines, and on the 3rd he managed to take some photographs in the afternoon despite the rain.

An urgent request reached 16 Squadron that day from the Canadian ground forces for fresh photos of the ridge before plans for their attack, due to be launched on the 9th, could be finalised. The air offensive proper was scheduled to start along the whole British front next day. The task fell to Garland, as the senior man in his flight after the flight commander. His determination to get his photographs was only equalled by the eagerness of the Huns to prevent him, their scouts diving on him again and again, firing incen-diary as well as ordinary bullets. (Often represented as being contrary to various Hague Conventions – which outlawed expanding bullets – their use was reckoned to be a cad's trick, and there were pilots, Mannock among them, who wouldn't use them, but both sides did.) Finally, when his observer's one-and-only gun jammed, Garland vir-tually hurled his machine at each attacker in turn in the hope that the pilot would choose to avoid certain death in a collision. Between attacks he dived, side-slipped and stunted, trying never to present a stable target. He must still have been doomed in the end had not five FE's come to his rescue. There were forty holes in his machine when he got back, but the photos looked good and were rushed to Canadian HQ by motor-cycle. He learned only much later, from the Canadian commander, General Julian Byng, in person how vital these photographs had been.

The air offensive duly opened on the 4th, the declared objective being to draw hostile aircraft away from the immediate battle area so as to leave the sky free for the corps squadrons. Of the original 'contemptibles', two were commanding squadrons in the front line – Willie Read, still running 45 Squadron under protest, and Harvey-Kelly, brashly confident in the superiority of the French-built Spad 7 with which his new squadron, No. 19, was equipped: it came to be regarded as the best French design of the war. Veterans Josh

Higgins and Gordon Shephard were commanding brigades. Other squadron commanders with names to conjure with included Arthur Tedder and Sholto Douglas (1½-strutters, 70 and 43 Squadrons respectively), and the ebullient Jack Baldwin, 55 Squadron, operating Geoffrey de Havilland's new nimble high-altitude Rolls-Royce-engined bomber the DH4, in which great hopes were vested. (Twenty-five years later, flouting 'Bomber' Harris's orders, Baldwin, as an air vice-marshal, was to take part in the first 1,000-bomber raid.)

The programme was timed to synchronise with a massive five-day bombardment by 2,800 guns, after which, on 9 April, the infantry would go over the top. But as had seemed all too likely in the previous forty-eight hours, artillery cooperation was greatly hampered by low clouds and rain. Despite this, as Garland noted, 'the air was thick with British machines.' Jamieson was among the lucky ones in finding a clear patch. 'Two trips, two shoots, successful,' he recorded; but some did not get off the ground at all. Alan Dore, noting 'a very stormy day, low clouds', flew over to his old squadron, No. 13, and found 'a few familiar faces amongst the men', but only two officer survivors of his era.

Smart, still attached to 16 Squadron, was booked for a shoot on the 5th, but noted: 'Quite hopeless owing to thick mist and low clouds.' It took him and others like him all their time to find their way about, but he did stay to witness what he called 'a fine bombardment by our guns'. Visiting the battery, a Canadian one, that afternoon, he was told by the major that the Hun 'will never stand the bombardment we are going to put up'. Smart concluded: 'They were certainly making things hot for Fritz.'

Elsewhere, throughout the five days, Fritz was making things even hotter for the Brits. Garland was lucky when taking photographs without escort when he spotted two of his BE2 colleagues briefed for the adjacent sector being attacked by three Albatros scouts in turn. Both went down in flames. 'One was Whitaker and the other Knight, who was with me yesterday. Both had observers.' All four men were lost. Garland managed to get all his photos, then 'scuttled back over to our side' as the Huns turned towards him. 'I came back safely but felt a bit off seeing those two go down in flames.' Next day, to his unashamed joy, he was transferred back to his first love, No. 10, as a flight commander, where his welcome was ecstatic. '*Quelle guerre!*' He was 20.

On 5 April Baring noted, somewhat tardily, 'Fighting in the air has begun.' It did in fact begin that day for the Bristol Fighters of 48 Squadron, which had arrived in France exactly four weeks earlier, giving them ample time, it seemed, to work up. Sooner or later they had to be blooded, to see what impact they could make on the air battle. The Brisfit was a sizeable machine for its time, 26 feet long and with a 40-feet wing span. The two crew sat back to back, the pilot with a synchronised Vickers, the observer with a Lewis mounted on a Scarff Ring with a swivel seat, firing on the flanks and to the rear. It was the observer's wide field of fire that was regarded as the bullpoint, especially as the Brisfit was erroneously thought to have inherent structural weaknesses which prohibited aggressive man-oeuvring. In any case a full understanding of the employment of the Brisfit in combat could hardly be arrived at except in action. The experience was to be dearly bought.

It was perhaps inevitable that the flight commander chosen to lead the first patrol should be a man who had already made a name for himself, a man whose fame in England eclipsed even that of Albert Ball. Over a period of many months, from January 1915 until September 1916, a total of 39 Zeppelin raids had been mounted against England, killing 439 people and injuring nearly a thousand, and the bearded commander of airships, Captain Peter Strasser, a fanatical believer in airships as a war-winning weapon, had mustered, for the night of 2 September 1916, an armada of sixteen for what he called 'the climactic raid', a decisive blow against Britain's capital city. All that threatened to hinder them over London was a mobile anti-aircraft force and half a dozen frustrated pilots in obsolescent machines – BE2c's – both rendered impotent by the height advantage that conferred virtual invulnerability on the raiders. Yet a young man named William Leefe Robinson, 'Robbie' to his intimates, had given Londoners the most spectacular heavenly conflagration of all time, witnessed by hundreds of thousands, by overcoming the odds stacked against him and shooting down the army airship SL11 over Cuffley, the first airship of any kind to be shot down over Britain. The sight of their comrades' incineration, cheered to the echo by Londoners, had so appalled the remainder that they turned tail.

A man who could do that, it was assumed, could do anything. Now here he was, seven months after his famous exploit, entrusted with the task by his commanding officer, Major A.V. 'Zulu' Bettington (from Cape Colony), of leading the first-ever Bristol Fighter patrol against the enemy.

Cynicism over the true worth of Leefe Robinson's feat was general in the RFC in France. Provided you could get the height, anyone could shoot down a Zeppelin: it was merely a matter of being in the right place at the right time. The hazardous part was finding one's aerodrome – or any aerodrome – and getting down afterwards, with the aid of a few flares in an otherwise darkened world. It was a predicament that led to many crashes, some of them fatal. But did its surmounting warrant a VC? Wasn't it a fact that once the psychological barrier had been removed, admittedly by Robinson, the feat had become commonplace – rather like, in a later age, Bannister's four-minute mile? Those unacquainted with the full story resented the publicity accorded the home-based hero, and wondered what qualified him to take command of a flight of the new Bristol Fighters in the front line.

In fact, Leefe Robinson was no stranger to France: he had flown with No. 4 Squadron in BE2c's as an observer before sustaining a shrapnel wound in May 1915 which had proved to be a 'Blighty' one. Recovering, and learning to fly, he had begun the lonely work of Zeppelin-chasing at night on Christmas Eve 1915, and persevered with many setbacks until his triumph of September 1916. But survival in the skies beyond the lines in April 1917 demanded special qualities of cunning and resource, not necessarily similar to those required for Zepp-chasing. Robinson had trained hard on the Brisfit in England, the work-up period in France had seemed adequate, and there is no doubt that he was better equipped to lead than most newly-arrived pilots: but this still fell far short of the ideal. Yet someone had to do it, and, to Zulu Bettington, Robinson must have seemed the obvious choice.

What followed was no fault of Leefe Robinson's: but blame must surely be attached to those who chose the route for this first offensive patrol. It seems that they were actually seeking a showdown with Richthofen: if so, they were notably successful. They met Richthofen where they would expect to find him, near Douai, where his *Jasta* was based. They hoped to give him a nasty surprise. But the tactical assessment that the Brisfit would be best suited to operating in close formation for mutual protection, like the FE2b, basing both offence and defence on the observer's gun, proved disastrously mistaken, and four of the formation of six were shot down, two by Richthofen. A fifth was badly shot about but got back along with the sixth. It was some consolation that Leefe Robinson, forced to land with his engine put out of action, survived with his observer to be taken prisoner. As a baptism of fire for the Brisfit, however, it was calamitous.

Richthofen was dismissive of the quality of the new British machine and pronounced his Albatros far superior; but after some technical and tactical adjustments, the Brisfit was to prove him culpably wrong.

No. 48 Squadron was not the only one to suffer in those first few April days. Heavy losses were also sustained by the Nieuports of 60 Squadron (ten in three days, all to *Jasta 11*) and the FE2d's of 57; in neither case could inexperience be blamed. A bombing offensive, beginning on 5 April and aimed at forcing the enemy to withdraw anti-aircraft defences and aeroplanes from the front line, also suffered costly setbacks. Good news came on 6 April when the United States declared war on Germany. Bad news was the loss of four Martinsydes: but they shot down two Halberstadts, and two of the pilots survived as prisoners.

The faster, high-flying DH4's of 55 Squadron made a good start in their first show by scoring direct hits with 112 lb bombs on an assembly point at Valenciennes and then, when swarms of Albatros scouts pursued them, outdistancing them comfortably. Daylight bombing was rarely granted close escort, but it was often loosely accompanied, or supported by offensive patrols, whereas the DH4's at high altitude were expected to take care of themselves. But any notion of invulnerability was quickly confounded when they lost three out of four in a raid on 8 April. Nevertheless pilots soon rated the DH4 the best bomber of the war and observers liked it for its dual control. A drawback was that pilot and observer were separated by the fuel tanks and were too far apart to communicate verbally.

An innovation was the night attacks by FE2b's of 100 Squadron armed with one-pounder quick-firing pom-poms, especially effective against ground targets; they succeeded in wrecking hangars and buildings on Richthofen's aerodrome at Douai, keeping Richthofen out of the air for a day or so.

Escort work, according to Alan Dore, remained 'a ticklish job'. Detailed to lead five 1½-strutters to protect six BE's bombing a rail junction at Don, Dore saw nothing of the bombers. As happened far too often, something had gone wrong with the timing. Returning against a near-hurricane, the Sopwiths were pinpointed by Archie and chased by fifteen Hun scouts. 'Our formation of five is well closed up and gunners ready. Just before crossing the lines they dive at us. Both my guns are jammed. I see one get on to my tail so stall and go down in a spinning nose-dive . . . We cross the lines separately . . . Thornton and his observer Blackburn fail to return.'[1]

Resentment and indignation amongst pilots at the obsolescent machines they were given to fly was not always suppressed. Returning from a deep penetration to bomb Tournai rail junction, a flight commander on 45 Squadron (also 1½-strutters) boiled over. 'Some say Sopwith two-seaters are bloody fine machines, but I say they're more bloody than fine.' At the time the brigade commander, T.I. Webb-Bowen, was visiting the disgruntled Willie Read to tell him that his request to return to his regiment had at last been granted by Trenchard. Webb-Bowen overheard the remark and had the man removed to Home Establishment forthwith. Yet Read, who was shortly to be succeeded by Major H.A. van Ryneveld, a South

---

1. Second-Lieutenant C.P. Thornton and Lieutenant H.D. Blackburn, killed in action 5 April 1917.

African, could not but be sympathetic. From October 1916 to early May 1917 the squadron lost twenty-three pilots killed and five wounded in exchange for three hostiles destroyed.

Balloon-busting, which exposed its practitioners to withering machine-gun and rifle fire, not to mention 'flaming onions' – balls of fire projected upwards in string-of-onions succession – was attempted by the Nieuports as part of the air offensive, but rapid reaction by enemy winchmen frustrated many attacks, and the ratio, in the space of four days, of five aeroplanes shot down for five balloons destroyed, with the balloon crews – but not the Nieuport pilots – escaping by parachute, was discouraging.

On 8 April Smart noted: 'Tomorrow the infantry go over to take the Vimy Ridge. Good luck to them, they have been marching past the aerodrome towards the lines all day, all of them looking very pleased with life and ready for anything.' Undoubtedly this readiness for action could be blunted over a period, but airmen, like soldiers, generally got a boost, rather than the blues, from the prospect of action. Even Garland's rejoicing at returning to 10 Squadron was tempered by regret. 'The pity is that tomorrow is the "push" and now of course I shall miss it.'

In the five days of the preliminary air offensive, from 4 to 8 April, the RFC lost 75 machines in action and 105 pilots and observers – 19 killed, 13 wounded and 73 missing. It was a destructive period, too, for accidents, partly because of the many inexperienced pilots on the squadrons and the stress they were under, 56 machines being wrecked. The wastage on some squadrons, particularly of observers, was catastrophic. 'Of the observers who came out with us from England – eighteen in number – not one remains,' wrote Dore of 43 Squadron. He added: 'We have eight of the original pilots left.'

On the eve of the attack, and the last day of the preparatory air offensive, Trenchard, despite acute bronchitis, toured the front-line in an RE8, with Baring tagging along behind in a BE. They visited eleven squadrons and talked to all the pilots. No. 56 Squadron, the first SE5 squadron, had arrived at Vert Galand that day, under an energetic organiser in Major R.G. Blomfield, born in Sydney, Australia. Harvey-Kelly, the squadron's first CO, had laid the foundations so well that the dapper 'Dickie' Blomfield found himself commanding some of the best available pilots, led by three experienced flight commanders. He himself was going to be the major-domo, fostering rather than leading.

By means of shrewd exchange postings, Blomfield enhanced the general expertise of squadron personnel. He assembled a group of musicians with London orchestral experience and inveigled a culinary wizard who before call-up had been a chef at the Ritz. Demanding high standards in all departments, he set out to mould his squadron into an élite force.

But first there was much to be done. The untried SE5's needed many modifications to make them combat-worthy, and during the working-up period in mid-April one young pilot was obliged to apologise to his parents for his slackness as a correspondent. 'I haven't written because we've been busy altering our machines. Dawn till dark we were hard at it.' This was the 18-year-old Maurice Kay, who as a trainee had disgraced and distinguished himself simultaneously by ignoring expert advice to stay on the ground, only to redeem himself, after crashing through the branches of a tree, by skilfully controlling his crippled machine and miraculously surviving.

Another young pilot, who had long pleaded to be allowed to get back to the fighting, was so disillusioned with the basic SE5 that he followed Trenchard from one airfield to another and begged for a Nieuport for lone forays. His publicity value in attracting recruits was such that he had been permitted to join 56 Squadron for one month only: his name was Albert Ball. At first, Trenchard prevaricated.

Ball had no illusions of indestructibility. He had told his father: 'No scout pilot who does any serious fighting and sticks to it for any time can get through.' But there was no doubting his delight at being back. 'They're giving the Ball', he said, 'another run.'

*   *   *

[31]

The Battle for Vimy Ridge duly began on 9 April, in abominable weather, with the promised attack by the Canadians. 'Infantry went over at 5.30 a.m.,' noted Smart. He was sent up to spot the flashes of enemy guns and advise the Canadian battery commander. 'Terrific wind blowing and as bumpy as Satan.' It was too much for his observer, who passed him a note saying he felt sick and wanted to go home. 'I passed him a note back reminding him there was a war on and telling him to think of the poor devils below.' But after ninety-five minutes Smart had to return for a change of observer. 'This chap was the real thing, he felt very sick in the bumps but did not say anything about it. We had a great time . . . and had the satisfaction of seeing several active enemy batteries strafed and silenced, thus making things easier for our infantry . . . Rumour has it that we have taken 10,000 prisoners and 16 guns, hope this is true.' The Canadians had indeed seized a section of Vimy Ridge, though only after three hours' heavy fighting. Near Arras, in the centre, the Third Army, by pushing the Germans back three-and-a-half miles, had achieved the biggest gain in two-and-a-half years of trench warfare.

Smart rated this day one of the worst for flying he'd known. Yet: 'I managed to do four and a quarter hours after having breakfast at 6.30 a.m. and lunch at 5 p.m. and nothing in between. Am on the early morning stunt tomorrow, shall be doing the same job again. Our shellfire today was worth seeing, the enemy lines were simply seething with bursting shells . . .' And Dore wrote: 'All along the Vimy Ridge a white line of bursting shrapnel told me that we had reached the summit. Below us the contact and artillery machines swept backwards and forwards like shuttles . . . Looking round I see some men on a road and wagons behind. Descend and shoot right into them receiving a few bullets in return.'

Other pilots, undeterred by the snowstorm, but often forced down to 300 feet, located targets for the artillery hour by hour as Smart had done, but they weren't all as lucky as he was, and casualties were heaviest among the corps machines. Yet enemy batteries continued to be registered and trenches photographed. 'Despite inferiority,' recorded Baring proudly, 'the work of the army was done and thousands of casualties saved.'

The RFC was pulling its weight despite the weather and the ever-present deterrent of flying through the barrage they were masterminding. Garland noted: 'Our own gunfire was a definite hazard . . . it is no exaggeration to say that the sky was thick with shells . . . Our planes had to fly in the thick of the shell fire for as much as three hours on end, not to mention enemy action aimed at our planes.' And Dore wrote: 'Once I felt the concussion of a big howitzer shell pass so near that the whole aeroplane shuddered as though struck. Later I actually saw a shell come up and pass by me on its way to the Germans.'

Smart was out of bed next morning at 4.40 and in the air at six. But after locating two active batteries: 'We ran into a most awful snowstorm, turned west and flew for ten minutes at a height of 600 feet absolutely blind . . . I got most horrible "wind-up" for there is a lot of high ground about here . . .' He force-landed as soon as he could and was told he'd just missed a chimney stack. 'The wind was huge and I had to get two Tommies to hold on to each wing-tip.' When they got tired, however, 'over she went, fortunately without doing any damage.' Examining his machine when he got back to the aerodrome he found it had been peppered with machine-gun fire and that his observer, especially, had been within inches of mortal injury.

Enemy small-arms fire, Archie, poor visibility, and high ground, were all familiar hazards, but there was nothing more intimidating than the unavoidable necessity of flying through the aerial minefield of 'friendly' shells. 'After a completely dud day and no flying,' wrote Smart on 12 April, 'we were all sitting in the mess at 6 p.m. when the CO rushed in and said "The Huns are shelling the Pimple."' This was a small hill recently taken during the push. One machine from each flight was ordered up and as Smart was first for duty in his flight he ran down at once to the aerodrome and ordered out his machine. 'It was raining hard and a thoroughly miserable evening, however we had to go.' When they reached Arras they were faced with an unforgettable sight: all guns on both sides in the district were firing away at frenetic speed. 'The whole ground, particularly on the enemy's side, was simply reeling with bursting shells, these together with the gun flashes presented a wonderful sight, there

[33]

seemed to be millions of spots of flame spread all over the countryside and it must have been as near hell as possible for those down below.' It was equally hell for those up above. 'The air was just stiff with flying shells and we got no end of bumps from them as they passed under and over us.' To some extent Archie was predictable, but the barrage was haphazard, and the BE's of 16 Squadron did not escape unscathed. 'One C flight machine was struck by a passing shell, both pilot and observer being killed.'

Next morning Charles Smart was transferred back to 5 Squadron. 'Everyone was very glad to see me and I was jolly glad to get back.' But euphoria was cruelly truncated. 'I got the afternoon off and walked over to 60 Squadron where I got an awful shock being told that George was shot down over Arras last Saturday. Poor old chap, he hasn't had much of a run. The news has depressed me terribly.'

George Smart had been shot down in flames on 7 April by Richthofen, who recorded that his victim had 'tried to escape six times by various tricks and manoeuvres'. Burnt to death, he was buried in a shell-hole close to the wreck of his Nieuport, with his broken propeller for a headstone. But when Charles returned after ten days' compassionate leave and tried to locate the grave he found the ground torn up by artillery fire and all traces of it eliminated. Charles applied for transfer to a scout squadron, thinking to avenge his brother, but he was still wanted where he was.

The dud day mentioned by Charles was a blessing for some. 'It has given us a rest, which has been much needed,' wrote Eric Routh, the harassed C Flight commander of 16 Squadron. Essential tasks could be attended to. 'We buried poor MacKenzie and Everingham.'[1] They had been shot down over ground taken during the push. 'Mac was looking most peaceful and quite normal, being shot through the back (probably died instantly or unconscious), but Everingham looked as though the end had not come quite so peacefully. He was not shot, but badly broken by the fall.' They had spun down from 4,000 feet: it was this agonising last minute or so that all but the

1. Second-Lieutenants Keith Ingleby Mackenzie and Guy Everingham, shot down by Manfred von Richthofen on 8 April 1917. MacKenzie was eighteen.

most unimaginative had experienced in morbid daytime fantasies or in nightmares, and it explained the difference between the death-mask of unconscious pilot and sentient observer. 'They were buried', recounted Routh, 'close to what was left of the machine. All around were hundreds of dead bodies, our own and the Huns. One dead man was leaning up against a tree, another had a cigarette in his mouth with a box of matches in his hand and looked very much alive, like a waxwork. Burying parties were at work, but it was a lengthy and tedious process.' Dore, too, taking advantage of the blank day, climbed the famous ridge. 'You could hardly put a pin's point between the shell craters . . . Devastation and mud . . . Ground littered with dead or portions of dead.' Reaching the crest, his party were immediately shelled, and Dore took cover in a trench. 'Realise I have lost the art of taking shells complaisantly.' It was better to be airborne after all.

Visiting 56 Squadron, Trenchard had tea with Blomfield and his star pilot, Albert Ball. He was so delighted to hear Ball speak with mounting respect of the SE5 that he gave in to his earlier request. 'He is giving him two machines,' noted Baring, 'the SE5 for his ordinary work and a Nieuport for his lone enterprises.' The squadron, still busy with refinements, expected to be ready to start patrolling within another few days.

Trenchard's visits sometimes met with cynicism from the men at the sharp end. He did sometimes reveal a capacity for stating the obvious. 'Boom came and inspected us today and talked a lot and told us all the work we had done previous to the 9th had been the cause of the success of the attack on the Vimy Ridge, this was stale news as we all knew that, and so does everyone else with brains.' Thus spake the long-suffering Routh. 'He also complimented us on the amount of flying, more especially in the rain and snow. He told us he was sorry we had casualties and that our machines were not quite all that could be desired, but "a working machine will never have a chance against a fighting scout".' It was a subject, wrote Routh, with some bitterness, 'on which we were all agreed'.

Routh was still going on about his *bête noire*, Sergeant Dangerfield, who had not returned from an evening patrol. 'Every time he's been out to the lines he's failed to return through some reason or other – either lost his way or had a forced landing. He is without doubt the most unreliable man I have.' Yet Routh had learnt to respect the man's ability to turn up like the proverbial bad penny, and he was quite upset when he had to report Dangerfield missing. It was no great surprise when, a week or so later, he was named as a prisoner. He had got down all right, as before.

With the capture of Vimy Ridge consolidated, ground patrols pushed vigorously forward, and on 13 April the weather improved. It was also a Friday, and it was not a lucky day for the RFC. Those who suffered most were the RE8's, the 'Harry Tate' as it was dubbed in rhyming slang, the machine ordered in 1915 to replace the BE range. It embodied most of the long-awaited two-seater improvements, pilot in the front cockpit with synchronised gun, observer behind with swivel gun, more powerful engine, faster speed and rate of climb. But from the beginning, production was dogged by misfortune, after which early models revealed a marked tendency to spin. Modifications in design were slow to impress and the machine acquired an evil reputation, which it was only just beginning to live down.

But now came a setback. Soon after eight o'clock that morning six RE8's of 59 Squadron set out on a photographic mission which called as always for accurate flying and a steady progression. Good support was being given at this time by three RNAS squadrons, flying Sopwith Tripes or Pups, but no close escort was detailed, reliance being placed on offensive patrols by FE2d's, Spads and Bristol Fighters. Two of the FE2d's were shot down, the Brisfits saw nothing, and the Spads were late. Intercepted by six single-seaters led by Richthofen, all six RE8's were shot down, ten of the twelve crew men being killed.

'BLOODY APRIL' – THE CLIMAX: BALL, BISHOP AND MANNOCK: MANFRED VON RICHTHOFEN

O N 16 April, along a 50-mile front on the river Aisne, 80 miles south-east of Arras, General Nivelle launched his controversial spring offensive, the massive assault that he had promised would destroy the enemy's forces and achieve a breakthrough that would win the war. Haig, Pétain and others believed that Nivelle had exaggerated his prospects and underestimated the enemy's strength, and this was almost certainly true; but security leaks arising from the distribution of plans down to unit commander level destroyed the vital element of surprise. Warned of the Allies' plans, the defenders were well prepared and enemy gunners in fortified positions inflicted frightful casualties when the French advanced. The eager *poilus*, buoyed up by forecasts of a virtual walk-over, were shocked into a dismay that quickly degenerated into demoralisation. There was a whiff of betrayal in high places, further setbacks precipitated widespread mutinies, and Nivelle was discredited. Within a month he had been succeeded as commander-in-chief by Pétain, with Foch replacing Pétain as chief of staff. The leading mutineers were executed, negative concepts were suppressed, and Pétain began the task of averting a complete collapse before rebuilding could commence. Meanwhile, Haig, one of the few privy to the truth about the mutiny, had to redouble the diversionary pressure.

Four days of bad weather on the British front so hampered the work of the corps squadrons that artillery preparations for a renewal of the offensive were delayed, but after an improvement on the evening of 20 April a full day's air cooperation on the 21st allowed the preliminary bombardment to begin. Despite their losses, 16 Squadron remained heavily engaged, and Eric Routh, led by senior flight commander J.P.C. 'Jock' Mitchell, took off with a young observer named MacKenzie (no relation of the pilot Ingleby Mac-Kenzie they had recently buried). After registering enemy trench junctions they penetrated more deeply to take photographs. 'On our way back we were attacked by three Albatros destroyers, two went for Jock and brought him down in flames, and the third went for me. I was hit in the hand by the first burst, but what with MacKenzie firing and my twisting and turning he did not get on to me again, though he had already succeeded in putting a bullet through my engine, camera and petrol tank.' Routh landed safely beyond Vimy Ridge but realised that the Albatros pilot was still firing at him. The chivalry of earlier years was by this time wearing thin, but even so Routh registered surprise: relations, he reflected whimsically, were becoming less than courteous.

'Directly we landed I shouted to Mac to get his gun on the Boche again, which he did from the machine and drove him off.' The Canadians were also firing 'for all they were worth'. Someone quickly bandaged Routh's hand. 'Poor Jock was not so fortunate as I was and I'm afraid is dead with his observer Rogers. One of them jumped out at about 500 feet, both were killed.' Routh added: 'I am afraid Mac is rather upset at the whole thing, and is rather shaken, but it made me laugh to see him after half a glass of neat whisky, it made him awfully tight and he was most amusing.'

The battle-hardened Eric Routh, as we know, could hold his liquor. But soon afterwards a minor accident when loading a French bomb ended his service with 16 Squadron after 126 days. The youthful MacKenzie's nerves did not recover.

Routh had been extremely lucky to survive so long. According to Garland, 10 Squadron had lent eight crews to 16 Squadron and only two had returned. 'If Durrant and I hadn't been posted back to No. 10,' wrote Garland, 'there's little doubt that we'd have been done in.'

Another victim of 'Bloody April', Lieutenant Norman Birks of 29 Squadron (now re-equipped with Nieuports from DH2's), had something to say on the subject of chivalry. The German sergeant pilot who shot him down visited him in hospital and apologised for continuing to shoot when Birks's machine was crippled and on the way down. 'If I'd left you alone you'd have got back over the lines,' was his excuse, which Birks agreed was true. Birks added: 'Until about 1917 it was considered "not quite the thing" by both sides to continue firing on a machine which was incapacitated. But this sense of chivalry was rapidly disappearing.' Boelcke, 'our brave and chivalrous foe,' for one, was credited with such acts of mercy. Routh would have agreed that the gloves were off.

When infantry attacks were finally launched on the morning of 23 April, there were 48 single-seaters patrolling the area, including 20 Sopwith naval Triplanes, 14 Nieuports (29 and 60 Squadrons), and, for their baptism of fire, seven SE5's of 56 Squadron. There were also 24 two-seaters – 1½-strutters, FE's, Armstrong-Whitworths, and RE8's – on line patrol, all aiming to keep the skies clear for artillery spotting and contact patrols. But with fighting continuous and fluctuating as the enemy counter-attacked, and enemy planes interfering when they could, requests by air observers for the lighting of flares on the ground to reveal forward positions were met with understandable reluctance and were mostly ignored. 'This', as the army commander reminded his corps commanders that evening, 'makes effective artillery support almost impossible.'

A combined reconnaissance and bombing operation, meticulously planned, got through unscathed, but there were losses amongst the FE's, and on the eve of the battle a Spad formation, bemused by identification problems (easy enough in the now crowded skies), mistook a group of hostiles for friendlies and suffered accordingly. Of eight DH4's of 55 Squadron setting out to bomb an ammunition dump, two crashed even before they reached the lines, and although the remaining six got through to their objective, they were savagely attacked on their way home, and before they could shake off their assailants they had lost one pilot killed and three observers wounded. Yet the Tripe pilots were asserting their superiority wherever they were engaged, the pilots of the Pups, recognising the strengths and limitations of their mounts, did useful work, and the Brisfit crews, revising their tactics, more than held their own. News of the SE5's, too, with their 150 h.p. Hispano-Suiza engines, was eagerly awaited.

The SE5, even more than the Brisfit, had had a disastrous inception. Owing to an unsuspected fault in the wing-tip structure, the prototype had broken up in mid-air, killing test pilot and spinning expert Frank Goodden. The resultant mood of despondency called for positive measures, and after remedial action had been taken Roderic Hill, replacing Goodden, set out to restore faith and confidence in a 20-minute display of handling and aerobatics especially for the benefit of the apprehensive pilots of 56 Squadron.

Diving, zooming, spinning, corkscrewing and looping, directly above their assembly airfield at London Colney, he demonstrated the reliability and robustness of the basic type, and the power of the 150 h.p. Hispano-Suiza engine, for all to see. The machine was armed with a synchronised Vickers firing through the propeller arc and a Lewis mounted on the upper wing. The many imperfections that remained had all proved susceptible to modification at squadron level, and at last the SE5, whose ancestry went back to Geoffrey de Havilland's SE2 in 1914, was ready.

In the months that followed, 56 Squadron, especially after the 200 h.p. Hispano-Suiza was introduced into their SE5A's in mid-June, were to eclipse all other scout squadrons in terms of victories; but on this first foray their pilots sighted nothing. Then Ball, patrolling alone soon afterwards in his Nieuport, picked out a pair of Albatros two-seaters and at once initiated his favourite form of attack. 'When I get to close quarters I generally pretend I am going to attack from above . . . then suddenly I dive under the machine, and if I am lucky I empty a drum into his petrol tank and he goes down.' One of the two-seaters escaped out of range, but Ball emptied half a drum of Lewis into the other and it staggered and began to go down. He followed it, still firing, and watched it crash. No one got out.

It seems that the surviving Hun had noted the red spinner that Ball always displayed on his propeller: anyway he reported the

characteristic method of attack, giving due warning that the Englishman Ball was back in business.

Fifteen minutes later Ball glimpsed another two-seater as it disappeared into cloud and dived after it. But in his eagerness he over-
shot, presenting the German with a fleeting but point-blank target.
The German escaped, and back at Vert Galand Ball found the wings
of his Nieuport were so riddled they had to be changed.

The first fortnight of Ball's permitted month in France had already
expired, so he had only a fortnight to achieve an ambition he had
conceived of passing the record of the Frenchman Georges Guynemer, which stood at thirty-seven. He was out to make up for lost
time, and he was off again two hours later, this time in his SE5, and
again his wonderfully keen eyesight, or his instinct, found him a
target others had missed. Stalking a white Albatros two-seater at
12,000 feet, and closing in under its tail, he had barely begun firing
when his Lewis jammed.

Landing at the nearest aerodrome, he cleared the stoppage and
within minutes was back on patrol. Above Cambrai he sighted five
green-painted single-seater Albatros scouts, patrolling with justifiable
arrogance, masters, as their pilots reasonably believed, of the sky.
Ball's tactics against scout formations seldom varied: he dived
immediately on the leader, opening up with his Vickers from close
range. By the time the formation had recovered from the shock, one
green Albatros was falling in flames. The others fired at him, but
they had lost their leader, and as Ball turned to face them they cleared
off home. Perhaps they too had seen the red spinner.

Testing his controls, Ball soared away and circled over Cambrai.
He sighted another Albatros two-seater and made his usual feint
attack, then pulled down his Lewis in Nieuport style and trimmed
his machine tail-heavy to leave both hands free. He fired half a drum,
then had to break off to avoid collision. He chased the pilot down
through the cloud layer, but when he saw him crash-land safely he
left him alone.

That night he wrote excitedly to the eighteen-year-old land girl he
had met and fallen in love with only a fortnight before leaving England. 'Have got my first two Huns. I had three flights and managed

to bring down one. This I did in my Nieuport. Next I went up in my SE5 . . . I got five shots in my right strut, four in the wings, and two just behind my head. This was done by five Albatros scouts. But I got one of them and set it on fire . . . Poor old chap inside.'

Ball's success gave a timely fillip to 56 Squadron, where the youngest pilot, Maurice Kay, not in the least overawed by his seniors, or by the enemy, was acclimatising well. In his letters home he gave a vivid picture of squadron life, in the air and on the ground. 'Ball has done himself great credit, making himself an even bigger name. Yesterday we did a lot of fighting, I had two flights. Had to give up each time with my man in my sights when my guns jammed.' Gun stoppages were a nightmare at first in the SE5, but Kay was philosophic. 'No matter, I put the wind up both . . . It was good fun – and the excitement was terrific!'

Kay continued: 'Things are going very well indeed . . . While I write this the piano is going strong, everybody is making quite a noise, I am thoroughly enjoying life. It is great fun . . . I must say again how ripping it is out here.'

This naive exuberance was checked only momentarily by bad news of a family friend in another squadron. 'Poor Heyworth, who is officially missing, is I'm sorry to say feared to be killed . . . He was seen to go down in a nose dive. It is very sad!! He was a good fellow!!!' Then he added, more soberly: 'I wouldn't say anything to Mr Heyworth about Heyworth being killed, when we only know he is missing.' (In fact, Heyworth had survived as a prisoner.)

Bad weather in the next two days gave Ball a chance to put the final touches to his hut, dig his garden, and tread in a few plants. Then, quite unselfconsciously, out came his violin. 'The chaps do laugh,' he wrote. His garden too, he said, always caused 'a lot of sport. When I am happy I dig in the garden and sing.'

Another succession of combats on the 26th brought him a third victim with 56 Squadron. 'It was dark when I returned', he wrote, 'and everyone thought I had been done in. You see, they do one or two jobs each day and I lead them, but during the remainder of the day I go up in my Nieuport and have a try by myself. This is the only way to get them. Just keep at them all day.'

The pace at which Ball was living, however, was bound to catch up with him, and in his letters home he confessed to a tiredness close to exhaustion. Often he went straight to bed after the evening patrol. This was in marked contrast to a future ace whose ambition was to overtake Ball one day: the Canadian Billy Bishop. Hearing that the short cut to a squadron at the front was as an observer, Bishop had volunteered. Undeterred by his experiences and injuries in the underpowered and unreliable RE7 and a subsequent grounding, he recovered to take a pilot's course under Garland and volunteer again for France, arriving to join 60 Squadron in March 1917. Like Ball an individualist, he differed in harbouring a personal vendetta against the enemy, perhaps because of what he had seen during his army cooperation work in the RE7. He revelled in spending seven hours or more in the air each day, and never seemed to tire: he was in his element. 'Far from affecting my nerves,' he wrote, 'each combat becomes more and more enjoyable.' And later: 'I had found the one thing I loved above all others. To me it was not a business or a profession but just a wonderful game.' Yet he resembled Ball in his aggression, his love of stalking alone, and in being no more than an averagely proficient pilot. He crashed so frequently while training that one of his instructors was heard to say: 'Get out of that bloody mess, Bishop, you ought to be flying a Harrod's bedstead!' But he was soon given a roving commission by Jack Scott, just as Ball had been. He also displayed qualities of leadership, and on 25 April he was promoted to flight commander.

If Bishop at 27 belied the theory that a scout pilot was too old at 25, a man in his thirtieth year, with defective eyesight, could hardly hope even to qualify as a pilot, let alone aspire to greatness. Yet this was the description that fitted Edward Mannock, a recent recruit to 40 Squadron (Nieuport 17 Scouts). Born, like McCudden, into a non-commissioned service environment but into a less stable family, Mannock knew deprivation as a child and had to take menial jobs on leaving school at 15. He later attained white-collar status but sacrificed it when he found office work depressed his spirit, becoming a telephone linesman. A cable-laying contract took him to Turkey, with good prospects, but when he realised in August 1914 that his work would benefit Turkey's ally Germany he downed tools. He was reviled and humiliated, and at the request of the Germans he was interned. Then, after breaking out of camp to get food for sick companions, he was punished with solitary confinement. When at length he was repatriated under an exchange of prisoners, he sought revenge.

Inspired by the exploits of Albert Ball, he applied for pilot training. 'You're too old,' he was told; but he had already made a study of the tactics of air combat, and he talked his way into a medical. An infection contracted in childhood had left permanent damage to one eye, but he is said to have kept the fault hidden by turning up early at his medical board and memorising the eye-test chart. Yet his colleagues have vouched for his exceptionally long sight.

Towards the end of his training, during which his maturity, leftist bias and half-Irish loquacity marked him out as a potential leader, he had the good fortune to be taught and befriended by McCudden, who by this time was working as a fighter instructor on an advanced pupils' course at Joyce Green. This was one of the first such courses. 'He was older than us', said a fellow pupil on his initial training course at Hounslow, 'and he was a thinker, and certainly no fool. Some of us learnt quite a lot from him on politics . . . Good chap, used to play the violin and sing mock opera with bogus Italian words . . . I never met him again. I got shot down, he became the ace of aces.' Thus when Mannock arrived in France in April 1917 to join 40 Squadron under Major Leonard Tilney, an Old Etonian who at 22 was eight years his junior and radiated the enthusiasm of youth, he was not quite the raw novice expected.

Indeed he was not what the squadron expected at all. An inch over six foot, with dark-brown hair and deep-set blue eyes, he was ten years older than most of them, yet as a new boy he was not expected to have opinions. In a community notorious for its studied reticence he talked, it was thought, too freely, and his self-educated, radical outlook irritated some. His intense hatred of the Germans, too, whatever the cause, was distasteful to men who were fighting a strictly impersonal war. In contrast, in his first few flights he showed no great eagerness to get to grips with the enemy. Unlike the boisterous Bishop, who went out of his way to seek action and gained almost immediate popularity with all ranks on 60 Squadron, Mannock met something approaching hostility.

Mannock was an idealist. He was fighting for social change as well as for military victory. But he was no rash, hot-headed youth. Too many novice pilots, he believed, were lost unnecessarily in their first weeks of combat. He had resolved on a cautious beginning. It was an attitude that was easily mistaken for cowardice. 'My feelings very funny,' he recorded after first crossing the lines, 'I had the wind up, I don't mind admitting.' He was still trembling after he landed, which did not go unnoticed. 'Now I can understand what a tremendous strain to the nervous system flying is.' Fear, then, was something to be reckoned with, something to be overcome.

Back with No. 10 Squadron at the chateau, Ewart Garland was getting his game of tennis again after patrols. But he was soon making nostalgic references in his diary to old friends wounded, missing, or killed. 'Poor old so-and-so,' 'Poor little so-and-so,' and so on. 'Directly we got back from the funeral,' went one entry, 'Bulmer and I went up . . .' On 26 April he noted: 'Someone in the squadron is brought down pretty well every day now.' But the 'playing fields' attitude amongst flyers, he believed, persisted, German pilots being referred to almost affectionately as 'the old Hun'. He found it interesting to talk to a couple of wounded Huns who had themselves been brought down: how did they feel? 'They were both only 19 years old, and said they had no desire to fight.' Nor , if it came to that, thought Garland, did he. He commented later: 'It seemed natural enough to me at the time, just turned 20, to refer to the German prisoners as "only 19"'.

On 28 April the infantry attack was renewed, with good communication at first between ground and air. But as soon as the enemy counter-attacked, the infantry, as before, stopped lighting flares, and reports from the air of their progress dried up. Meanwhile the enemy pilots, aided by low cloud, and concentrating on the weakest vessels, destroyed or severely damaged twelve corps machines, of which ten were BE's. Leading his flight, Ball shot down an Albatros two-seater, but this was an isolated riposte.

'Bloody April' rose to an awesome climax as the weather on the 29th improved and the air fighting intensified. The day began with a scrap between six grey Albatros scouts and an offensive patrol of three SE5's of 56 Squadron, led by flight commander C.M. 'Billy' Crowe, with Canadian Jack Leach and Maurice Kay in tow. FE2d's of 57 Squadron joined in, but lost one of their number almost at once, pilot and observer surviving to be taken prisoner. They were more than avenged when Leach got on the tail of an Albatros that was chasing Kay and set it blazing, the pilot, rather than waiting to be consumed in the fire, plummeting, arms and legs whirling, into space.

Leach had seen Kay flip into a spiral to escape the Albatros and had assumed he was safe. Sadly, there were to be no more letters home from the boyish Maurice Kay. The last act of the doomed Albatros pilot, unseen by Leach, had been to shoot him down.

At Vert Galand, Harvey-Kelly, commanding 19 Squadron, had been asked by Wing HQ to put up a Spad section to scout for Richthofen, who had been spotted leaving Douai. A and B flights were already out on offensive patrols, and there was no way of contacting them, so C Flight, which had just returned from an abortive dawn patrol under sub-leader W.N. Hamilton, was called upon. Hamilton's companions were to have been two young second-lieutenants named Applin and Harding, but the prospect of getting to grips with the Red Baron was too attractive for Harvey-Kelly to miss, and Harding was stood down. Then Applin was delayed, leaving Harvey-Kelly and Hamilton flying in tandem.

Richthofen, of course, was not alone, and soon his flight of six red Albatros scouts was sighted and joined by the remaining five grey ones. Reinforcement was on the way, too, for the Spads, Richard Applin having chased bravely after them and located them at 5,000 feet east of Douai.

When six naval Triplanes hove in sight, Harvey-Kelly, despite his lack of height and the odds against him, did not hesitate. Vigorous action could turn the tables: that was their best chance. And the

Major-General Sir David Henderson, Director-General of Military Aviation: according to Trenchard 'the true father of the Royal Air Force'.

an Henderson, MC (7 victories), son of ir David. He was killed in a flying ccident in June 1918.

Charles Smart and Jimmy Larkin first and second from the left, Hendry fourth, in front of an RE8. 'We now call ourselves the Circus.'

Alan Dore, 34, formerly a major in the Worcestershire Regiment, then observer, pilot and squadron commander in the RFC.

George Downing. Of his pilot he wrote: 'Guess I'd go anywhere with him . . . It was glorious sport!'

The youthfully enthusiastic Maurice Kay. 'Ball has done himself great credit . . . the excitement was terrific!'

P.B. 'Bruce' Prothero always flew in a kilt. 'You wouldna have me taken prisoner in disguise would you now laddie?'

They're giving the Ball another run.' Leaving or France, hatless as always, to join 6 Squadron, 7 April 1917.

No rash heroics for Jimmy McCudden. He stalked his prey, but could be content to fight another day.

P.G. Taylor (later Sir Gordon) with his air mechanics. For him, flying became a vocation, hence the knighthood.

Eric Routh (21) of 16 Squadron (BE's). 'Why was every ham-fisted pilot sent to me?'

2nd Lt R.F. Glazebrook, when a prisoner, witnessed how a dedicated German surgeon broke down when his young RFC patient died.

Oscar Greig. Rated his 37 days on FE2b's of 25 Squadron 'the most unpleasant of his service,' worse than his subsequent capture.

William Leefe Robinson, VC. First man to destroy a Zeppelin over Britain – but he suffered for it later as a prisoner.

Edward 'Mick' Mannock. 'He planned every attack like a chess player.'

W.A. 'Billy' Bishop. 'To me it was not a business but just a wonderful game.'

Starting on his 19th birthday, J.T.P. Jeyes developed a successful partnership, in RE8's, with an observer from his old school.

Arthur (later 'Bomber') Harris. 'With your favourite mechanic, you were just a team together.'

Gwilym H. Lewis (12 victories) in his SE5A. 'Everything is spoiled at the time by being so frightened.'

Arthur Rhys Davids (centre),
Keith Muspratt (left) and
Maxwell Coote (right).

All on this page flew with 56 Squadron, and, according to
McCudden, were 'as splendid a lot of fellows as ever set foot in
France'.

Leonard Barlow   Dick Maybery

Triplanes would be along in a moment. No sense in waiting for them: that would give the enemy time to think. He followed his golden rule: get your blow in first.

Going for the rearmost Albatros, he signalled for Hamilton to aim for the centre, a manoeuvre designed to prevent the leader attempting to gain a height advantage. Applin followed. But the odds were too great. Richthofen zoomed before diving on Applin, whose Spad exploded and broke up. He was Richthofen's 49th victim. Harvey-Kelly, too, was surrounded, his final executioner being the German ace Kurt Wolff. Only Hamilton, who was shot down by the Red Baron's younger brother Lothar, lived to tell the tale. Harvey-Kelly survived for three days but died in a German hospital.

The absence of any news of the three Spads and their pilots cast a gloom over Vert Galand. The loss of the lovable Harvey-Kelly, the first RFC man to land in France, severed one more link with the armada of August 1914.

Earlier that month H-K had told Trenchard that the current stock of German pilots were like 'floating meat', and it seems possible that he had reached the stage of over-confidence which was one of the most dangerous for experienced pilots. Trenchard might perhaps have divined this from the remark. But H-K had acted entirely in character. His expectations that the Triplanes would come to his aid were well founded, and at least one of the enemy formation was shot down. Later, Billy Bishop, escorting the FE's of 11 Squadron on photo reconnaissance, spotted one of the enemy scouts and dived on it out of the sun. Firing in bursts of three, he watched it go into a spin before bursting into flames. If this went some way towards avenging Harvey-Kelly, the afternoon, during which Richthofen recorded his 50th and 51st victims and completed five in one day, went, like the rest of April, overwhelmingly to the enemy.

Although Richthofen's Circus proper had not yet been formed, the four *Jastas* based at Douai, the 3rd, the 4th, the 11th and the 33rd, were combined on 30 April to form a single group, capable of operating *en masse*, and were promptly dubbed 'Richthofen's Circus' by the RFC. Simultaneously, smaller enemy scout formations sought targets at low level over the battle front, while two-seaters spotted for the German artillery and machine-gunned Allied trenches. 'Bloody April' thus ended with the future course of air fighting firmly delineated. But with Brisfit and SE5 pilots gaining in experience and confidence, and with the introduction of the Camel, together with the gradual replacement of the BE's by the RE8, the superiority the Germans had enjoyed that spring was at an end. Never again, even in the crisis months of 1918, was the RFC to be so afflicted or to suffer such casualties. These amounted, in April alone, to 151 machines brought down, as against 119 German, with 316 aircrew dead or missing. The dead included those who, although mortally wounded, regained the Allied lines.

The expectation of life of a newly-arrived pilot in April 1917 had fallen to seventeen days, and an accusing finger was inevitably pointed at Trenchard. Although he retained the unqualified support of Henderson and Brancker, and certainly of Haig, there were voices, both in Parliament and in the RFC hierarchy, which questioned his policy of aggression at all costs and asked whether his pursuit of it were not both obdurate and profligate. 'Is the work being done, even in wartime,' William Joynson-Hicks, MP for NW Manchester, wanted to know, 'at too great a sacrifice?' Harold Balfour, unnerved after being shot down and crashing into the lip of a crater on Vimy Ridge ('he is said to be temporarily "loony"', wrote Alan Dore), later dubbed Trenchard's policy 'aerial attrition', and wondered whether a little more subtlety might have reduced casualties and served the army just as well.

Sending 'untrained lads' over the lines was inexcusable on any grounds, in the judgement of Brigadier-General P.R.C. Groves, an energetic RFC staff officer who had distinguished himself in operations in the Middle East. 'It was a squandering of resources, especially in an aerial arm where efficiency and survival depend upon adequate skill.' Keeping formation, clearing gun jams quickly, outmanoeuvring the enemy, engaging him from the best angle, breaking off combat when necessary, knowing how and when to shoot – these were some of the essentials listed by Groves. But he was writing in retrospect. Of more immediate significance was the stand taken by Lionel Charlton, then serving in the Directorate of Military Aeronautics at the War Office – and the response of the brass hats to it. To Charlton, one of the RFC's original flight commanders and holding a DSO, to detail men for action in France when they could only just about fly, and knew nothing beyond that, seemed little short of murder, and he resolved to put his foot down. He made it a rule that no pilot should be sent to France who could not satisfy him or one of his assistants that he was qualified in every possible way. Translating this resolve into action on the spot, he cancelled the posting of three youths who were patently undertrained. Despite his seniority, in less than half an hour he had been overruled – presumably by Henderson, under pressure from France.

A strong supporter of Trenchard was Jack Slessor, then a flight commander on 5 Squadron. He applauded him for not reverting to the defensive, despite intense pressure, thus avoiding the mistake made by the French at Verdun. 'The essential point', wrote Slessor, 'is that the requirements of the army in reconnaissance, photography and artillery cooperation must always be met.' Although the Germans had air superiority they had been hotly engaged east of the line over their own aerodromes, and Slessor knew of no instance of a photograph being required and not being obtained, or of a shoot being left undone, despite continual harassment from enemy machines. This was a proud boast, but it cost many lives. And having said all that, Slessor still suspected that some of the most arduous and hazardous work, such as photography, which always drew fierce opposition from the Germans because they knew its importance, was superfluous, and that cover twice a week was all that was strictly necessary.

Fred Winterbotham (who later made his mark in Military Intelligence), joined 29 Squadron (Nieuports) under Major H.V. Champion de Crespigny that April and noted that pilots were arriving and disappearing daily. But he did not blame Trenchard. 'The RFC was of course subject to orders from Army Command, who seemed blithely unmindful of the tremendous losses of highly trained pilots and valuable aircraft which the air photography entailed, and which the Germans were anxious we should not carry out.'

Inevitably there were mutterings within the squadrons against

[49]

Trenchard, but he still inspired a fierce loyalty amongst his crews. One of his youngest pilots, 18-year-old Bertram Wood, another recent arrival on 29 Squadron, wrote on 8 April: 'It does make me wild to see articles in the papers running down our Flying Corps on account of the casualties. If you only knew the work we do compared with the Hun, you would realise how ridiculous this is.' Bert Wood, or 'Woodie', of Grimsby, whose lucky mascot, a Lincoln Imp, adorned an inter-plane strut of his Nieuport, had quickly absorbed the ambience of sympathy with the infantryman which informed all RFC thought. Despite his fair-skinned, almost effeminate good looks, and his aura of aestheticism as the naturalist and poet he was, he proved a dashing and skilful pilot and a brilliant patrol leader, credited with eighteen victories after three months in France, with an MC for his air fighting and a Bar for his low-level strafing. A career which must surely have led to even greater honours was later cut tragically short in a flying accident while he was engaged in the air defence of London. He had left his lucky mascot on his machine in France, where it survived.

Trenchard, in his own defence, could point to his continual pleadings and warnings of lack of resources throughout the second half of 1916, and again in 1917, of which the last had been a mixture of recrimination and despair. 'You are asking me,' he had told the Air Board, 'to fight the battle this year [1917] with the same machines I fought it with last year. We shall be hopelessly outclassed.' Nothing could have been clearer than this. He had continued: 'Something must be done. I am not panicking, but the Hun is getting more aggressive. I warned you firmly as far back as last September, and the Chief [Douglas Haig] warned you in November, and I warned the Air Board personally on 12 December. All I can say is there will be an outcry from all the pilots out here if we do not have at least these few squadrons of fast machines I have asked for as absolutely necessary.'

The Air Board, set up on 11 May 1916 under Lord Curzon, a former Viceroy of India and a member of the inner Cabinet, was seen as a forerunner of an Air Ministry. It had naval, military and Parliamentary representatives but no executive powers. It had since been strengthened and reconstituted under Lord Cowdray, and it now included: Godfrey Paine, the Fifth Sea Lord, first commandant of the Central Flying School and one of the earliest of naval flyers; Sir David Henderson, Director-General of Military Aeronautics; William Weir, Controller of Aeronautical Supplies; and Percy Martin, Controller of Petrol Engines; with Major J.L. Baird as Parliamentary Secretary. It functioned principally as a Ministry of Supply, helping to eliminate competition between the two services, but it was many months before its efforts were reflected in France, and meanwhile the supply position remained acute.

It was at the December 1916 meeting of the Air Board, which Trenchard attended, that the Admiralty had agreed to lend four additional naval squadrons to the RFC 'at this moment of great emergency'. They were to prove invaluable, but they were not enough. All Trenchard could do was brace himself for the inevitable casualties. They had to be expected, and they had to be ignored. The 150,000 casualties suffered in the Arras battle by the army were more than enough justification. No sacrifices were too much for these men.

For the RFC, one of the most poignant losses in the ground battle was that of the massive figure of Colonel C.J. Burke, of the Royal Irish Regiment, known to every participant in the Channel crossing of August 1914, which he had led (although pipped on the post by Harvey-Kelly), as 'Pregnant Percy'. Promoted beyond routine operational flying, and hearing that the Royal Irish were short of officers, Burke had insisted, in the summer of 1916, on returning to his regiment. He was killed leading his men on the first day of the Arras offensive, 9 April 1917.

PARCELS FOR PRISONERS

T HE puritanical disdain of Bob Smith-Barry for anyone he suspected of making preparations against possible capture was generally regarded as idiosyncratic. Most men took a more fatalistic view. But Smith-B, or S-B, as he was commonly known, having borrowed a machine from one of his flight commanders, had been scandalised to find a package neatly stowed in the cockpit containing all manner of comforts, from silk pyjamas to cigarettes. 'One of my pilots is preparing to be a prisoner!' he had exclaimed, and he had scattered the contents of the package irascibly across the sward. But on most squadrons, crews carried an irreducible minimum of razor, toothbrush, soap, and a wallet of francs.

On a long-distance bomber squadron towards the end of the war, Willie Read had a batman who volunteered to become proficient on the Lewis gun solely to accompany and succour his 'gentleman' on bombing raids. A valet in peacetime, he always went aboard with a little suitcase 'in case we land the other side, sir.' Food and drink while airborne and something extra for emergencies seemed no more than prudent husbandry.

Spartan if not harsh conditions were expected in captivity, but the initial greeting was often surprisingly friendly, especially when aerial adversaries met on the ground. One of the crew of an 18 Squadron two-seater bomber badly shot up over Bruges was observer-turned-pilot Robert Ingram; he managed to land on the beach at Ostend. 'For three days we were the guests of a German squadron and were extraordinarily well treated. It has come as a great surprise.' One of the German pilots turned out to be an ex-Dulwich schoolboy and a graduate of Merton College, Oxford, and he offered to drop letters from Ingram over the lines, addressed to his CO and his girl friend. They got the letters. But a Belgian who saluted him on his way into captivity was 'very badly roughed up by the Germans'.

Maurice Marcus Kaye, also of 18 Squadron, was pulled out of his burning FE2b by his observer, Sergeant F. Russell, although both had been quite badly wounded. They had been escorting a photographic machine west of Cambrai. While Russell, as was customary, was whisked away separately, Kaye found himself being driven to hospital in the company of the man who claimed to have shot him down, one Wolter Niesen.

Niesen kept calling to the driver, '*Langsam, langsam*', to spare Kaye's injuries on the bumpy road. Grateful though he was for this consideration, Kaye soon realised that Niesen had a more selfish motive: he wanted Kaye to sign a statement that it was he, Niesen, who had brought him down. Kaye obliged, only to discover, much later, that he had been Niesen's first and only victory, and that his signature would qualify Niesen for the coveted *Ehrenbecher* or cup of honour. But thanks to Niesen and a German surgeon – and not least, in the first place, to observer Russell – Kaye's life was saved. 'In POW camp the Germans were strict but they treated us with respect,' recorded Kaye, 'and we got our [Red Cross] parcels.' Segregation between prisoners by rank meant that Kaye never saw his rescuer again.

Arthur Whitten Brown, shot down near Aachen with his pilot Harold Medlicott, was completely incapacitated by his injuries, until a series of operations, eight in all, set him on the road to rehabilitation. 'I have been in three hospitals,' he wrote, 'and received the kindest treatment and consideration.' Both men had made contingency plans for escape; Medlicott was later shot dead in the attempt. Brown's post-war achievement with John Alcock in making the first direct air crossing of the Atlantic in 1919 is commemorated in a statue at Heathrow.

Second-Lieutenant J.E.P. Howey, one of several observers who got their machine down safely on the German side after their pilot had been killed, said of his captors: 'They were all as kind as possible.' He was taken to the Mess, his damaged ankle was put in a splint, and he was given food, drink and a smoke. One of the pilots who shot him down landed nearby, shook him by the hand, and cheered him up by assuring him he had had no chance.

Canadian test pilot Ben Lefroy, after transferring to a squadron, crashed in no man's land and lay there unconscious, a target for both sides. When he came to, a German was bending over him. 'Can I have a cigarette?' asked the German. After rummaging in Lefroy's pockets he pulled out a silver cigarette case, took one for himself, gave Lefroy one, lit both, then closed the case and put it back in the Canadian's pocket. His rummaging had disclosed Lefroy's identity. 'I bet you wish you were in Vancouver now.'

The first responsibility, on being shot down, was to destroy the machine, using the incendiary torch always carried. Lieutenant G.W. Armstrong, intercepted by six scouts during a bombing raid on Roulers, was shot down despite the spirited return fire of his observer, Hubert Pugh-Evans, who kept firing until they actually hit the ground. The crash-landing was successful until the machine ran into a ditch, which turned them over. As with Eric Routh, the German pilots continued firing on them throughout, 'churning up the ground on all sides like a plough'. Armstrong was trapped but Pugh-Evans got him out, and between them, with German soldiers running towards them, they set fire to their BE2c.

Edward Pennell, earlier a pioneer pigeon dropper when he was working with agents in 1915, and now flying a Martinsyde of 27 Squadron, bombed the railway junction at Hirson from 1500 feet, climbed back to 14,000, and then had mechanical trouble and lost height alarmingly. After nursing his engine as best he could he force-landed alongside a wood, which he judged was on the Allied side of the lines. To his horror he saw a gaggle of troops, patently German, emerging from the wood. With his torch inaccessible, he set fire to his fuel tank with revolver and Very pistol, under the noses of the Germans, who watched the blaze apathetically. Then from the wood came a second group, whom Pennell recognised as *poilus*. He had landed on the right side after all! The Germans, dumbly indifferent, were the prisoners of the French.

'My lovely plane,' he moaned, 'which I had burnt! I felt like weeping!' 'Biffy' Borton, his monocled squadron commander, was almost choleric – until Pennell suggested he might have done the same in similar circumstances, to which Borton had to agree.

Second-Lieutenant E.L. Edwards, an observer on 43 Squadron, shot down in a 1½-strutter on a photo recce after his guns had jammed, was immediately surrounded by enemy infantry; neither he nor his pilot had any chance to burn their machine. But they steadfastly refused to answer any questions about their role. For this they suffered a period of solitary confinement. Indeed the obdurate Edwards resolved to make life as difficult as he could for his captors, and later he was awarded 108 days' solitary for disobeying an order and insulting the commandant. He was repatriated after the war.

Interrogation on capture could be searching, accompanied by threats, and it wasn't unusual for a prisoner to get fourteen days' solitary for giving unreliable information. Few prisoners could tell the Germans much anyway, because they knew so little themselves.

Harold Tambling, a Cornishman whose father was an Admiralty overseer on the Clyde, wrote, after his capture, to a Glasgow firm of outfitters with a list of requirements that included shirts, collars, underwear, socks, gloves, pyjamas, towels, and silk ties. The manager thanked him for his order and said he was sending the goods by parcel post in two packages. 'You'll notice prices have increased a little, but the quality is keeping up the old standard. Things are going on here much as usual, business is very good with everyone.' The men in the trenches would surely have read this with incredulity. The packages duly arrived.

Second-Lieutenant H.C. Wookey, a Brisfit pilot in 11 Squadron, shot down near Cambrai in October 1917, was court-martialled and sent to a criminal prison, his crime being to have carried propaganda leaflets, which the Germans declared to be illegal. This was, perhaps, an indication of the effectiveness of this type of warfare, so often ridiculed. Eventually the British Government, after threatening reprisals, effected his release, and he followed the usual route via Brussels and Karlsruhe to Holzminden. To avoid further such incidents, the practice was abandoned, the prevailing wind being utilised to carry these leaflets into enemy territory by balloon.

Lancastrian Sidney Attwater, whose exploits with posthumous VC winner Tom Mottershead are recorded elsewhere,[1] had no chance when, on a dawn photo recce in an FE2b, with an aircraftman second class named Leigh whom he knew as a good gunner, he met the Richthofen Circus. 'Leigh got one down,' said Attwater afterwards, 'and so did I, but there were no clouds to hide in.' The next thing he remembered, some German girls were giving him a drink. When he looked round for his gunner, he 'saw the old bus burning like mad.'

It was a relief when he spotted Leigh. His face was badly gashed and one eye looked damaged beyond repair; but otherwise he appeared to be in one piece. The area was packed with Germans, who marched them off. As a POW, according to Attwater, he 'had a pretty rough time'.

A prisoner who had an even rougher time was Lieutenant A.D.G. 'Grey' Alderson, of 3 Squadron. Shot down in March 1918 and seriously wounded, he was plied, when barely conscious, with questions he couldn't answer. Eventually the interrogation officer gave him a pen and a postcard, to write a message home. With great difficulty he managed to scrawl: 'I have been captured by the Huns, will write, Love, Grey.' When the interrogator returned an hour later, Alderson was told he was going to be court-martialled.

Orderlies came in and arranged a table and chairs in the centre of the ward, and he was guarded by two sentries instead of one, both fondling fixed bayonets. What could he possibly have done? A stamping of feet and a clanking of swords heralded the arrival of a German general and his staff. After the charge had been recited in German

1. *The Royal Flying Corps in France: from Mons to the Somme* (Constable, 1994).

it was translated by the interrogation officer. Alderson had insulted His Imperial Highness Kaiser Wilhelm II by his use of the term Hun.

The bemused Alderson was quite unable to follow the proceedings, no notice was taken when he tried to protest that he had intended no insult, and eventually he lapsed into a coma. Suddenly the general, in a frenzy of rage at his apparent indifference, strode over to his bed, called him a *schweinhund*, tore the postcard into fragments, and threw them in his face.

Alderson's worst deprivation was that they had confiscated his pipe. Transferred to a hospital in Douai, he was subjected to excruciating pain in the wagon, which was callously driven, he believed deliberately. His wounds had not been treated, and he feared they would fester. But in Douai Hospital a nurse spoke to him with transparent kindness in perfect English. She talked of happier days when she had been at school in England; she had only returned to Germany from a sense of duty just prior to the outbreak of war. Alderson was the only prisoner in the hospital; all the others were wounded German soldiers. They called him *der flieger*, treated him as one of themselves, and shared their food parcels with him.

Still he received no treatment. But the nurse was engaged to the senior surgeon in the hospital, and she pleaded with him to do what he could to save Alderson's life. An immediate operation was performed, and he recovered.

An even more critical operation, on a wounded patient who looked and was no more than a boy, this time in a prison camp hospital, was not so successful, despite the most devoted attentions of the German surgeon. The story was told forty years later by the man who had been in the next bed, formerly Second Lieutenant R.F. Glazebrook, who, like so many others of his time, had hitherto resolved not to inflict his war experiences on his family. 'I will never forget the German doctor bursting into tears when his patient died,' he recalled, 'and how he cursed the warring nations for sending their children to war.'

*   *   *

Perhaps the most famous British prisoner was William Leefe Robinson, and it seems that he was made to suffer for it. He had been responsible for the death of a German hero in the airship commander Herbert Schramm. He planned escape from the beginning, his attempts landing him in solitary confinement. Transferred to camps where security was stricter, he ended up in Holzminden, where he was harried and even persecuted. He became the focus of the malevolence of a notorious camp commandant in Karl Niemeyer, who is said to have used every instrument of cruelty against him short of physical violence. Robinson got home safely a month after the armistice, but in his weakened state he succumbed to the influenza virus which claimed millions of lives immediately after the war, 150,000 in the United Kingdom alone.

The contrast between Harold Tambling and his Glaswegian gents' outfitter, and the harsher treatment meted out in camps under men like Niemeyer, was stark. And as the Germans themselves felt the stranglehold of the blockade, conditions in the camps deteriorated. Ewart Garland, by then back on a bomber squadron, was one who realised, by the end of the war, that he had badly misjudged the conditions in these camps. 'I was soon engaged in picking up Allied POWs straggling and staggering along the roads a few days after the armistice. Many died of exhaustion and all were skeletons.'

These men still had to face a final interrogation by MI9 on their return to the UK: they had to show that their capture was genuine, that they had not wantonly given themselves up. From this it can be inferred that there were some who did. If anything discreditable was unearthed, the perpetrators were sent for short sharp shock correction at a so-called Patriotic School.

It was not until 28 July 1919 that Harold Tambling was 'presented with the compliments of the authorities', the writer, loftily impersonal, being 'commanded by the Air Council to inform him that his statement regarding the circumstances of his capture by the enemy having been investigated, the Council considers that no blame attaches to him in the matter.'

For men like Harold Tambling, after months of airborne hazard and years of incarceration, this could only come as an affront.

CHARLES SMART AND ALAN DORE;
VON RICHTHOFEN THE UNSURPASSED;
MANNOCK REHABILITATED;
'REMEMBER BALL'

J UST as the RFC could only function in France under the protection of the ground forces, so the army itself depended on a secure home base; and this security had come under increasing threat from Germany's espousal of unrestricted submarine warfare. Starting with a modest pre-war force of some twenty U-boats, the Germans, on the outbreak of war, had begun an urgent construction programme, and by early 1917 they had built up a sizeable fleet. From 31 January, one outgoing British and Allied ship out of every four leaving the UK was doomed never to return, while the crews of American and other neutral ships were refusing to sail to British ports. A million tons of Allied shipping was sunk in the month of April alone, a rate which spelt defeat if it were allowed to continue. But with the introduction of the convoy system in June 1917, long resisted by the Admiralty because of their strategic preference for offensive rather than defensive measures, and with the help of new anti-submarine techniques, backed up by intensive RNAS patrols, losses were dramatically reduced. A shortage of escort vessels weakened the new system at first, and it was not until the end of the year that it became fully effective, but eventually, with the growing support of the American Navy, maximum protection was given. Soon new ship construction was keeping pace with losses, and before the year was out the Allies were sinking U-boats faster than Germany could build them. But in May 1917, as Haig and his army commanders, complemented by Trenchard, planned for an Allied summer offensive that must inevitably be dominated by the British, the outcome of the war at sea, and therefore the security of the BEF in France, was still in doubt.

Haig's plan, which had been gestating for many months, aimed to end the stalemate on the Western Front by breaking out of the Ypres salient, capturing the high ground on the eastern flank, and, by advancing north to take the Flemish ports of Ostend and Zeebrugge, denying them to the U-boats. He would then be poised to drive the Germans out of Belgium. Meanwhile, to divert attention from his preparations in Flanders and from the French collapse, and to buy time while the French recovered, he renewed his action on the Arras front. Trenchard too was working on proposals for the redistribution of his forces for the summer offensive, but the RFC likewise was still deeply involved around Arras. Although there were factors which fostered genuine hope for improvement – the new machines and their air and ground crews were rapidly acclimatising – the lowering skies of April did not immediately dissolve into a sunlit May.

One man who could attest to this was Sergeant-Observer H.G. Taylor of 25 Squadron, the man whose first reconnaissance sketch had been described as 'bloody marvellous' by Oscar Greig. Formerly a machine-gunner on the Somme, where he had faced death every second, not knowing when it might come, he was grateful for the stand-down periods when he could count at least on a few more hours to live. Returning from leave on 1 May to be met by a host of new faces, replacements for those killed or missing in his absence, he found that his best friend on the squadron, an observer like himself, had died from his wounds after a raid the previous day and that he was to act as a pall-bearer that morning at his funeral. Furthermore, he was to take the dead man's place as observer to a Lieutenant Berry King, a Jamaican, aged twenty-six; King had somehow escaped injury and was to be given no rest. It was a further shock, though, to be briefed that same afternoon to take off on a bombing raid with King that evening in a formation of six FE2b's.

Standing up in the open cockpit of the pusher, facing the tail,

where attack generally originated, held no terrors for Taylor, for all
its apparent insecurity: he felt perfectly at home. Their target was
an ammunition dump, and they had dropped their bombs and were
on their way home when they sighted a formation of nine Albatros
scouts, with two other hostiles in attendance. Three of the Albatris
immediately dived on Taylor's machine and within seconds he had
stopped a succession of bullets which 'blew one thigh to pieces and
paralysed one arm'. Bullets were brushing his hair, his gun was
smashed, and their fuel tank was pierced, blowing petrol all over the
nacelle. By this time Taylor was slumped on the cockpit floor, bleed-
ing profusely. Then came oblivion. He did not know it, but his
principal assailant had been the German ace Kurt Wolff, the con-
queror of Harvey-Kelly. The shock of hitting the ground revived him
briefly: they had crash-landed on Arras racecourse, and somehow
King had again escaped injury.

Losing consciousness again, Taylor woke up on a stretcher
amongst masses of wounded infantrymen on the floor of Arras
Cathedral, which was doing duty as a casualty clearing station. The
only way the surgeons could save his leg was to leave it permanently
stiffened, and pieces of bullet were still being removed from his thigh
fifteen years later. In his old age the leg was amputated.

There was still no rest for Jamaican-born Berry King: he was airborne again forty-eight hours later, accompanied by his third
observer in five days, named as 'Trumpeter Lawrence', which suggests that volunteers had been called for to fill the gaps. If so, it
was first time unlucky for 29-year-old James Lawrence, of Cupar,
Fifeshire, and third time unlucky for King. Returning from a similar
raid on the same target, they had no chance when their machine
caught fire and nose-dived out of control.

Charles Smart, also back from leave, was sent to St Omer to learn
to fly RE8's, a move to which he strongly objected. 'No end of
experienced pilots have killed themselves on their first trip in these
machines.' And of his conversion training he was similarly dismissive.
'The course of instruction consisted of a three-minute lecture from
a man who stuttered and a seven-minute flight as a passenger ... I
cannot say I like the machine, it is much too heavy and cumbersome,

more like a flying steamroller than an aeroplane.' But he was not so prejudiced as to fail to appreciate its speed advantage – 105 m.p.h. against the 90 m.p.h. plod of the BE2e.

The renewal of the infantry attack, scheduled for 3 May, was preceded by intensive air cooperation with the artillery, accompanied by the bombing of aerodromes and other military targets by Martinsydes, DH4's and FE's, the latter bombing by night as well as by day. There was also a pre-planned assault on enemy kite balloons. While the artillery put down an extra-special barrage on the German trenches, Nieuport pilots of 40 Squadron began a hedge-hopping approach to the balloons, surprising the winch crews before they could haul the balloons down. Eight balloons were caught out by the ruse, four were destroyed and the remainder damaged, without loss to the Nieuports, although many were hit.

Despite clear skies, bomber and corps crews alike reported less opposition than previously, partly because of a change in enemy tactics, which concentrated their fighters into massed formations at set times, generally morning and evening, leaving periods of comparative inactivity of which advantage was taken. Another factor was the departure from the front on 1 May of Manfred von Richthofen. Postcard portraits of him were being circulated throughout Germany, newspapers featured his exploits, and wherever he went he was mobbed. He had become a propaganda pawn, his name a byword, and the German High Command may well have felt that his loss would be a staggering blow to morale. In any case the landmark of 50 victories called for some gesture, and they prevailed upon him to cooperate in producing a book on his exploits.

Representations of Richthofen as a cold, calculating killer who exposed himself to as little personal danger as possible, selecting easy prey while leading strong formations that amounted to a personal bodyguard, fail to give him proper credit for professionalism. No doubt compared with Mannock, who generously passed opportunities (or the credit) to underlings when he himself had enemies at his mercy, he was vain and acquisitive. He is said to have been jealous even of the success of his younger brother Lothar, though 'even' may be redundant here, since jealousy between brothers is not uncommon.

But however that may be, in the context of the battle he was fighting, the elder Richthofen was unsurpassed. He combined the hunter's instinct with the alertness of the hunted.

The German Air Force was generally outnumbered, hence the need for economy. Its pilots scrapped only when they had the advantage, and preferred, as Richthofen himself had put it, to 'let the customer come to the shop'. All the great RFC patrol leaders stressed the importance of seeking the advantage before attacking, and of not being ashamed to live to fight another day. Also, as the fighting progressed, they concluded that the initiative in any attack must always lie with the flight leader. Formation-keeping during combat, rather than individual pursuit of targets, was mandatory. 'The natural consequence of this order', as Sholto Douglas later observed, 'was that it was usually the flight commander who shot down the enemy machine.' As the formation leader he was usually the most capable, and with his flight behind him to protect him he could concentrate on the job in hand. This, in simple terms, was Richthofen's method, but it did mean that his absence left a bigger gap than that of the average patrol leader. Lothar, whom he left in charge, was possibly the greedier killer (he was already credited with twenty victims), but his devil-may-care temperament was less suited to the group philosophy.

Manfred's flamboyant arrogance and apparent immunity might be resented, but the painting of the machines of his *Jasta* bright red, and the variety of patterns and hues of other *Jastas*, had a definite psychological effect. 'A good deal of harm was done', wrote Slessor, 'by pilots returned wounded or time expired to the UK, nerves not at their best, talking wildly about the famous Red Albatros circus and their deeds.' As with the Fokker Scourge two years earlier, new pilots arrived with an exaggerated fear of the enemy. The circus would rarely attack, in Slessor's experience, except in superior numbers, and even a well-handled RE8, with its gunner swivelling a Lewis in the rear seat, could cause a formation to break off. Nevertheless the techniques adopted by Richthofen, other things being equal, became standard in the Allied air forces. Only McCudden, and later Mannock and one or two others, could compare with him.

[63]

This is not to devalue the inspirational aggression of men like Bishop and Ball. In a force whose ethos it was to take and maintain the offensive they were an essential part, as confirmed by the new pilots on 56 Squadron, who, like the unfortunate Maurice Kay, responded eagerly to Ball's leadership. 'Captain Ball is surpassing his previous efforts and has already accounted for six Huns off his own bat,' wrote a young pilot named Roger Musters. 'He came back the other day with a huge hole right through the tail of his machine. He got out and immediately got into another machine and was off again. He really is a marvel.'

On the evening of 2 May, when twenty-five RFC scouts went out to seek their German counterparts over Douai, most of the individual combats were indecisive, but Ball shot down an Albatros two-seater and watched it crash. It put him ahead of Guynemer, with thirty-eight victims, and that night Trenchard visited Vert Galand to congratulate him. The feat was riotously celebrated in the Mess that night; but Trenchard was alarmed by Ball's expression of utter fatigue, and he feared he was burning himself out.

'Would you like two weeks in England?'

Ball shook his head. There was work to be done, and at least he would stay until his allotted month was up. The party that followed helped to revive his spirits, and soon he was back at the top of his form. 'Everyone is very pleased,' he told his Land Army girl-friend Bobs. 'I am now one in front of the Frenchman . . . Just longing to be with you again, and when I have made my total 40 I will come. I have only two more to get.' This was on 3 May. Four days to go.

The infantry attack that began that morning was fully prepared for the tactics of counter-attack that both sides now favoured, based on lessons learned in the Somme battles, and this led to suitable RFC squadrons being employed in a new role. They were to scour the ground from low level in advance of positions taken in the initial assault and report any obvious enemy concentrations to the artillery. But with both sides employing similar tactics the battlefield became too chaotic for lucid description, though there were exceptions, notably among observers in the 1½-strutters of 43 Squadron. They spotted enemy troops massing for a counter-attack on Oppy, taken that morning but hidden from the artillery by the Vimy Ridge – and were rewarded for their vigilance by being ordered to go out and stop them.

The Sopwith 1½-strutter was already obsolescent, being outclassed above 10,000 feet by the new German scouts, but it was useful at low level, and by increasing the size of their formations from three to five, closing up, and improving their shooting, they had some success in their new role. They were described by Alan Dore, also returned from leave, as 'the tanks of the air'. 'At 11 o'clock we learn that Huns are massing at Mauville Farm. Flying low I cross at 1,500 feet with a missing engine. At Neovireuil I dive to 600 feet and fire with front guns at Huns. I can see into the trenches and village. Dare not go lower. Engine hardly takes me over the ridge. My other four machines do finely.' Unimpeded by engine trouble, they fired their guns from between 50 and 300 feet. 'Other low-flying attacks on isolated bodies of men', notes the official history, 'were made by the same squadron in the afternoon.'

Another man in his thirties, Charles Smart, still for the moment flying a BE2e, with the faithful Hendry (now awarded an MC) as observer, also found himself over Oppy, on a contact patrol. 'We had to go up and fly amongst the shell barrage and spot our infantry flares to see where they had got to. The shell fire was simply terrible.' A heavy ground mist and the smoke from bursting shells forced them down to 900 feet in order to see. 'Shells were whipping through the air in thousands, bumping us about all over the place.' Nevertheless they marked the position of one of the flares and dropped a message over Division Headquarters before returning to the lines. 'Just as we got over Oppy we got an awful bump and a crack, one of our own shells carried away the right lower wing-tip leaving it hanging in shreds of canvas and wood. I thought all was up but found I could still fly the machine by keeping the stick right over on the left-hand side.' With gentle handling Smart managed to crawl back to his aerodrome and land. 'This is the worst trip I have had up to now and I feel more than a bit shaken.'

He didn't expect to be flying again that day – but was told to take up two observers one by one in an RE8 to give them the feel of the gun position. 'Orders are orders so I had to go up.' Next day he began his new career in RE8's by acting as escort to a machine on photography. He had done his sixty-first and last show – and very nearly his last show of all – on BE's. Two-thirds of these had been with Hendry. He was getting adjusted to the new machine and noted: 'RE's do climb fairly well, we got to 8,500 feet in twenty minutes.'

'The fine weather continues,' noted Dore on 4 May, 'and gives us all a great amount of work.' Enemy activity, too, increased, and Ball shot down an Albatros two-seater. Flying was curtailed on the 5th, partly because of thunderstorms and partly to give the crews a rest, but it did not stop Ball going out in his SE5 at six o'clock that evening. Crossing the lines at 8,000 feet, he spotted two Albatros DIII scouts 1,000 feet above him, heading across his path. Climbing to get above and in front of them, he deliberately exposed his tail to tempt them, and the Germans accepted the bait. By timing his next manoeuvre, a steepling figure of eight, to a nicety, Ball turned the tables on them completely, getting underneath one of the surprised enemy pilots and pulling down his Lewis. While he was changing a drum the German spun away, but Ball rapidly overtook him, and with bursts from both Vickers and Lewis at point-blank range sent him spiralling down.

Now he had to cope with the pilot of the second Albatros, who had closed in and started firing. So determined was the German to avenge his comrade that he was developing a head-on attack which threatened the end for both men. With the Hun hurtling straight at him, Ball held his ground, firing his Vickers, yet still the Hun came on. As the two machines closed, Ball sat there as though paralysed, his thumb frozen on the gun-button. A week ago his sense of preservation would have saved him. Now it was blunted.

The shattering, mutilating shock of the inevitable collision was something his senses seemed to absorb. He was awaiting the long spiral into oblivion when he found he was sailing on with reduced velocity into an empty sky. The collision had taken place solely in his imagination. At the penultimate moment he had shot the German down.

He descended to 3,000 feet to get his bearings, and there beneath him, not 400 yards apart, were the mangled wrecks of the two machines whose pilots had set out to destroy him. 'Flushed in face, his eyes brilliant, his hair blown and dishevelled,' wrote the recording officer afterwards, 'he came to the squadron office to make his report.' He was so overwrought that he found dictation impossible, and for a long time all he could do was mutter incoherently. 'God is very good to me . . . I was certain the Hun meant to ram me . . . God must have me in his keeping.' It was midnight before he could sleep, and he was up again at four, but mercifully the weather was bad and he was able to busy himself in his garden.

The squadron went on an offensive patrol that evening, and Ball went with them, but he had chosen to fly in his Nieuport, and he could not keep up with the SE5's. Yet he took on four red Albatros scouts over Douai, dived straight into them with his customary verve, broke up the formation, and shot down one of them, watching it crash near a cross-roads. The others recognised his red spinner and made off.

Earlier that day, 6 May, the commander of 9th Wing, Cyril Newall, had called for a full report from Blomfield on all Ball had done with 56 Squadron. This was to include: his combat reports; what other pilots had seen him do; the condition of his machine on returning; any confirmation of machines destroyed; and any other points Blomfield might think of. The request arrived on 7 May, Ball's thirty-first and last day in France, if the month was to be adhered to. Although Trenchard's offer, on 2 May, of two weeks in England is hard to reconcile with a fixed stay of one month, it seems likely that Newall had it in mind to relieve Ball and that he was seeking material on which to put him up for a further award. Since he already had a triple DSO and the MC, the award in prospect must surely have been the VC. Many people were asking why the award hadn't been made already.

Mannock, with two other pilots of 40 Squadron, had his first scrap with a Hun early that morning, 7 May. Between them they drove an intruder off, but it was only a decoy: lying in wait were the scarlet scouts of Richthofen's *Jasta 11*. Mannock did as much as anyone to shake them off, but he got separated from the others, and he was the last to return. His colleagues feared he must have gone down and they had time to reflect that he had fought his corner, and to regret their coolness towards him. Thus when he landed he was greeted with unaccustomed warmth. All was forgiven and he was 'Mick' to them now. Then at nine o'clock that same morning seven pilots of 40 Squadron, Mannock among them, took off in an attempt to repeat their balloon-strafing success of five days' earlier. As before, an artillery barrage was put down on adjacent enemy trenches and the Nieuports hedge-hopped to the lines. This time, with surprise less likely to be achieved, four more Nieuports were briefed to patrol overhead while twelve naval triplanes gave top cover.

Leading the attack was a new flight commander with a reputation for pugnacity, W.E. Nixon, himself only twenty. At a colourful briefing he directed each of his pilots on to individual balloons. Mannock's target was on the extreme left of the line, where the enemy fire was even fiercer than before, and Mannock found himself peering through an inferno of tracer as he raced towards his target. Holding his fire, he was convinced that if his engine kept going he couldn't miss. After emptying an entire drum from his Lewis he pulled up over the top and saw his balloon writhe before spurting smoke and flame. Ducking his head below the cockpit coaming, he rammed the throttle open and headed for home.

All the strafing pilots sustained damage to their machines and all wrecked them in forced landings or crashed them back at base except Mannock, who somehow achieved a smooth landing. But when his rigger showed him the damage to his plane he shuddered. In his diary he wrote: 'I don't want to go through such an experience again.' He was shocked, too, when he learned that Nixon, trying to divert an attack by German scouts, had been shot down, a victim of Lothar von Richthofen. But Mannock had had a good day.

The habit of the German scouts based at Douai of patrolling in strength morning and evening issued an implicit challenge to the SE5's, and in the absence of the Red Baron – which was known – planned interceptions were encouraged by Wing HQ. A morning patrol on 7 May failed to make contact, but that evening ten SE5's of 56 Squadron, with six Spads of 19 Squadron, tried again. Also airborne in the vicinity were a few Pups and naval Triplanes. One of the SE5 pilots was Cecil Lewis, and he described vividly the tall voluminous peaks of thunder-cloud, fraught with valleys and ravines, that they were obliged to thread their way through. In these conditions it was impossible to keep together, and when Ball, leading the SE5's, sighted the scarlet wings of *Jasta 11* and urged his pilots into action, his three flights, chocolate-coloured in contrast, became separated, while all but one of the Spad pilots lost touch completely. An eerie light, bilious in the west but darkening in the east, pervaded the scene, and visibility was worsening. Soon it began to rain. Nevertheless the skirmishing was bitter and there were losses on both sides. One such was Roger Musters, the young man who had written so enthusiastically that Ball was 'a marvel'. The remaining SE5's reformed over Arras, where another dog-fight started.

Ball emerged safely from the resultant mêlée and fired another attack signal which glowed brilliantly in the gathering dusk. Then he chased a red Albatros into cloud. Almost certainly the pilot was Lothar von Richthofen. Flight commander Billy Crowe, of 56, spotted them and followed Ball into the cloud. When he came out on the far side, both Albatros and SE5 had vanished.

That the two met in combat seems certain, and that they could have shot each other down more or less simultaneously is feasible. Lothar is known to have force-landed soon afterwards with engine failure, possibly resulting from a clash with Ball. At about the same time, Ball was seen to crash.

According to a message dropped later at Vert Galand, Ball had been shot down by 'a worthy opponent' – Lothar von Richthofen – and no doubt the Germans believed it. But the claim is irreconcilable with Lothar's own account of the scrap, which identifies a triplane as his adversary. An alternative claim that Ball was shot down by a machine-gunner mounted in the tower of a church in the village of Annoeullin, a mile or so from the crash, also gained some credence. But neither of these claims was supported by eye-witnesses.

A young German lieutenant stationed at Annoeullin, Franz Hailer, heard the sound of engines and saw an aeroplane emerge from the cloud. It was flying, he said, upside down. It then disappeared behind a row of trees before crashing into rising ground. 'We examined the wreckage,' wrote Hailer later, 'and we all came to the conclusion that the aircraft had not been shot down from the air or by anti-aircraft fire, as the dead pilot had no marks or scratches and had not been wounded.' This was hardly conclusive, as the machine had been wrecked and the engine may well have been hit. Hailer himself had gained the impression, when Ball flew over, that his propeller had stopped.

The mystery that veiled the exit of so many of the aces also shrouded Albert Ball. It seems likely that he was alive when he over-flew Annoeullin, and that he was killed when he crashed. 'The doctor couldn't find any bullet wounds on the body,' said Hailer, 'although the back and one leg were broken.' Could it be that, in cloud con-ditions colourfully described by all who flew that evening, Ball was a victim of turbulence, or of losing orientation? It seems a possible explanation.

But whatever the truth, Albert Ball was dead, and the VC that was probably in the pipeline was awarded posthumously. More sig-nificantly, the spirit of aggression that he personified had become the lodestar of the RFC, and later of the RAF. Many fighter pilots of World War II were brought up on a slogan from World War I:

He must fall,
Remember Ball.

'In the ranks of the great fighter pilots,' said the Official History, 'Albert Ball yields place to none'. He had forty-four confirmed vic-tories, perhaps many more, and he was still not 21 when he died. He was quite irreplaceable. But it is curious that the day of Ball's death should have coincided with Mannock's coming of age as a scout pilot.

THE GOTHAS AND THE SMUTS
REPORT: 'SPORTING AUDACITY'

A GREAT many pilots were arriving in France from the UK in
this period, including some who, like Mannock, could soon
be said to have arrived in more senses than one. Among them
was a former Norwich schoolboy named Philip Fullard, an outstanding sportsman and scholar who had played centre-half for Norwich
Reserves on the one hand and won an Exhibition to Brasenose on the
other. Learning to fly at his own expense in 1916 at the age of 19, he
gave up his Exhibition to join the RFC. Because of his exceptional flying skills he was soon made an instructor, and he was still under twenty
when he was posted to France. Although familiar with the Sopwith
Pup, he found himself, with the bizarre logic of the services, joining
No. 1 Squadron on Nieuports, a machine with which pilots arriving
from the UK were totally unfamiliar, since there were none available
in reserve squadrons at home. Within six weeks of his arrival he saw
eighty-four pilots pass through the squadron, many of them because
they couldn't cope and were posted elsewhere, but all too often because
they became casualties almost before they had unpacked their kit. Fullard, who harboured no false modesty, had boasted, to reassure his
parents, that the RFC 'would not let a dud man go to scouts', but he
himself found the Nieuport unwieldy after the Pup. The biggest drawback, undoubtedly, was the lack of prior training on the type.

For all his natural abilities, Fullard had learnt that success had to be worked for, and, in No. 1 Squadron under Major A. Barton Adams, he found himself amongst kindred spirits. By exploiting the Nieuport's strengths and allowing for its limitations, by a meticulous attention to armaments, and by developing a discipline in formation flying that was in itself a deterrent to attack, even by superior numbers, they succeeded despite the marked superiority of the Albatros DV and the Fokker Triplane, both of which were introduced that summer. Fullard scored his first two victories in May 1917 and five more in June, and he was soon promoted to flight commander. Nine more in July and twelve in August brought him an MC and Bar, and with confidence and compactness as their watchword, every pilot in Fullard's flight gained five victories or more. He suffered a blank September through breaking a blood vessel while stunting a Nieuport on test, but another fourteen that autumn brought him a DSO and took his score to forty-two. He then broke a leg playing football and had to be sent home when the injury didn't mend.

Looking back on his six months with No. 1 Squadron, Fullard admitted to neither stress nor strain, and he insisted that any good instructor ought to make a good scout pilot, a somewhat singular view. He attributed his success – again in unorthodox fashion – not to superior marksmanship, nor to getting in close, nor to surprise, nor to luck, nor to an aggressive nature, but to sheer flying skill. (Compare with McCudden's: 'Good flying has never killed a Hun yet.')

The squadron's loss when Fullard went home has been compared to 24 Squadron's when they lost Hawker. Letters to relatives written by squadron commanders were inevitably couched in appreciative, even fulsome terms, but in Fullard's case there were no sorrowing parents to be soothed; yet Barton Adams wrote: 'No. 1 Squadron will lose its finest and most stout-hearted pilot ... He was the "crack" pilot in France.'

Attempts to reset the broken leg failed repeatedly, ending Fullard's operational career, and eventually the leg had to be plated. Meanwhile – as contemporaries might perhaps have been consoled to hear – he completely lost his nerve for flying.

Not all the men reaching scout squadrons in France were embryonic Fullards, however, and it was distressing for both pilot and squadron when their unsuitability was recognised. A young man named Stuart (L.S.) Campbell, posted to 56 Squadron, had already experienced a similar rejection. He was waiting at CFS for a posting to France when he was instructed one night by his flight commander to take up a BE12, fly to Bath and return. He had no experience whatsoever of night flying and the BE12 was a single-seater, so there was no place for an instructor or observer. 'It was a bitterly cold night with heavy storm clouds,' wrote Campbell, 'and when over Devizes I ran into a murderous snowstorm. The only sensible thing to do was to turn back whilst the lights from the Upavon sheds were still visible.' This he did, to be told by the flight commander that he was 'not suited to being a night-flying pilot.' This, it seems, was his qualification for posting to a crack scout squadron. But it was soon apparent at Vert Galand that he wouldn't make a scout pilot either, and his fate was to be transferred to 27 Squadron on Martinsydes. 'Its role was long-distance daylight bombing,' recorded Campbell, 'and it was, without question, an absolute death trap when up against fast-moving Albatros scouts.' In its ceaseless war against enemy communications the squadron was averaging three raids per day, but escort by the Pups of 66 Squadron met with such remarkable success that after a dismal April not a single Martinsyde was lost in May. The Pup was chosen because it was slow enough to stay with the Martinsyde, a somewhat dubious distinction; indeed, once the Martinsyde had dropped its bombs it was actually the faster. Nevertheless by timing their supporting action to a nicety the Pup pilots generally fought off interception.

Eighteen-year-old Gordon Taylor, one of the Pup pilots guarding the Martinsydes, was an Australian. Despite a nervous wreck of an instructor at Netheravon whose sole aim was to send his pupils off solo as soon as possible so he didn't have to fly with them, killing in the process the compatriot Taylor had travelled with from Australia, Taylor himself, a natural flyer, was at home in the air from the start. He soon resolved that if he survived the war he would make flying his career.[1] No. 66 Squadron was formed at Filton, Bristol, where

1. Which he later did, to become, both solo and with fellow Australian Charles Kingsford-Smith, a pioneer of trans-oceanic and air route flying. Both were knighted.

[73]

Taylor 'gained some measure of fame,' it was said, 'by flying under Clifton Suspension Bridge.' It was further said that the squadron commander, Owen Boyd, 'turned a blind eye to the incident, feeling rather that the reputation of his squadron had been much enhanced.'

Under flight commander J.O. 'Jock' Andrews, formerly a stalwart of 24 Squadron with Lanoe Hawker, VC, Taylor prospered. Determined to put his trust in the Pup or perish, he looped it six times over Filton and satisfied himself and others of its structural integrity. A mock duel with Andrews at 6,000 feet earned him the appointment of deputy flight leader, and with the judicious Andrews leading he actually enjoyed the cerebral challenge of outsmarting the Hun in an inferior machine. When Andrews went home in July with a DSO to add to the MC he had won on DH2's, Gordon Taylor, having himself won an MC, replaced him. The B Flight commander went home at about the same time: his replacement, on a three-week attachment, was Jimmy McCudden.

The attachment was intended as a refresher course: after four months as a fighter instructor at Joyce Green, McCudden sought and was granted an opportunity to bring himself up to date on the latest trends in air fighting, ostensibly for the benefit of his pupils, although he was also looking ahead to his third tour of operations. Dispassionate, astute, and analytical, McCudden had appreciable fighting experience, but this was confined to two-seaters as an observer and to the DH2 as a pilot. His only operational experience in a tractor scout came that summer in his personal Pup, the machine in which he toured training stations to lecture and demonstrate. In this he joined Home Defence squadrons in chasing after the Gotha bombers, which mounted their first big raid on London on 13 June. On that raid, in broad daylight, 162 civilians were killed and 432 injured, and of 92 machines which went up to intercept, none got close enough to do any damage.

In the clamour for improved home air defences that resulted, Haig was forced by the War Cabinet to transfer two of Trenchard's best fighting squadrons, No. 56 to Bekesbourne near Canterbury and No. 66 to Calais, to cover both sides of the Dover Strait. Trenchard strongly resented this misappropriation, as he saw it, and would have refused it if he could. In one of his pep talks to his pilots he delighted them with the opinion that 'it does politicians good to be bombed occasionally.' On paper he pointed out that, to be effective, any system of defensive patrols would require a far greater effort than could feasibly be mounted, and that the most effective counter would be to clear the enemy from the Belgian coast, which happened to be one of the main objectives of Haig's coming offensive. This would increase the distance the Gothas had to travel and oblige them to traverse territory occupied by the Allies. He also correctly forecast that the Gothas would simply turn to attacking towns and bases behind the British lines. After a fortnight or so of useless patrolling the detached squadrons were returned to normal duty, whereupon the Gothas at once resumed their assault on London. This led to renewed demands by the Cabinet: first, for two first-class fighting squadrons, as before, and second, for a reprisal bombing raid on Mannheim, a diversion Haig had already rejected after the June attack. Haig promised to send two scout squadrons at once, but he warned that the fight to establish air supremacy prior to the summer offensive had already begun, that it would be the severest test yet, and that his entire campaign depended upon it and would be seriously jeopardised by both demands. Whether or not his predicament was overstated, the Cabinet settled for a single Sopwith Pup squadron, No. 46, which was released in turn after seven weeks. They abandoned the Mannheim project for the moment.

More significantly, the concept of an independent Air Ministry, already urged by Winston Churchill and others as a logical coordinator of the competing demands of the two air services, was flushed into focus by the attacks on London and the desire for reprisals, leading to the appointment of the South African statesman and visionary Jan Christian Smuts to enquire and report. Smuts, who had acted as the South African representative at an Imperial War Conference in April 1917, had since been co-opted by Lloyd George to the War Cabinet. In the meantime a project for the provision of forty long-range bomber squadrons to attack German cities sent Trenchard scurrying to northern France in search of possible bases, though he was doubtful of the wisdom or practicality of either project. The unobtrusive and farsighted David Henderson, as Director-General of Military Aeronautics, and as the RFC's first leader, joined Smuts as an adviser.

Henderson, whose training manual published in 1907 on the acquisition of information about the enemy ('The Art of Reconnaissance'), had replaced his own earlier manual on Field Intelligence, recognised the aeroplane as a fresh challenge, and he learned to fly in 1911 at the age of 49 to study and report on its practical applications. A graduate of two Scottish universities, he combined a quiet persistence with a rare quality of gentleness, together with an indifference to personal aggrandisement. Perhaps because of this, his contribution to the birth, first of the RFC and later of the RAF, has been underrated. Trenchard called him the true Father of the Air Force.

McCudden left for France on his refresher course in mid-June and found himself on the same airfield as 56 Squadron. He had visited them twice when they were at Bekesbourne and renewed acquaintance with an old friend from his days with 29 Squadron, G.H. Bowman, now a flight commander, and he rated them the best outfit he'd seen. The atmosphere created by Blomfield, with his international orchestra and cuisine, was unique, while the pilots were an exceptional bunch, and the new SE5A, to which the pilots were converting, was proving noticeably faster, with improved ceiling. Although McCudden's record of five confirmed victories might appear modest, it had been achieved in a difficult period, recognised by his MC, MM and *Croix de Guerre* awards, and Blomfield invited him to join one of 56's sorties under A Flight commander Captain P.B. 'Bruce' Prothero, promising to get him transferred 'as soon as a chance arose'.

The red-haired Prothero, as McCudden soon discovered, was an extrovert. A true Scotsman, with a burr hard to decipher after a dram or two, he insisted on wearing a kilt at all times. When he returned from a patrol his knees would be blue from the cold 'and the hair thereon would stick out like bristles on a hog', according to Canadian colleague V.P. 'Versh' Cronyn. One day Cronyn asked him why he punished himself in this way, to which Prothero replied: 'You wouldna have me taken prisoner in disguise, would you now, laddie?' Sadly he was shot down and killed five days later, his place being taken by Gerald Constable Maxwell.

Another vacancy for a flight commander was in fact already imminent, through the impending transfer of Captain Ian Henderson, MC, only son of Sir David Henderson, to instructor duties. Still only 20, Henderson had seven victories.[1] Thus McCudden, after a final sortie with No. 66, some more Gotha-chasing, and ten days' leave, returned to France on 14 August as the new commander of B Flight.

Despite the vital work of the corps squadrons, it was the scout pilots protecting them who caught the public imagination, and this was exaggerated by a system of decorations which rewarded the spectacular rather than the routine. The achievement of scout pilots was readily measured in their scores, whereas corps pilots were less easy to assess one against the other, while qualities of leadership were in less demand. The contrast in recognition caused much bitterness, as was inevitable, and Trenchard deplored it, yet the life of a scout pilot tended to be shorter, providing justification. A higher level of physical and mental fitness was required of scout pilots, for whom sudden and frequent changes of altitude were commonplace, and they had to be imbued with a spirit of aggression – a burning desire not merely to get to grips with the enemy, but to bring him down 'in the greatest possible numbers'. This competitive instinct, the ambition to shine above his fellows, was accepted as a vital ingredient. No one put his finger more imaginatively on the temperament of RFC scout pilots than Trenchard's opposite number General von Hoeppner, who wrote of their 'sporting audacity'. They too had to suffer at various times from inferior machines and unpopular policies. Enough has been said in praise of the men of the corps squadrons to emphasise their worth; but the fighting squadrons got the best of what was going, both in mechanical and human terms.

When McCudden joined 56 Squadron he was amongst equals. Half a dozen of the pilots had more victories than he did. Men

1. Ian Henderson was killed in a flying accident in Scotland on 21 June 1918.

like 'Beery' Bowman, so called because of his florid complexion, Constable Maxwell, Dick Maybery, Arthur Rhys Davids, Leonard Barlow and the Canadians Reginald Hoidge and 'Versh' Cronyn would have stood out in any company. Compare this with the experience of flight commanders in corps squadrons, many of whom were struggling, as Eric Routh had done, with demonstrable inferiority in both man and machine. Jack Slessor, still not twenty, returned to France on 1 May 1917 to take over A Flight of No. 5 Squadron on RE8's, which he was flying for the first time and which to his surprise he 'rather liked'. 'Pember is a rotten bad pilot,' he wrote, 'he will have to go home if he crashes again.' 'Pember twisted off his tail fin and bent his axle again. I wish the CO would get rid of him.' 'Hodges destroyed another RE8 and retired to hospital, he will have to go now, thank Heaven.' His replacement was 'a good fellow but a rotten pilot – he did in his centre section today on his first flight.' 'Hanman seems a footling person . . . lands badly.' There was grief for a pilot shot down in flames, and a complaint of a lack of protection. 'I don't know what's the matter with our Tripes and scouts these days.'

There were still compensations in the occasional day off. 'Went to Amiens with Joyon and Duncan and Owen, had a great time. Amiens rather a good spot. Lunched at the oyster shop and dined at the Grand and filled in the time with Charley's Bar.' A guest night in the Mess two nights later improved morale – but the quality of the new pilots remained abysmal. 'The flight is in ghastly shape now.' Pember, having weathered all Slessor's disdain, and having finally transgressed by losing formation, had fought well when attacked – but had been lent to 10 Squadron, Garland's unit.[1] 'Hanman is still in hospital, and Lomas is going home. Nerve all gone to pot, fainting in the air etc.' Slessor, inevitably, was getting all the flying he wanted and more. As for the unfortunate observers, there were only two qualified men left.

In mid-July Slessor noted: 'Two new pilots just rolled up. Not bad but not up to much.' But next day: 'The new pilots are pretty bad.

1. E.H. Pember, formerly of the Royal Artillery, survived to be promoted to Lieutenant, but was killed in action on 30 September 1917.

One got into a spin and nearly killed Stone.' Stone was one of the two surviving qualified observers, already badly shaken by three similar escapes. Duncan, one of the men who had accompanied Slessor to Amiens, 'crashed badly amongst the transport lorries getting off. The other new pilot, Ashton, wrote off 8683. Stone with him again. I think his nerve has gone badly now. No wonder, he has had five bad crashes, all with new pilots.'

It was going to be a long time before Smith-Barry's revolutionary training methods, begun early in 1917 at the Gosport School of Flying, would be reflected in new arrivals at the front. As late as 1918, Gerald Dixon, during pilot training at Catterick, had never heard of Smith-Barry or his teachings. Meanwhile, raw pilots continued to arrive at the squadrons, filling empty chairs but driving harassed flight commanders to distraction. A more mature newcomer, Fred Winterbotham, posted to Nieuports on 29 Squadron, complained of 'pilots arriving and disappearing daily'. But after seeing action he commented, as others had done before him, on 'the strange *détente* between those who fought in the air'.

'HALF A PARACHUTE IS BETTER THAN NO PARACHUTE AT ALL'

THE principal reasons advanced by the British for the failure to incorporate parachutes in the equipment of aeroplanes in the First World War were:-

1. That pilots, given a means of escape, would be tempted, when under threat, to abandon their machines prematurely.

2. That although it was right for the crews of kite balloons to be offered a means of escape because they were vulnerable and couldn't hit back, aeroplane crews were equipped to defend themselves.

3. That the parachutes available were altogether too bulky for stowage in the tiny cockpits of the time, and too complex and cumbersome for external fitting; that their weight (28 lbs) would have detracted from aircraft performance; that they would have become entangled with the tailplane or some other obstruction on release; and that they were unreliable anyway.

4. That most fatal crashes occurred on take-off and landing, or when stunting at low level, when height was insufficient for a parachute to open.

Whatever one may think of the slur on the fighting instincts and resolve of pilots implicit in the first excuse, the other three scarcely bear examination. Many of the machines shot down were so poorly armed as to be almost as vulnerable as kite balloons; urgent priority could surely have been given to the design of parachutes for aeroplanes and of cockpits to accommodate them; while the last excuse could only have been advanced by men whose knowledge was confined to training units in the United Kingdom.

There is no doubt that the RFC authorities were almost pathologically opposed to the notion of parachutes in aeroplanes, and that they went so far as to discourage efforts to develop them. A pilot's job was to stick to his machine. Curiously enough there is also little doubt that a kind of macho bravado existed amongst pilots which scorned the safety angle and stifled any concerted pressure for the development and issue of parachutes, either from squadron and flight commanders or from the pilots themselves.

Tom Mapplebeck, brother of Gibb, who flew at the time of the Fokker scourge, said he 'never thought about parachutes'. Harold Tambling, of 22 Squadron (FE2b's), said the same. 'Puggy' Shone said: 'We never thought about parachutes seriously as part of our equipment, because the additional weight would have affected the performance of our aircraft, and we accepted that the powers that be really believed that it might affect our morale if we were equipped . . .' Harold Balfour denied that there was ever any controversy about parachutes in the squadrons in which he served. Hugh Walmsley said he loathed the idea of parachutes, because of the discomfort they inflicted on the wearer; even when they were introduced in the mid-1920s he didn't wear them. Jack Slessor recalled: 'The first time I really thought about a parachute was in about 1924, I suppose when I was told I was going to have one.'

Against this, there were pilots who vilified the authorities *at the time* for failing to provide them, others who sought to procure their own. Among the more vociferous was Arthur Gould Lee. Arriving in France in May 1917, he was moved to sympathy with colleagues and enemies alike when he saw them in unrecoverable situations three miles up but with plenty of time to get out. Although he conceded that there was no room for a parachute in the tiny cockpit of his Sopwith Pup, he cited many other types, particularly the more vulnerable, where a parachute should have been mandatory. Why weren't machines designed from the beginning to take parachutes?

Lee believed that every pilot would have sacrificed a little in performance for a chance of escape *in extremis*. So far from weakening resolve, it would, he thought, have been a great boost to morale: 'To know you had a sporting chance from a break-up or a flamer would make you much braver in a scrap.' The same point was made by the inventors of parachutes.

The use of a parachute to retard a fall from a height had long been envisaged, but one of the first to pursue its practical application in the twentieth century was Edward Maitland, the veteran airship and balloon pioneer of the original No. 1 Squadron at Farnborough. Maitland became so concerned for the safety of his balloon crews if war came that he made a parachute descent himself from a balloon as early as 1908, and he continued for many years to study and experiment with parachutes for lighter-than-air craft, making the first descent from an airship in 1913.

Parachute descents from aeroplanes were made before the war in Britain, France and America; but it was as a life-saving device in kite balloons that the parachute became a recognised wartime accessory, the first suitable British parachutes being designed by the firm of C.G. Spencer. Spencer himself made a demonstration jump from an airship at the Royal Naval Air Station at Kingsnorth on 17 December 1914, an experiment so successful that 'it completely changed the views of all who saw it'. The airship positioned itself as directed by Spencer, who jumped from 1,000 feet. The parachute opened within 100 feet and Spencer came gently and safely to earth despite a brisk wind, landing almost exactly where he had intended. Soon afterwards his firm were invited to tender. Thus when the operation of kite balloons in France was taken over by the RFC, they inherited the C.G. Spencer Static-Line (Automatic) Parachute.

Another inventor, retired railway engineer E.R. Calthrop, was meanwhile developing a more sophisticated and practical model. This was both smaller and lighter. No doubt he had an eye to profit, but he expressed a noble intent: 'To Reduce the Unnecessary Wastage of our Airmen'. Despite pre-war rebuffs from both the Admiralty and

War Office when he offered to test his parachute in their presence, he persisted. In October 1915 Mervyn O'Gorman, the flamboyant Superintendent at Farnborough, proposed to the Directorate of Military Aeronautics that an experienced balloon jumper be engaged to carry out experiments with a Calthrop parachute, but a Minute from the Assistant Director, enquiring of Henderson, the Director-General, whether experiments were to be continued, was annotated emphatically: '*No, certainly not!*' This uncompromising negative was still being quoted a year later to stifle further initiatives.

Much of the blame for this attitude has been assigned to Trenchard, though Henderson was the one who expressed it so forcibly. Yet it is surprising that Trenchard didn't campaign for an urgent programme of research and development. He seems, at least, to have had no part in the shameful declaration by the Air Board on parachutes for the RFC.[1]

It is the opinion of the Board that the present form of parachute is not suitable for use in aeroplanes and should only be used by balloon observers.

It is also the opinion of the Board that the presence of such an apparatus might impair the fighting spirit of pilots and cause them to abandon machines which might otherwise be capable of returning to base for repair.

Here it was at last, in plain, brutal language: the RFC, and presumably the RNAS, could not be trusted with parachutes. This was to turn the whole question on its head. What about the pilot himself returning to base for repair, an outcome which a parachute might achieve? Few machines in which a pilot dived from a height to his death were repairable; why not at least try to save the pilot, and the observer if one were present? The salvaging of the machine was not and never was crucial, except perhaps when a test pilot might stay too long in a vain effort to preserve a prototype. Apart from the human reasons for putting life before hardware, once a pilot had got

1. *The First Great Air War*, by Richard Townshend Bickers (Hodder, 1988).

past his first few shows his value became immense and his replacement infinitely more difficult than the replacement of his machine.

Encouraged by Maitland, Calthrop persisted, and he resumed trials of his parachute at the naval air station at Polegate. By 21 August 1916 the Admiralty were pronouncing the trials 'most satisfactory', and they proposed to adopt the 'Guardian Angel', as Calthrop named his parachute, for use in kite balloons and airships. The tests were all made from an airship, first with weights, then with dummies, and finally with a volunteer parachutist, Sir Bryan Leighton. Leighton jumped from 9,000 feet, the parachute cushioning him and opening in two-and-a-half seconds. In a personal report to Commodore Murray Sueter, Head of the Admiralty's Air Department, Leighton observed: 'I am quite sure I could do the jump from a BE type of aeroplane' – but the offer was ignored. Maitland believed that the Guardian Angel 'represented a distinct advance on the Spencer', but his report was more reticent than Leighton's, recommending the parachute as 'a thoroughly reliable one and fit to be taken into use for lighter-than-air craft of all descriptions (aeroplanes and seaplanes excepted) forthwith.' Nevertheless the Spencer type was retained for kite balloon work. It had become familiar, and it was also thought that the Calthrop might deploy too near to what might be a burning balloon. So Calthrop was disappointed again.

His persistence seemed about to pay off, however, when the Guardian Angel was used in the first British military live descent from a heavier-than-air craft, by Captain Clive Collett, a 30-year-old New Zealander in the RFC, in an experimental flight in a BE2c from the test flying and research establishment at Orfordness. After twenty drops from the same machine using dummies, Collett made his jump from 600 feet on 13 January 1917.

A report on Collett's jump, by Vernon Brown, who was one of the pilots involved, makes it clear that the Guardian Angel, as then constituted, demanded skilful piloting to ensure a safe exit by the parachutist, the dummy drops having disclosed that canopy and rigging lines were liable to snag in the tail skid unless a banked turn was being flown. This was scant reassurance for a pilot and observer jumping from a crippled machine, and once again Calthrop was disappointed. An alternative prototype, designed by a Captain Mears, was similarly rejected.

Less than a month after Collett's historic descent, an extract from a Minute addressed to the Secretary of the Air Board settled the matter: 'The heavier-than-air people all say that they flatly decline to regard the parachute in an aeroplane as a life-saving device which is worth carrying in its present form.' The crux of the matter lay in the last four words: further development was needed. But the Air Board gave no lead, basing their inaction on factors which reveal a breathtaking callousness:

1. Safety was not really considered important.
2. The ignorance and prejudice of pilots, and the fact that a good proportion of accidents occurred on landing, take-off, and stunting close to the ground. [This was the desk-bound Home Establishment attitude again.]

Not only were the Board antipathetic to parachutes for the RFC, they were also dog-in-the-manger about letting anyone else have them. In March 1917 the Board considered an application from the Russian Government for '100 Calthrop's Patent Safety Guardian Angel Parachutes', but this did not influence them to change their stance. 'In view of the opinion of the Naval and Military Flying Services that this device has little chance of being used in aeroplanes, it was decided in the first instance to enquire for what purpose the Russian Government required the parachutes.' This question, bordering on impertinence, was soon answered: the parachutes must be adaptable for both airships and aircraft. At this the Board consented to an order, not for a hundred but for twenty, with the proviso that 'the Russians should be informed that the Board could not agree to their being supplied for aeroplane purposes, for which they were not considered suitable for the British Air Services.'

Trenchard himself was far more sympathetic to the introduction of parachutes for his crews, and he suggested that trials should be conducted in France, asking for twenty Calthrop parachutes for this purpose, but this was refused. Yet when he asked for twenty parachutes for dropping agents behind the lines he got them. If this was a ruse to go ahead with the trials against orders, there is no evidence that they ever took place.

One of the early RFC pioneers, however, took up the fight. This was Charles Longcroft, who was already a major when he took part in the Channel crossing of August 1914. He had taken a leading part in some of the earliest reconnaissances, led No. 4 Squadron, and finally commanded a brigade. Mild in manner, but clinical in mind, and no respecter of persons, he told his seniors: 'I and my pilots keenly desired parachutes.' To the objection that parachutes would impose too great a strain on the pilots themselves he replied that their principal use would be to escape from a burning machine, surely sufficient compensation for any minor inconvenience. As for the notion that pilots might jump prematurely, he simply did not believe it.

Soon afterwards, on Maitland's recommendation, a Parachute Committee was formed, which included representatives of the Technical, Airship, Supply and Air Inspectorate Departments, the Establishment Branch and the Kite Balloon Section; but practical difficulties with the models available persisted. One progress report opined that 'half a parachute was better than no parachute at all'; but it was also said that unless an aviator had confidence in his equipment it was more likely to disturb his peace of mind than to enhance it.

Pressure for more rapid progress was about to be applied from an unexpected quarter: in the last summer of the war, the Germans started using parachutes. They had previously introduced them for their airship crews, but their weight reduced altitude, the airship's most effective defence, and they were withdrawn. The aeroplane type was named after its developer, Otto Heinicke, whose parachute was similar to British models. It was packed in a sack strapped to the pilot, and a 50 lb break cord attached to the machine was designed to jerk the canopy out of the sack once the pilot was clear of the tail surfaces of the plane. Air could be spilled from the canopy on landing. The parachute was by no means foolproof, nor was it universally fitted, and escapes from crippled or burning aircraft did not always succeed.

The most publicised escape was that of Ernst Udet, the second highest ranking German ace, who owed his life to Heinicke's invention (as, later, did Hermann Goering). Udet jumped on 29 June 1918 following a clash with a French Breguet, though after unfastening his safety-belt and standing up in his seat he was blown aft and his parachute harness snagged on the forward tip of the rudder. With the strength of desperation he broke off the rudder tip, only to find himself tumbling over and over, convinced that his parachute had failed. He was down to 250 feet when it opened, and he sprained an ankle on landing. Yet he would surely have endorsed the view that 'half a parachute was better than no parachute at all'.

Curiously enough, neither the French, nor the Americans, who might have been expected to provide this kind of luxury – if luxury it was – for their pilots, had produced a practical parachute by the war's end. After the final plunge of the American ace Raoul Lufbery on 19 May 1918, when witnesses saw the pilot jump to escape the flames and plummet to earth, Colonel Billy Mitchell, the American air commander, commented: 'If he had had a parachute he could easily have been saved.' But the US Government still refused to issue the parachute, thus far imperfect, that they were developing. Yet the British, goaded by the protection being afforded their enemies, seemed about to move swiftly at last. The greatest proselytiser was a former Royal Marine, by then in his forties, Major T. Orde Lees, who risked his neck in a number of spectacular jumps, none more so, in November 1917, than from the top of Tower Bridge. His frequent visits to France eventually brought, on 16 September 1918, the following declaration from the Headquarters of the RAF in the Field: '*All single-seaters are to be fitted with parachutes forthwith.*'

By this time the Camel was regarded as obsolescent, so it was decided to convert only SE5A's and Sopwith Dolphins and Snipes. Orders were to be placed – with Calthrops – for the requisite number of parachutes. The two-seaters were not forgotten: the Brisfit and the DH4 and DH9 bombers were also to be adapted for parachutes. The Armstrong-Whitworth and the RE8, for the same reason as the Camel, were not.

All this sounded positive and expeditious. But other points in the

Headquarters letter of 16 September on the Adoption of Parachutes suggested that much was still to be done. The weight of the parachute was, if possible, to be reduced – but not if it meant reducing the size of the canopy. All parachutes were to be fireproofed. Because of the number of man-hours required to pack and repack, service and maintain the Calthrop parachute, experiments were requested with a view to simplifying the design. Trials were requested to determine the difference in performance between fitted and non-fitted machines. And so on. Clearly all this would take months. 'Forthwith' was an idle boast.

Nothing more was achieved before the Armistice, and it is implicit in subsequent events that the notion of parachutes in peacetime did not appeal and was pigeon-holed. It was not until the mid-twenties that the Irvin Air Chute, a free-fall type of American design, was introduced.

Sholto Douglas was only one of many who later learnt 'to my disgust' that it had been official policy 'to deny us the use of parachutes'. He wrote of the great comfort it would have been to have had such a means of escape, not to mention 'the saving of many men from horrible deaths.'

OVER AND UNDER MESSINES

ALTHOUGH spasmodic air fighting over the Arras front continued into June, Trenchard, by the first week in May, had already worked out the redistribution of his forces in support of Haig's long-gestating Flanders offensive. The objectives of this offensive remained as Haig had devised them: to break out at what he considered the enemy's weakest point, the Ypres salient, protect his eastern flank, and advance north to the Belgian coast. Few shared his optimism that the campaign would succeed as planned, but major offensive action of some kind had to be undertaken that summer, if only to buy time while French morale recovered from the mutiny. The magnitude of this catastrophe was still a well-kept secret, not only from the enemy, but also from the British War Cabinet. But if Haig failed to act decisively, the French collapse might be total. There remained the frightening possibility that the BEF would be stranded by the U-boat campaign, which still demanded urgent attention. In any case, for Haig to keep his armies idle, and abdicate the initiative to the enemy, was unthinkable.

These were the factors that determined Haig's strategy for the remainder of 1917, from the preparatory Battle of Messines (7 June), to the main assault at 3rd Ypres (beginning 31 July). Various subsidiary battles were to follow in August and September, culminating in the final reckoning in October and November at Passchendaele.

Essential to the launching of the main offensive was the prior capture of the dominating heights of the Messines ridge, rising in places to 260 feet, from which British preparations could be monitored by the enemy. For Trenchard, as for the BEF, the planning for this preliminary operation took precedence.

The RFC now had forty-five squadrons in action in France, plus five naval squadrons on loan, a total of 881 aircraft in all. Of these, some 300, a third of them fighters, were earmarked for the Messines front. Of the naval squadrons, three were Sopwith Triplanes; but in the RFC squadrons there was still a dearth of modern machines. There was only one SE5 squadron, No. 56, only one complete Brisfit squadron, No. 48 (though No. 11 was soon to join it), and only one DH4 squadron, No. 55. Squadrons that had been raised to twenty-one machines and sometimes twenty-four for the Arras battle had had to revert to eighteen because machines to replace those lost or damaged beyond repair were not forthcoming. The RE8 now outnumbered the old BE2 by two to one, but there were still five BE squadrons operating daily. For much of that summer, Nos 43, 45 and 70 Squadrons were still flying the outmoded Sopwith two-seater, re-equipment of all three squadrons with Sopwith Camels not being completed until September. It was to the pilots and observers of these three squadrons that Trenchard particularly addressed himself on his final round of visits before the Battle of Messines.

As always he was brutally frank. After praising them for their successes, he told them he knew only too well that their machines were outclassed by the latest enemy fighters. He promised he was doing all he could to get them better equipped; but meanwhile, knowing of his efforts and of his sympathy with their predicament, he would rely on them to do their best. This meant, he stressed, that they must go at the enemy with all their might to achieve the vital task of keeping the sky clear of enemy aeroplanes, not merely over the lines but far behind them, to a depth of some 10,000 yards. Once again Trenchard was appealing to the aggressive instincts of his pilots to bridge the quality gap, of which they were only too well aware.

What was the reaction to Trenchard's apology and exhortation? There were always cynics and critics. Few were more critical than

Arthur Gould Lee, but of Trenchard he wrote: 'He is a fine man, with a terrific personality, who knows how to impress and inspire us. To have a few words of praise of our work was an enormous encouragement. Trenchard is a leader after the hearts of service pilots, and although we don't like some of the things we have to do, such as Distant Operational Patrols in obsolete machines, everyone in the RFC looks up to him as a great commander.'

The RFC's primary tasks at Messines, in simple terms, were for the corps machines, under the protection of the fighting squadrons, to give the maximum help to the British artillery in registering targets and directing fire, and for the fighting squadrons to prevent the German Air Force from registering our own battery positions. So successful were they that when the bombardment proper opened on 31 May the corps squadrons enjoyed almost complete freedom of movement and were rarely attacked. Of thirty-three machines reported missing in II Brigade between 15 May and 9 June, twenty-nine belonged to the army wing and only four to the corps wing.

The preliminary bombardment of the Messines ridge, which had begun on 21 May, was much more concentrated and detailed than for previous battles. For the RFC, cooperation with the artillery included finding the targets and directing the fire for the 2,400 field guns that had been assembled on a ten-mile front. Among specific aims was the obliteration of the barbed wire entanglements fronting the German trenches to clear the way for the advancing infantry. Graphics and charts carried by the corps pilots proliferated so alarmingly that Charles Smart (RE8's, No. 5 Squadron), complained, on 2 June, that he would have to take a secretary up with him. 'It nearly drove me frantic trying to remember where each lot of ground strips were situated and whose turn it was to fire and on which target.' He lined things up eventually, but admitted it was a very worrying business. 'Archie does not help you much in the thinking line either.'

Day bombing, mainly by the Martinsydes of No. 27 and the DH4's of No. 55, helped to hamper and divert enemy air activity, the Martinsydes with Pup escort and the DH4's from high level, but it was the night bombing of the FE2b's of 100 Squadron that inflicted the most damage. The DH4's also flew photographic reconnaissances

[91]

up to 21,000 feet. But as Trenchard had foreseen, the Sopwith two-seaters were outclassed, and they suffered accordingly. Eight machines of 45 Squadron on a photo recce were challenged by five Albatros scouts, with more German pilots joining in as the scrap evolved. The Sopwith crews did not need Trenchard's blandishments to fight for their lives, and one of their attackers was sent down in flames. But two of the Sopwiths were lost, a third was forced down behind the lines, and two more were so crippled that they were wrecked in forced landings.

Exceptional skill was often shown, of necessity, by the FE2b crews, but they were up against it when seven of No. 20 Squadron were attacked by fifteen Albatros scouts. One of the pusher pilots was mortally wounded by the red-painted leading Albatros, but another, after a running fight, got in a burst at close range that pulverised the Albatros, which broke up in mid-air. Lieutenant Harold Satchell and his observer, Second-Lieutenant T.A.M.S. Lewis, had shot down the German ace Karl Schaefer, whose score had reached thirty at the time of his death.

Meanwhile a system of eavesdropping on the signals of intruding enemy machines by army intercept stations, fixing their position and notifying the fighting squadrons, had proved so successful in previous months that many similar stations were established solely for the purpose of reporting the movements of hostiles. The hope that these messages might be transmitted direct to airborne machines was never realised for lack of equipment, but alternative signalling methods proved adequate, and interception rates were greatly improved.

Other tasks of almost equal significance were discharged daily once the battle started. Contact patrols, working low over the heads of the infantry in the attack area, sought continually to report progress to the relevant headquarters, often returning to deliver fresh instructions in weighted and streamered bags. Yet there were still times when the ground forces showed a frustrating reluctance to reveal their positions. Equally important were the persistent machine-gun attacks on enemy airfields, transport, and troops. This low-level ground strafing, which had been begun successfully at Arras, developed at Messines into an established part of air support for the advancing ground forces, to be used extensively in July and August at 3rd Ypres and subsequently. But it exposed its practitioners to withering fire.

Alan Dore, who had taken command of 43 Squadron after the solid Sholto Douglas injured himself when hitting a horse on an emergency take-off (the horse it was that died), despatched seven two-seaters at 4 a.m. on 7 June to strafe troops and transport behind the Messines Ridge. 'The dull rumble of guns reaches me as I see them off in a grey light. It is a dangerous mission. Then telephone messages come through . . . One [Harriman] is down with petrol tank shot through . . . D'Arcy is wounded and lands his machine in splinters. Rutter comes back not at all.' At one point Harriman had almost despaired of surviving, while D'Arcy, although wounded, had shot down a balloon and damaged another. 'D'Arcy goes on long after he is wounded and lands in a faint.' Rutter, one of the flight commanders, who had treated Dore and others to dinner two months earlier to celebrate his birthday and the award of an MC, had been one of the last three remaining of the original thirty-six officers of 43 Squadron. 'His loss is another link snapped.'

Nieuports of No. 1 Squadron, Sopwith Pups of 66, FE8's of 41, and a Spad and an SE5 from 19 and 56 respectively, all joined in the low-level mayhem. The strafer in the SE5 was Second-Lieutenant Leonard Barlow, born in Islington and about to celebrate his nineteenth birthday. He dived at a German aerodrome and peppered the hangars from twenty feet, spotted a nearby train and hosed it with both Vickers and Lewis (having wired them up so they could be fired from the same button), and riddled rolling-stock in the nearby station yard. He still had enough ammunition – and aggression – to perforate the sheds of a second aerodrome on his way home. Of an ingenious turn of mind, he was known as the gadget king.

The most spectacular weapons employed for the actual taking of the ridge were the mines that had been laboriously laid by tunnelling companies over many months under the German front line, to depths of up to a hundred feet. Twenty-one of these were planted at intervals, and the nineteen that were successfully detonated at 03.10 on 7 June aggregated nearly a million tons of high explosive, the boom being heard 130 miles away in London. Ten thousand Germans are believed to have been killed, and 7,000 more were stunned and captured. The Allied infantry were able to advance rapidly, and by 09.00 they had seized the ridge. For once the German casualties were heavier than the British, and next day an enemy counter-attack was repulsed. Yet Messines, although brilliant in conception and execution, was still no more than a local success. Several days before the engagement ended with a final push on 14 June, Trenchard was already bent on consolidation for the main struggle ahead.

Addressing his brigade commanders – there were now five of them, one for each of Haig's armies – on 10 June, Trenchard wrote: 'I would ask that as far as possible you do your best to point out to your Armies that it is of the utmost importance that the Flying Corps should avoid wastage in both pilots and machines for some little time.' Nothing could have been more revealing of the dependence of Trenchard and his brigadiers on the restraint and good sense of the various army commanders. He continued: 'My reserve at present is dangerously low, in fact, in some cases it barely exists at all, and the supply from home is not coming forward sufficiently freely to enable us to continue fighting an offensive in the air continuously.' In this respect, as he was careful to remind them for their own use, they were worse off than the infantry. 'As we have no reserve squadrons it is necessary to do everything to avoid losses.' But as always with Trenchard, there was a sting in the tail. 'It is of the utmost importance, however, that the offensive spirit is maintained in the Flying Corps.' Take it easy on the one hand, but keep up the pressure on the other.

Proud of their successes at Messines – and mourning their losses – pilots and observers felt they hardly needed this form of cajolery. Equally extreme, perhaps, was the conclusion of an X Corps staff officer in a memorandum on *Lessons of the Battle*, though it sounded harmonious to an airman's ear. 'The success [at Messines] was due to a great extent to the excellent work of the artillery which made the work of the infantry exceptionally easy as there was practically no wire left.' Clearly the work of the corps squadrons, mostly RE8's and BE2's, favoured by good weather and the suffocation of enemy interference by the army squadrons, had been decisive. The RFC had achieved its primary task.

There was still room for individual initiative, and it was a scout pilot, during the build-up to the battle, who conceived one of the most daring exploits of the war. This was Billy Bishop, of 60 Squadron. Fred Winterbotham, of 29 Squadron, based on the same aerodrome, and also flying a Nieuport, records that 'a boisterous young Canadian' asked him, on the evening of 1 June, 'can I join your patrol tomorrow?' This was the dawn patrol. It had been a favourite ploy of Albert Ball to get in an extra patrol in this way, and Winterbotham agreed without further thought. Bishop, who had already cleared his exploit with his squadron commander, Jack Scott, arranged an early call, pulled his flying suit over his pyjamas – normal practice for the dawn patrol – and took off with 29 Squadron just before four o'clock. It was a misty morning, with a drizzle of rain, but when they were well over the lines Winterbotham caught a glimpse of Bishop peeling off steeply and diving down towards Cambrai.

Bishop's plan was to make a lone surprise attack on a German aerodrome at the moment when they were rousing themselves for the business of the day. He hoped to do spectacular damage. After losing himself for a time in cloud, he found himself overflying a German airfield well inside hostile territory, but found to his chagrin that it was deserted. His luck soon changed as he sighted a second aerodrome, which was pulsating with early morning activity. This was Estourmel, on the outskirts of Cambrai.

Several machines were already lined up in front of the hangars with their engines running, just as Bishop had imagined they might be. He counted six Albatros III's and a two-seater. Diving to 200 feet, he began machine-gunning the line of aircraft, but was challenged at once by a barrage of small-arms fire from the perimeter defences. Turning back on a reciprocal course, he saw one Albatros already starting a take-off run. Dropping to 60 feet, he caught it with a 15-round burst just as it left the ground and saw it crash.

Meanwhile a second Albatros was already airborne and Bishop pursued it. The accuracy of his shooting was already legendary, but this time he missed. Yet the virulence of his attack so disorientated the German pilot that he crashed into a tree.

Two more Albatros pilots took off in opposite directions, intent on trapping their tormentor, and Bishop, still under withering small-arms fire, had no alternative but to stay and fight. Here the agility of the little Nieuport served him well. He had to climb to 1,000 feet to engage them, but he shot one of them down and the other withdrew, giving Bishop a chance to escape.

Bishop was no automaton, and the tension of the previous minutes had left him dazed and nauseated. Also he had run out of ammunition. When a formation of hostiles suddenly appeared directly above him, he unshipped his gun – which was now useless to him – to gain speed, then dived at full power for the lines, braving the inevitable barrage. When he landed back at base, the hundred or more bullet holes in his wings and fuselage were eloquent of all he had faced.

Bishop's subsequent report was forwarded by Jack Scott to Wing Headquarters, who lost no time in spreading the news. Although there could be no witness to corroborate a lone attack of this kind, Bishop's personal account was accepted, and Trenchard called his exploit 'the greatest single show of the war'. A Military Cross had been gazetted seven days previously, a DSO was already in the pipeline, and on 9 August, more than two months after his lone raid of 2 June, Bishop was told by Trenchard of the imminent award of a VC.

The lapse of time suggests that Bishop's claim was carefully checked and confirmed, though it is not clear how this could have been done, and some air historians have never been wholly convinced. Of the fifty-one VCs awarded to airmen in two World Wars, Bishop's, based on personal evidence only, uncorroborated by witnesses, or by Allied or especially in this case by German records, is unprecedented. More brashly self-assertive than most of his squadron colleagues, and sometimes accused of hyperbole, even of 'bullshit', he was nevertheless immensely popular with seniors and juniors alike, and this, and the support of Jack Scott, and of Trenchard himself, was crucial. But it is worth noting that Bishop's claims throughout his career enjoy formidable verification – from his Combat Reports, from Squadron Records, from Official Communiqués, and from his letters home.[1]

A Bar to his DSO followed him when he returned to Canada on extended leave on 1 September 1917, by which time his official score was forty-seven. And he would be back.

1. Philip Markham, *Historical Research Section of the Friends of the Canadian War Museum, Ottawa, Ontario.*

[97]

SUNNY DAYS IN JUNE: THE COLD AT HIGH ALTITUDE

A PLEASING picture of the hot, sunny days of June 1917 has been painted by the author Norman Macmillan, a pilot on 45 Squadron. He recorded how a grassy path led uphill from the hangars at St Marie Cappel to a little footbridge, emerging into a sizeable meadow surrounded by trees. Tents lined the eastern and northern perimeters of the meadow, and the Mess marquees, one for each flight, dominated the western side. When pilots and observers were not on duty they lazed on camp beds in the shade of the trees, drowsily aware of the hum of bees and the calling of birds, with camp dogs, panting in the heat, sprawled at their feet. Sometimes the heady resonances of summer were smothered by the rumble of a homing flight from some sister squadron or the muffled booming of distant guns. It was totally unreal, yet it was better to savour the moment than to dwell on what Macmillan called 'that other life', the life that lay behind them and might or might not lie before them. It was folly to think about that.

Only that morning they had been patrolling above the battlefront in their Sopwith two-seater scouts (1½-strutters) at 12,000 feet, photographing an amorphous world of scarred and cratered earth, with a farrago of explosions blinking menacingly at them the while. Yet the pall of smoke that defied the naked eye would have been partly penetrated by their cameras.

Through recurring casualties, and the departure to Home Establishment of seasoned survivors, Macmillan had become one of the squadron's senior pilots, and he cooperated enthusiastically in taking care of newcomers, giving them conducted tours of the lines, sending them off with an experienced observer, and positioning them next to the leader on patrol, with one or more protecting machines behind. But in spite of this paternalism, it was still the tyros who formed the bulk of the casualties. Nothing changed that. But if they could survive those first precarious weeks, a longish career could follow.

This was certainly the experience of Charles Smart, whose dedication to the task in hand was enhanced rather than diminished by time. Smart had been engaged on several trench-bashing shoots in the Oppy area, a German strong-point six miles north-east of Arras on which a second infantry attack was planned, the first having failed after heavy fighting. 'I understand the attack on Oppy comes off tomorrow evening,' noted Smart. 'I have put myself down for the contact patrol job, I must see the show through . . .' His narrow escape over this same target six weeks earlier, when his wing-tip had been shredded by a 'friendly' shell, was to prove insignificant compared with what lay in front of him now.

The attack was launched at 19.10 on 28 June under cover of the usual shell barrage, and Smart, with Lieutenant Currie as observer, took off at 19.30 with instructions to call for flares by klaxon horn at 20.00 to find out how the attack was going. He was also to drop messages from Corps Headquarters. 'I did not like the look of the weather as we took off,' he wrote afterwards, 'but of course the job had to be done at all cost.'

At about 19.50 the storm Smart was expecting broke. 'In a few seconds I was fighting for my life with every muscle and sinew in my body. The gale was like a mighty whirlwind, lightning flashed and rain came down like a deluge, clouds and thick mist came up and blotted out everything. My machine bounded up and down like a mad thing and was quite out of control most of the time. Our job simply had to be done so I dropped down to 400 feet till we could just see the ground . . .' They crept along a road through their own shell barrage, but could not call for flares as they could see nothing.

[99]

Six times they flew back and forth along this road, until a break in the mist just as they crossed the lines finally fixed their position – and brought a blizzard of machine-gun fire. 'Currie thumped on his klaxon horn and as if by magic a row of red flares appeared on the ground below us right along the line of our objective. Currie nearly went mad with excitement . . .'

Their next task was to find their pre-arranged dropping stations, where flares would be lit to guide them, drop their messages, and fight their way back to their aerodrome. There they found that the gale had demolished three hangars and the machines inside them and ripped off the roof of the Mess, while a thunderbolt had dug a hole in the aerodrome four feet deep. The ground was so waterlogged that as soon as they came to a standstill their machine sank up to its axles. Amidst general astonishment that they were still in one piece, they were hauled out of their machine, revived with an egg flip (egg, brandy and milk), and driven at breakneck speed to Corps Headquarters to report.

Back at the aerodrome they learned the good news that the commanders at all three dropping stations had telephoned to know if they were all right. The bad news came when the squadron commander, Major E.J. Tyson, asked if they felt equal to doing the same job again in a few hours' time, taking off at 03.45. 'Of course we said "Yes", although personally I felt as if I never wanted to see an aeroplane again . . .' By the time they had calmed down they decided it was too late to go to bed, so they sat up smoking until it was time to go up again. Fortunately the storm had abated and they were able to report that the infantry were still hanging on.

'I got to bed at about 6 a.m. quite exhausted,' wrote Smart. But at nine o'clock they were awakened by an orderly with the message that Gordon Shephard, their brigade commander, wanted to see them. Surely not another show? 'The General was awfully nice and said the usual thing about upholding the honour of the Flying Corps etc.' So all was well. The General Officer Commanding also congratulated them, saying that 50 per cent of the success achieved was due to No. 5 Squadron RFC. Oppy was only a small show, as Smart realised, with limited objectives that were not as it happened attained.

He was told by Major Tyson that he had been recommended for a decoration, but he didn't expect anything to come of it. Personal congratulations also came from the divisional commander, who told Smart that their messages were the only news that came through from the front line that night, that the phone wires were all cut, and that the barrage was so fierce the runners could not get through. The general also recorded his astonishment that a machine could be kept in the air in such weather. Smart's MC came through a fortnight later.

The episode, both in the air and on the ground, was a stark reminder that the summer months, although they might be idyllic at times, as Norman Macmillan recorded, could not always be relied on for campaigning. The weather could sometimes turn nasty. It was a threat, though, that had to be ignored if a major breakthrough was to be attempted that year.

The preliminary bombardment that was due to begin on 8 July was itself delayed, bad weather restricting flying until the 11th. Every delay brought the autumn and winter nearer. Meanwhile Haig, who had not yet received acceptance of his plans from the War Cabinet, was being pressed, as already recorded, to release squadrons for home defence. With nearly a million Allied soldiers crammed into the Ypres salient, the Germans could not but be aware of the impending attack, and they assembled in similar strength. Also based at aerodromes opposite Ypres was the newly-formed Richthofen Circus, a hunting group of four *Jagdstaffels* the essence of which was mobility, individual *staffels* being capable of being switched at short notice to sensitive areas. Richthofen, whose presence at the front had been rated by Ludendorff as 'worth three divisions', had returned in mid-June, and the old magic was beginning to work. The task that faced him was to prevent the RFC from regaining control of the air before the battle commenced.

On the morning of 6 July he was out with his *staffel* when he spotted a formation of FE's. They were fighting FE2d's of 20 Squadron, and they were engaged at once by up to forty German fighters, led by Richthofen. Four Sopwith Tripes of 10 (Naval) Squadron were providing top cover for the FE's and they drove down four of the hostiles without loss to themselves; but although the FE's fought tenaciously they suffered losses, two being shot down and the observer being wounded in a third.

The streamers that denoted the leading FE acted like a magnet to Richthofen, but he was up against a skilful flight commander in Captain Douglas Cunnell and an experienced gunner in Second-Lieutenant A.E. Woodbridge, who had already driven off several challengers. Recognising Richthofen's scarlet Albatros, and knowing he would have no chance against its superior armament if he let it get close, Woodbridge opened fire early in the hope of driving it off. Richthofen had not even flipped off his safety-catch when he was struck by what he would have called a lucky hit on the left side of the head. As the Albatros spun viciously earthwards, Richthofen instinctively switched off his engine to prevent a fire, meanwhile fighting for orientation. Temporarily blinded, he pushed back his goggles, but he was falling through a veil of darkness from which there seemed no escape.

Richthofen had sent so many good men to their deaths that he knew no one was indestructible. But as he gathered up his energies he was suddenly conscious of light and shade, and finally of colour. He was down to 2,500 feet, but his comrades were protecting him from further indignity and he managed to get his Albatros down. He was still barely conscious when they rushed him to hospital. The wound refused to heal quickly, and this put him out of the reckoning for a few weeks at least, during which the struggle for air supremacy over the battlefield would be fought. If Woodbridge's hit was a fluke, it was a significant one.

Six days later, on 12 July, as the weather cleared, air activity of an unprecedented intensity developed over the Ypres front. Although the Allies had a numerical advantage, the Germans were doubling and trebling the strength of individual formations, and British casualties were inevitable. Among them was Douglas Cunnell, whose gunner (Lieutenant Albert Bill, not Woodbridge this time) got an Albatros before flying the FE2d back to base when Cunnell was killed. Yet German losses generally exceeded the British. Enemy pilots thought twice before crossing the Allied lines, but the RFC's overall task, as at Messines, of keeping the skies clear for the corps machines, and denying reconnaissance access to the enemy, had yet to be achieved.

In pursuit of the desired ascendancy, an air battle was fought on 26 July near Polygon Wood, five miles east of Ypres and two miles behind the lines. A typically massive German hunting formation was matched by an equal number of RFC single-seaters, so that an estimated ninety-four fighting machines became locked in combat at various levels. The *casus belli* was a flight of German two-seaters, lurking on the German side at 5,000 feet, waiting for an opportunity to cross the lines and reconnoitre the Ypres area. Three thousand feet above them, thirty protective Albatros scouts were being challenged by seven of the new DH5's, tractor replacements for the outmoded DH2 pushers. Five thousand feet above them in turn, ten Albatros scouts were fighting off thirty British scouts of various types. Higher still, up to 17,000 feet, seven naval Triplanes were slugging it out with another ten Albatros scouts. None of these exchanges, however, was decisive, but the engagement must be accounted a defeat for the British. While they were absorbed in the mêlée, four of the German two-seaters sneaked across the lines and completed their reconnaissance.

More successful was a deliberate enticement the following day in the same area, when eight of the FE2d's of 20 Squadron crossed the lines in close formation to set a trap for the Circus, to be sprung by a posse of avenging fighters drawn from British squadrons within reach. It was typical of the self-confidence of the crews of this pusher squadron that they embraced the idea with enthusiasm. Circling nose to tail as was their wont for mutual protection, they held off a swarm of some twenty Albatros scouts while simultaneously luring them towards the fighters. SE5A's and Triplanes both scored victories, more than offsetting their own losses, but the day was won by the FE crews themselves. Mounting three Lewis guns to a machine, two for the observer and one for the pilot, they claimed six hostiles destroyed, with some justification. Two were seen to go down in flames, a third broke up in mid-air, and three more crashed, while the only casualties sustained by the FE's were a wounded pilot and observer.

[103]

Slowly the squadrons were recovering from 'Bloody April' and all it entailed. The Australian Francis Penny, whose pilot training had been interrupted when he had been shanghaied to help fill empty cockpits on 12 Squadron as an observer ('I've just come from there,' an informant had told him, 'I reckon you'll last about six weeks'), had lasted long enough to be sent back eventually to England to complete his pilot training. He had just about qualified when another urgent appeal, this time for pilots, sent him scurrying back, again to 12 Squadron. In his absence, RE8's had replaced the BE's, and this was not the only change: the array of new faces was daunting. Yet in many ways life with the RFC in France continued to be comparatively luxurious.

No. 12 Squadron had a new commander, Major C.S. Burnett, who was accustomed to having a whisky and milk before breakfast. The milk had to be fresh, not condensed. Penny, reckoned, as an Australian, to be accustomed to cattle, got the job of acquiring a squadron cow, and after fitting up a vehicle as a cattle truck he began scouring the countryside. Eventually he found a farmer willing to sell a likely looking animal. A nearby cavalry regiment provided suitable fodder, and an airman who admitted to having worked on a farm was appointed cattleman and milkmaid. Fresh milk in the Mess was much appreciated – and the major got his whisky and milk.

Meanwhile the Germans, copying the night bombing of their aerodromes by the FE2b's of 100 Squadron, reciprocated in kind, sometimes with dire results. But at 12 Squadron the only casualty was the cow, which was reported missing. Very sensibly, she had decided to make her way back to the more peaceful atmosphere of the farm. Next morning Penny remounted the cattle-truck, and he and the airman/farmer set off in pursuit. They found the cow grazing happily by the roadside, and with some difficulty persuaded her back into the truck.

A contrast which the infantry did not have to endure was that between the summer temperatures at ground level and the cold at higher altitudes. Frank Ransford, commissioned in 1914, was another recruit from the trenches, and by July 1917, after transfer-

ring, he was posted as an observer to FE2b's. He tells of reporting
for orders on summer mornings in full flying kit – thigh boots,
lambswool leather coats, fur caps, mouthpieces, goggles and scarves,
essential protection in open cockpits, but unbearably sweaty on the
ground. Not all transferred infantrymen took kindly at first to the
vertiginous peculiarities of the FE, but Ransford settled quickly. 'I
take my seat in the front edge of the nacelle, facing my pilot, as I am
responsible that no one dives on our tail . . . I sit there as easily and
comfortably as if I am sitting in a deck chair.' Perched right on the
edge of the nacelle at 100 miles an hour at perhaps 12,000 feet,
anchored to nothing, holding on to nothing, he experienced no fear
of falling out. Every succeeding flight made him feel more at home
and increased his confidence in pilot and machine. But for all his
care with guns and ammunition, he was under no illusions about
the FE's vulnerability, and spoke of 'the joyful sight of an escort',
seldom granted.

Yet another recruit from the infantry, Lieutenant A.D. Light, had
seen the army order that all RFC applications must be forwarded,
whether recommended or not, and he told his brigadier his nerve
would fail him if he stayed in the trenches much longer. It was an
escape route for officers that was rarely available for other ranks. The
brigadier knew his man and gave him a good report, and although he
was told he was too old at twenty-six, he joined 48 Squadron under
Zulu Bettington that summer as an observer, after a spell at the
School of Aerial Gunnery at Hythe. Within a week of his leaving the
line his replacement was killed, and he was lucky, too, in joining 48
Squadron. Although said to be too old in 1917, he flew as an air
gunner in flying boats more than twenty years later in the Second
World War.

THE PRANKS OF SIBLEY AND SHONE

No. 48 was a truly remarkable squadron. After its disastrous start, it had quickly acquired a reputation commensurate with its status as the first Bristol Fighter squadron. Besides the inimitable Zulu Bettington, the three flight commanders were all distinguished in their way. New Zealander Keith Park, at 25, was described by contemporaries as 'like a Greek god', and he was revered by those who flew with and alongside him; but he might perhaps be said to have his greatest days to come, as AOC 11 Group in the Battle of Britain. Brian Baker, then just 20, and dubbed by contemporaries, for reasons now obscure, 'the corporal-major', also had a brilliant career ahead of him. But of the third flight commander, Samuel Sibley, 'Squibs', as he was known, it might be said that, even among the giants of 48 Squadron, he was something special. As for his nineteen-year-old observer, P.N.M. 'Puggy' Shone, he was incomparable.

Haig's plan for developing his campaign inland from the Belgian coast, once the Roulers—Thourout railway link was in Allied hands, meant the transfer of a number of squadrons to support the British Fourth Army in that area, and one of these squadrons was No. 48. Already suffering from shell shock, Shone, as an infantryman, had re-applied for the RFC in the spring of 1917, directly he heard that anyone who had been turned down on minor medical grounds and still wanted to transfer could do so. Shone had slightly defective vision in one eye. 'Sorry I can't give you a choice between pilot and observer,' he was told in France by a certain Major H.O.D. Segrave, later to be associated with speed records on land and water, 'but we're very short of observers, so that's what you'll have to be.' 'I don't mind,' replied the accommodating Shone, 'as long as I get in.'

Returning to England to report with eighteen others to the Gunnery School at Hythe, he was thrown around in an Armstrong-Whitworth FK8 'Big Ack' for ten minutes, only keeping in by holding on to the Scarff Ring. Of the eighteen trainees, nine were lifted out after their ordeal in an appalling state of air sickness and returned to their units. But not Shone. He was posted to 48 Squadron. Park's regular observer was on leave, so for a time Shone flew with him ('a delightful man,' was his verdict). When Park's observer returned, Sibley, on Park's recommendation, asked for Shone.

Sibley had joined 24 Squadron in its early days at Hounslow under Hawker and served with him in France – a worthy apprenticeship – until a crash, in August 1916, interrupted his career. To Puggy Shone, he seemed out to make up for lost time.

Sitting back to back in a Brisfit, with no artificial aids to intercommunication, pilot and observer had to have an understanding, and Sibley and Shone worked out their own code of taps and signs for various tactical situations, so that eventually they became instinctive. They soon became not merely close friends but, in Shone's words, 'an absolute team'. Sibley taught Shone how to handle the Brisfit, lest he be incapacitated. 'Come on, Puggy,' he would say, returning from a patrol, 'you take over.' Shone eventually turned down the chance of a pilot's course to stay with Sibley.

The main job of a Brisfit squadron at that time was the offensive patrol, and in the summer of 1917 they would be off the floor by 4 a.m. and formed up at about 14,000 feet by the time they reached the line, when they started looking for trouble. 'We nearly always got it, within a very short time.'

They were doing a daily average that summer of one long OP and one short OP, the former involving a penetration of about twenty miles, the latter about five. The average life of a pilot/observer combination, during the fighting in May/June/July for what was euphemistically known as air supremacy, was twenty hours. Before their partnership was broken, Sibley and Shone had done 150. Long before then, according to Shone, the RFC, with the help of the RNAS, had regained the ascendancy.

'We knew exactly what we would do in any and every dogfight,' boasted Shone. But he admitted that he had very little recollection of what actually happened. Two bangs on the back of Sibley's flying helmet was Shone's signal that he had spotted hostiles. Sibley then led his flight into the best possible position for attack, and when Shone fired a red light, it was every man for himself.

Team work was the main but not the only factor. Armament for the Bristol was a Vickers for the pilot firing through the propeller arc and a Lewis for the observer; later a second Lewis was fitted. Shone angled his second Lewis at approximately 45 degrees to the ground, as it often happened when they met an enemy formation that two hostiles would dive together at their tail, the first firing from about the same level, the second continuing the dive until he attacked from somewhere below. Shone found he just had time to fire at the one coming straight for him and almost simultaneously loose off a burst at the chap underneath. By loading his guns – they all filled their own drums – with tracer he made sure the hostiles could see they were being fired at. It had a most salutary effect.

Something of the temperaments of these two men may perhaps be gauged from their nicknames. They had no illusions, but they enjoyed themselves, off duty and on. Grounded because of the weather, they went into nearby Dunkirk for a meal and some shopping. Sibley stopped by a fruit stall. 'Look, Puggy, I've got an idea. All those blasted Huns who sit out on the promenade at Ostend with their girl friends – I really don't think we can allow that to go on.' It was a scene they had glimpsed many times as they photographed the coastline to prepare for the amphibious landing that was planned. 'Let's get a big bag of oranges, and one day when we've got some broken cloud on the way back from a show, we'll come down nice and low over Ostend and throw these oranges at them. What do you think?' 'Squibs,' said Shone, 'it's a brilliant idea!'

[108]

Within a few days the conditions were favourable, the oranges were ripe, perhaps a shade over-ripe, and Sibley came down to fifty feet parallel with the promenade. Rows of Germans and their girl friends were socialising happily when suddenly Shone stood up and began hurling oranges at their feet, one after another as fast as he could. 'We watched these chaps falling off their chairs, jumping up and rushing into the cafés behind them, their girl friends in pursuit, convinced they were the victims of some frightful new weapon. Why we didn't crash, because we were laughing so much, I really don't know.'

Later they played a similar trick on a German aerodrome. They got hold of an old football, painted it bright red, attached long streamers to it, waited for reasonable cloud cover, and dropped it from 500 feet on a line of Albatros scouts, some with their engines running. Their aim was accurate, the football behaved like a bouncing bomb, and there was a gorgeous moment of chaos as mechanics ran for cover and pilots tried to taxi their aeroplanes clear. It would have been easy enough to give them a few bursts with a machine gun for luck – but that would have spoiled the joke.

Chivalry, according to Shone, was not quite dead: messages dropped in metal canisters asking the fate of missing men nearly always got a reply, dropped from machines sent over at maximum height. And there was still at least one pilot/observer combination too squeamish to shoot down a machine in cold blood. On their way back from a show, in broken cloud, Sibley and Shone, to their amazement, saw an unarmed enemy two-seater training machine emerging sedately from the sanctuary of cloud, pilot and instructor looking in the opposite direction, completely oblivious to their peril. 'I tapped Squibs, but he kept on an absolutely level course. He made a gesture, and I knew what he meant. It was our duty to shoot the plane down, but we couldn't do it.'

The same thing happened again a few days later, only this time the German crew had got lost over the Allied lines. 'Sibley motioned them down and we landed at our own aerodrome with our capture. We gave the crew a jolly good lunch and plenty to drink before notifying wing headquarters.'

It was not that life on this part of the front was significantly easier than elsewhere. Photographing the whole coastline from Nieuport to Ostend and beyond had been a major and precarious task, quite apart from their offensive patrols. Confidence in their machine and in each other was a part of it, but their keen sense of the ridiculous did not always protect them from fear. 'There was no tour of duty,' noted Shone. 'You went on until you'd had it. You did not admit to your closest friends that you'd got to the point where you doubted if you could go on.'

Early in September Sibley's flight was involved in a tremendous scrap. Two Brisfits were lost and Sibley's machine was in a sorry state, main spars splintered, ailerons, rudder and elevator damaged, engine running roughly. Only superb handling by Sibley got them back. As they passed Ostend and neared the trenches Sibley alerted Shone and pointed down, indicating that, once they had crossed the lines, he would have to attempt a landing on the beach. On touching down the fixed undercarriage collapsed and the Brisfit somersaulted, finally coming to rest upside down. 'I undid my safety belt,' said Shone, 'turned on my back and undid Squibs's belt for him, and he gently slid out.' Bruised and bludgeoned, they crawled away and sat exhausted on the beach. 'Sibley then made one of the absolutely classic remarks of World War I. "You know, Puggy", he said, "the trouble with this war is that it's so bloody dangerous."'

Not surprisingly, the crash reactivated Shone's shell shock. His older brother Geoffrey, a pilot on 56 Squadron, was killed on 19 October, and he realised that his nerve had gone. He was reduced to instructing his batman, when calling him for the early morning long OP, to wake him up with two stiff whiskies. 'Without them I wouldn't like to think what I might have done.' Soon afterwards, in another fierce engagement, their machine was crippled again, and they had barely crossed no man's land when they crashed. Under fire at first from all sides, they were rescued by one of their own batteries. Sibley recovered quickly but Shone spent the next ten months in hospital and convalescing. On 14 February 1918, with a new observer, Sibley was shot down and taken prisoner, but both men survived the war.

*　　*　　*

Less spectacular, but still of prime importance, was the work of the corps machines. Lieutenant John Theophilus Percival Jeyes joined 21 Squadron on RE8's on his nineteenth birthday, 3 June 1917. The experienced observer he was given to get him started was soon posted home, to be replaced by a beginner, Second-Lieutenant M.L. Hatch; they soon discovered that they were both old boys of Oundle School. Maurice Hatch was the senior by several years and had actually been Jeyes' school prefect, but he gave Jeyes great encouragement by showing confidence in him and acknowledging him as skipper. 'We soon found that we could work together in the air,' wrote Jeyes, 'which was a great thing for us both.' Jeyes believed that boys from an engineering school like Oundle had a better chance of coping with the practical side of aviation than boys from the more illustrious colleges. (Against this, the record of Old Etonians in the RFC seems exceptional.)

The routine of artillery cooperation remained much the same, with wireless playing a much larger part than in the early days. After their various pre-flight checks and procedures came the task of getting airborne from their small airfield, with Jeyes holding the machine down low over the grass and pulling up swiftly to avoid the hop poles beyond. Even near the front line, French peasants were always at work. Jeyes would then circle while Hatch unwound the trailing aerial and made a check call to the wireless station on the aerodrome. If he reeled out the aerial too quickly it would snap, and they would have to land to repair or replace it – a tricky procedure when they had bombs on board, as they often had. The work of fixing the aerial would take about fifteen minutes, and then they would have all their pre-flight checks and procedures – and the take-off – to go through again. It would then take about an hour, with the loads they carried, to get to 7,000 feet.

On the way to the lines they would start calling the battery they were to work with, and the battery would put out ground strips to acknowledge that they were ready for action. For the next hour or more they would be monitoring and directing the battery's fire, which meant continual manoeuvring of the machine so they could see the battery's shells bursting. So absorbed did they become in their work

[111]

that they sometimes forgot how vulnerable they were, and reminders from Hun machines and Archie could shock them into sudden awareness. But thanks to the fighting squadrons, and to their own growing competence, the two ex-Oundle schoolboys continued to work successfully together. 'We used to think we were being overworked,' wrote Jeyes, 'especially after Dawn Patrols and two other patrols in the same day, lasting approximately three hours each patrol and usually getting attacked by Hun aircraft, and always ack-ack at us when we were photographing enemy lines and unloading 25 lb bombs on them . . .

'When flying in formation, and one [machine] is shot down and the others left, it is really frightening to carry on . . . But one soon forgot one's fears and got busy with immediate problems.' They survived all vicissitudes, mostly together, for the rest of that summer and far into the autumn and winter, being posted home at last in January 1918, the only known instance of a team of Old Boys 'Playing for the School'.[1]

Before the end of July 1917, two more squadrons, Nos 11 and 22, had completed conversion from FE2b's to Bristol Fighters, and 70 Squadron had swapped their Sopwith two-seaters for the first of the RFC's Sopwith Camels. Although the Camel was inferior in speed and rate of climb to some of the later German models, the gyroscopic forces produced by its 130 hp Clerget rotary engine gave it an ability to flip round to the right with an extraordinary turn of speed and complete a full circle while other machines were turning only 90 degrees, disconcerting for enemy pilots to say the least. Everyone loved the Camel once they had mastered its peculiarities, but it remained, in essence, 'a fierce little beast'. A switch in training from an Avro to a Camel could be altogether too abrupt, resulting in many accidents, and not until the cockpit of trainer Camels was modified in 1918 to take an instructor behind the pupil was the death rate among the latter reduced.

Meanwhile the new machines had played their part in redressing

1. Maurice Hatch also flew frequently with Second-Lieutenant Basil E. Catchpole, MC, DFC, later a flight commander on this Squadron.

the imbalance of March, April, May and June, so that the Fifth Army was able to record by the end of July that the enemy 'has shown less individual activity and does not cross our line as often as he used to'. The large formations in which he had begun operating had been repeatedly repulsed, nearly always on the enemy side of the lines, while counter-battery work, supported by air reconnaissance, had actually caused a further postponement of the battle, because the enemy had been forced to withdraw many of his batteries and time was needed for our own forces to adjust. Haig knew well enough that the establishment of ascendancy in the air was a vital contribution to the battles ahead, and on 28 July he passed his 'very hearty appreciation' and 'best congratulations' to Trenchard. Three days later he began his Flanders offensive.

THE THIRD BATTLE OF YPRES: 'ALL FOR TWO SHILLINGS A DAY'

H AIG'S attack, aimed north-east from the Ypres salient by Gough's Fifth Army on a front of seven and a half miles, with the French First Army on his left and Plumer's Second Army on his right, opened at dawn on 31 July, the British Government having finally approved Haig's plans on the 20th. The results of the first day's fighting were encouraging, much of the first German defence system being overrun, but the pre-arranged plan for RFC cooperation was negated by low cloud and rain. The problems of the air observers were exacerbated by the infantry's failure to light flares when requested by klaxon horn to do so, and many corps machines were hit and put out of action through crews having to sweep over at low level to try to identify uniforms. Fifty-eight contact patrols were flown in the course of the day by the corps squadrons, and only by dogged persistence did they succeed in keeping pace with the general progress of the attack.

Typical of their tenacity were the crews of the RE8's of No. 6 Squadron. The pilot of the machine entrusted with the initial patrol was killed, and the observer of the relief plane was wounded. The long-stop detailed was a newcomer, Second-Lieutenant Nicholas W. Wadham, for whom this was his first experience of action. His Canadian observer, Harry Quigley, wore the ribbons of the Distinguished Conduct Medal and the Military Cross, but these awards had been won first as a private in the Canadian Infantry and second as an officer with the Canadian Engineers, and his experience as an observer was less impressive. Wadham set off in some trepidation, but at least his observer was likely to be cool under fire.

With cloud down to 500 feet over the battlefield they had to fly under it, and they had been over the lines no more than minutes when an 18 lb shell drilled what Wadham called 'a perfectly neat hole' through the peak top of his engine cowling. Understandably, he was 'extremely frightened', but the reaction of his battle-hardened observer astounded him: he 'appeared to think it was the best joke in the world'. Totally unconcerned, he rallied Wadham and actually kept him over the lines for another two hours, giving him agonies of suspense but teaching him an operational equanimity he might never otherwise have acquired, and they came back with a valuable report. 'I gradually came to see the affair', noted the chastened Wadham, 'more from his point of view. That shell', he concluded, 'must have gone right through the prop without touching it and then over the top plane, for nothing was hit except the cowling.' It was a bizarre example of reverse synchronisation. 'No wonder Quigley thought it funny.'

The army squadrons, too, were impeded by the weather, and the patrols they attempted proved abortive. They reverted to bombing and harrying aerodromes and communications centres. This change of tactics, dictated by the conditions, was anticipated only just in time, fighting squadrons being up most of the previous night fitting improvised bomb-racks and 25 lb bombs, generally four to a machine, with little idea what the result might be to the airworthiness of the machines. The Spad pilots were spared the gamble because it was found impractical to fit bomb-racks to their machines, but not so the pilots of the newly delivered SE5A's, who found themselves, with much misgiving, putting the experiment to the test in battle.

Few matched the verve and aggression at any time of the head-strong Lieutenant R.A. 'Dick' Maybery, of 56 Squadron. Twenty-two years old and a native of Brecon, he had begun the war in the cavalry and was known as a dead shot. His combat report for this opening day has been widely quoted. Taking off at 04.45, Maybery

[115]

crossed the lines at 500 feet 'underneath very thick clouds', just as Wadham had done. The smoke from the artillery barrage made it impossible to see ahead, so he steered south-east and came down to 200 and then to 30 feet. Sighting Courtrai, he headed for the Circus aerodrome at Heule, but was spotted and attacked by two Albatros scouts. He tried to frighten them off with a few gun-bursts, but combat, in his heavily loaded machine, had to be avoided. He saw a Spad machine-gunning a ground target that was invisible to him, suddenly realised he was alone, sighted Courtrai again in improving visibility, found the aerodrome at Heule, zoomed to 200 feet, and circled the 'drome to pick his spot. 'I then flew east, turned and came back along the line of the southernmost sheds and dropped my first bomb, which hit the third shed from the east and exploded. This caused immense excitement . . .' Turning first to the left, he flew along the line of the easternmost sheds and dropped another bomb, which hit the first shed from the south and exploded. He next flew straight at the sheds at the town end of the aerodrome and dropped his third bomb, which went through either the roof or the door of another of the sheds: he could see smoke, and he felt and heard the explosion.

He had one more bomb to drop, and as he came near, approaching this time from the north, a machine-gunner opened up at him from the rear of the sheds. He pulled the bomb release, but nothing happened. He was still looking for the explosion when he found his bombing run had taken him close to the railway station at Courtrai. This seemed a worthwhile target and he pulled the bomb release again, hopefully. This time the bomb fell away and exploded between a goods train and a shed.

He had no bombs left, but he was not quite finished with Heule aerodrome. The same machine-gunner fired at him, and another whom he could not locate, but he silenced the former, and the latter evidently thought it best not to reveal his position. He then flew twice across the aerodrome, so low the second time that he actually brushed the ground with his wheels as he fired both guns at the sheds.

Incredibly, he was still not finished. Flying straight on to Cuerne, another Circus aerodrome, he machine-gunned the sheds before attacking, as opportunity targets, two military-looking horsemen, witnessing their dishevelment when their horses bolted. An attack with both guns on a column of infantry 200 strong scattered them to the verges of a road, and after changing drums he attacked them again. Sighting a German two-seater at 200 feet, he zoomed without being seen and shot it down, seeing it crash. 'Only one man got out.' Not until he ran out of ammunition for the Lewis, and the Vickers jammed, did he recross the lines and return.

Many other pilots reported similar experiences, among their targets being aerodromes, transport and troops. In giving their own troops a helping hand, three pilots and one observer were killed, two two-man crews were shot down and taken prisoner, and the pilots and observers of four more crews escaped with wounds. Despite the conditions, twenty-three combats were recorded and eight victories claimed.

Yet Trenchard's doctrine of the offensive, and his constant theme that the aeroplane was not a defensive weapon, was still not fully understood by army commanders, or by their subordinates, who did not appreciate the RFC's achievements in depth because they could rarely see them, and they called for local protection whenever a strafing German intruder appeared. Trenchard was obliged to prepare a paper for circulation among the General Staff clarifying the role and limitations of the aeroplane in battle.

Haig's remark to Trenchard, before the Battle of Neuve Chappelle in March 1915, that 'If you can't fly because of the weather I shall probably put off the attack', suggests that the 1917 Flanders offensive might never have been begun if the weather in the remainder of that summer could have been foreseen. 31 July had been bad enough, but the first four days of August were marred by continual rain, stormy and unsettled conditions followed, and counter-battery work, reconnaissance, and all forms of patrolling, on which the ground forces now relied so heavily, were impeded if not choked altogether. The battle area, already churned up by the preliminary bombardment

[117]

and with its drainage systems mutilated, turned, in the words of Haig's subsequent despatch, into 'a succession of vast muddy pools. The valleys of the choked and overflowing streams were speedily transformed into long stretches of bog, impassable except for a few well-defined tracks, which became marks for the enemy's artillery.' For the Allied soldier, to leave these tracks was to court death by drowning, a fate that befell men and pack animals alike. 'In these conditions,' as Haig himself wrote, 'operations of any magnitude became impossible.' The fine weather that Haig relied on for the ground to recover came too little and too late, and the succession of minor battles of the next few months developed into a war of attritional slaughter. Nearly all the ground gained was eventually lost, the prior condition of the capture of the Roulers–Thourout rail link for the opening of the Nieuport offensive was never fulfilled, the main German line was not even reached, and criticism of Haig for persisting right through to November has since been widespread. Meanwhile the RFC, still an integral part of the Army, fought and suffered with it.

Pilots whose patrols were rendered sterile by the weather usually sought to contribute something positive by coming down low on the return flight to strafe enemy trenches. This form of harassment was becoming routine, but the crews, too, were vulnerable. Alan Dore records how men in the Allied trenches witnessed the end of a Sopwith two-seater of his squadron, No. 43; they saw the tail come off and the observer either jump or fall out. Dore motored out to the front next day to recover the bodies. 'We buried their poor mangled remains amid the desultory shell-fire that always greets you near the trenches.' The pilot's name was Second-Lieutenant L.A. McPherson, and his observer, or more accurately gunner, was a second-class air mechanic named Frederick Webb, another two-shillings-a-day volunteer. A study of squadron records reveals how vital to the work of the RFC these largely anonymous and unhonoured volunteers were.

The same squadron, still under Dore, and still waiting for their Camels, registered – despite heavy losses – a remarkable success in mid-August in a subsidiary attack on Hill 70, near Lens, before the Ypres operations proper were resumed. After the night and day bombing of aerodrome and communications targets on 13 and 14 August by Armstrong-Whitworths, Martinsydes and DH4's, Dore noted: 'Tomorrow [15 August] is the day of the attack. For several days past we have been preparing for it. I attend the conference at Canadian Corps Headquarters [First Army] . . . We are to try to spot counter-attacks and send out machines to fire at troops from the air.'

Dore took off with the rest of his squadron for an advanced landing ground at 04.45 next morning, his crews being employed all day in groups of three at a time, watching the zone through which the enemy must pass to counter-attack. Their brief was to look for movements, to machine-gun any congestion of enemy infantry, to engage enemy artillery, and to attack any intruding enemy aeroplanes. Dore could see at once that the attack was going well, but he could also see several of his machines on the ground, 'two having evidently collided'. He landed and managed to recruit a doctor for the injured men. Of the rest of his squadron he recorded that one of his flight commanders, Captain Collier, had had his fuel tank perforated but had got home on his gravity tank with a wounded observer; Hood had dived at and fired on some enemy guns; Veitch after many adventures had strafed a battalion, a battery, and various smaller groups; and best of all, an observer named Croll, flying with a Lieutenant Thompson, had identified the signs of an enemy counter-attack. This, believed Dore, was the RFC's first success of this kind. The bad news was that 'Maplestone returned wounded in the foot; Hargreaves made a good landing but died a few minutes later; Moore and Snelgrove did not return.' Both, it transpired, had been killed.

These casualties, in the words of a First Army report, 'were slight in comparison with the value of the work done by the squadron'. Eighteen flights, at 1,000 feet or under, were flown by 43 Squadron that day and a total of 5,000 rounds fired, an enemy two-seater was destroyed in combat, and a pilot named Gedge, attacked by twelve single-seaters, drove one down out of control. The outstanding success was the frustration of the enemy counter-attack. The General Officer Commanding First Army thanked Dore personally, and

Trenchard wired his congratulations. Soon afterwards Dore went on leave, his first for four months. 'Very glad to get away after the strain of the last few days.'

Other squadrons successful that day included No. 40, still flying Nieuports and operating from the same advanced landing ground as No. 43; their orders were to go up in pursuit of low-flying enemy machines that had been sighted and reported by wireless from one of the strategically placed observation stations. One of their flight commanders, recently promoted and awarded the MC, was Mick Mannock. Two of the hostiles were destroyed, three shot down out of control, and many others were damaged or driven off. It was directly attributable to the work of 43 and 40 Squadrons that the corps machines remained unmolested all day.

The RE8's of 16 Squadron, now under Peter Portal, DSO, MC, also earned high praise, first for their work in engaging hostile batteries and infantry concentrations, secondly for providing up-to-date photographs of the enemy lines, and thirdly for their contact patrols. 'Perfect liaison was maintained and we were instantly informed of the situation.'

The main battle that ensued on the Ypres front – of Langemarck, as it was known – failed in its objective, but the RFC bombed their targets successfully, strafed enemy troops remorselessly and recorded movements accurately. RE8 crews particularly distinguished themselves, the counter-battery work of No. 9 Squadron standing up exceptionally well to subsequent analysis, while the observers of 7 and 21 Squadrons showed no fear of interfering Albatros scouts, destroying two and possibly three on the first day without loss to themselves.

It was an RE8 crew – of 59 Squadron – who were called upon, at seven o'clock on the evening of 18 August, to register a vital target for a siege battery, at a point where the enemy wire defences had been insufficiently cut, holding up the advance. This particular crew, like many others, had taken time to settle down, mutual appreciation only coming from experience of each other in action. On their first flight together, the pilot had actually reported his observer, through a misunderstanding, for failing to open fire. 'As we taxied across the aerodrome,' wrote observer Lieutenant Richard F. Sheraton, 'the pin on the left wheel sheared through and the wheel came off just as we were leaving the ground.' Sheraton saw it happen and warned his pilot, Lieutenant John A. Craig, but the reaction of both men was the same. 'It was vitally important that the shoot should be proceeded with, since dusk was approaching and there would be no further opportunity that day.'

After a successful shoot – the area was captured next morning – Craig and Sheraton returned to face what seemed a certain crash landing. Twice Craig circled the aerodrome in preparation, giving time for the assembly of an anxious but ghoulish crowd. 'The whole personnel of the squadron appeared on the aerodrome,' wrote Sheraton, 'since the RE8 was notoriously nose-heavy and prone to catching fire.'

Darkness was falling as they approached, heightening the drama. 'I felt our sole remaining wheel touch terra firma, and everything went quite smoothly until the axle dropped and cut into the soil. Immediately this happened, the whole world appeared to turn upside down and the plane went over on its back.' There was no fire, and both men scrambled out unhurt, but they had given the ghouls a run for their money.

'On 30 August,' concluded Sheraton, 'our Brigade sent a letter in acknowledgement of the work which Craig and I did on the 18th, when we continued our flight to range the enemy guns after losing a wheel taking off.'

'THE OBSERVERS OUT HERE ARE VERY PLUCKY CHAPS'

Captain Leslie Horridge, No. 7 Squadron

T HE shortage of experienced observers, mainly because of their vulnerability in combat, was often acute, and those who volunteered to fill vacancies inevitably took time to adjust. 'Starting out one morning with a new observer who had only that day arrived at the squadron,' wrote Brisfit pilot Frank Ransley of 48 Squadron, 'we had no sooner crossed the lines when we met an unusually heavy barrage of anti-aircraft fire which took me all my time to dodge. As soon as I had a chance I looked round to the back seat to see how my new observer was taking things. He was on the floor in a faint.'

Turning back to base with the idea of getting a seasoned replacement, Ransley felt a tap on the shoulder from a still pallid observer who was nevertheless pointing eastwards, anxious to redeem himself. 'Once more the anti-aircraft fire let us have it,' recorded Ransley. 'I looked round and the poor chap had fainted again. This time I took him right back to the aerodrome.'

Either the man was unsuited to aerial warfare, decided Ransley, or he should have been given his baptism of fire by degrees. Had it not been for the disproportionate casualty rate of observers, no doubt he would have been. 'I always had great sympathy and admiration for the observers in two-seaters,' Ransley wrote later. 'They not only had to face the perils of war but also the possibility of having to put up with the vagaries of a bad pilot.' This particular volunteer left the squadron the same day – without, according to Ransley, having unpacked his kit.[1]

From the earliest days, preparation for the specialist role of observer was patchy, and recruitment came mostly from volunteer infantry and gunnery officers already serving with their regiments at the front. Opportunities to transfer to the RFC were advertised, and the rule was that all applications must be forwarded to Headquarters. The chance to fly, and to escape from the Flanders mud, were among the attractions. Many of the aces started their careers in this way. They found the work frightening initially but intensely rewarding, particularly when cooperating with the artillery, giving them the satisfying feeling that they were assisting in hitting back at the Hun.

One might have thought that Archie would hold few terrors for men who had experienced bombardment in the trenches, but Leslie Horridge, who had faced both, did not agree. 'In an aeroplane there is always the feeling that it is a personal matter. They are not firing at a line of trenches but at you.' Sergeant-Observer H.G. Taylor had made a similar point. 'In the trenches you face death every second, not knowing when it might come . . . In the air you could see death coming.'

Highlander Jock Andrews had progressed from regimental officer to observer before becoming a pilot on DH2's with Hawker. Even as an observer he had relished the relaxed discipline and easy cama-raderie of squadron life; but for him, as for many others, this did not compensate for the feeling of inferiority inherent in the relative status of pilot and observer. There was no formal training for observers until 1917, such training as was offered was sketchy, and there was no career structure; for men like Andrews it was simply a step towards becoming a pilot. Promotion was negligible, the pay was less than that of the most recently arrived pilot, and decorations and mentions in despatches for observers were rare. The ironic consequence, as it seemed to Andrews, was that as soon as an observer became really proficient he went off to train as a pilot.

1. Frank Cecil Ransley, OBE, DFC, *Croix de Guerre*. He died in December 1992.

The meagre training available to observers meant that they learned their trade the hard way, in action over the lines. The coveted 'brevet' had to be earned. Once earned it could not be forfeited: it virtually amounted to a decoration. Robert Ingram, who had had a year in the trenches, completed 62 hours' flying before he was graded as a qualified observer and could proudly put up the half-wing. Ten flights over the lines was an absolute minimum, according to D.R. Goudie, in addition to the passing of various tests, the most important being a 'practical', under the critical eye of the brigade machine-gun specialist. Like pilots they enjoyed no simulated training, and many probationary observers didn't live long enough to qualify. 'We went up with an experienced pilot,' wrote E.D.G. 'Ted' Galley, 'and that's all the instruction we got.'

Some men felt perfectly at home almost immediately. After his first trip up the line, with a pilot named Cooper, Bob Ingram wrote to his family in Wimbledon, 'I can't tell you how I loved it. With a man like Cooper one feels as safe as in a bath chair on Wimbledon Common.' But he would not always have the admirable Cooper for a driver. Others acclimatised less readily. Quartered over the lines by ugly black clusters of Archie, they panicked. Airsickness, too, was a problem, causing some to be sent straight back to their regiments.

There was a reversal of roles when an observer became more settled: he would be expected to accompany a new pilot to the lines and familiarise him with the topography. Sometimes the new man would be apprehensive, sometimes over-confident. On one such indoctrination, according to Galley, the following conversation took place.

'What's that over there?'

'That's a Hun.'

'Good – that's what we're after!'

And the newcomer, determined to start his career in spectacular style, made straight for it. Nothing Galley could do would stop him. Fortunately it was only a harmless two-seater, which soon sheared off.

If Galley thought over-confidence was the worst fault, he changed his mind when a new pilot proved too nervous to take evasive action, flying dead straight with a Hun on their tail. Twice Galley was shot down in this way. The second time he was injured, but it got him home on a pilot's course.

Other recruits from within the BEF were the volunteer rankers, mostly air mechanics, whose extra two shillings a day was doubled to four shillings when they were graded 'proficient'. (Officers got a flat daily rate of flying pay of eight shillings.) A few of these men, McCudden among them, graduated to pilot, and many were decorated, but here again there was no career structure, and the prospects of advancement were poor. Yet neither corps nor army squadrons could have functioned without them. Charles Smart's diary entries are full of commendations of these men, and their casualty rate was high.

Recruits from the UK were often snatched from pilot training to fill empty observer cockpits. At the School of Aerial Gunnery at Hythe, they were liable to be handled roughly. O.L. Beater, a captain in the Royal Dublin Fusiliers, was scandalised by the slackness of discipline in the RFC, volunteers doing much as they liked when not flying. Many of them were 'noisy and obscene, their minds and language at an extremely low ebb'. When Beater's turn came for a trial flight, the pilot did his best to make him air-sick. The stench of burnt castor oil and doped fabric was nauseating enough anyway, and soon half his course had been rejected. But Beater qualified, spent many months with Trenchard's bombing force near Nancy, made and lost many good friends, won the DFC, and went home on a pilot's course – to be returned eventually to the artillery as 'hopelessly dud'.

Many of the methods of recruiting observers involved deception. D.R. Goudie, volunteering for pilot, was determined to resist a transfer to observer, but he was told he was medically unfit for pilot because he was long-sighted. He might misjudge his height on landing and possibly kill himself, or wreck the machine, or both. Yet he was also told that after six months in France as an observer he could come home and qualify for his wings. In the course of that six months, it seemed – if he survived it – his long-sightedness would undergo a miraculous cure.

[125]

Like Beater, Goudie found much at Hythe to alarm him. One evening in a Folkestone hotel, a popular rendezvous for airmen, he met a man with a Charlie Chaplin moustache and a rubicund nose who got so drunk that he fell down the stairs and they had to put him to bed. Next morning Goudie was horrified to see last night's Chaplinesque drunk, now apparently sober, waiting to take him into the air. At 2,000 feet, without warning of any kind, there was a sudden inrush of air, he felt himself being whirled around helplessly, he was not strapped in, and after hanging on desperately to the bracing wires from inside his seat he felt himself being forced through the floor of the cockpit, or so it seemed, and he waited resignedly for the end. After the landing he asked the pilot if he had been looping the loop and he agreed that he had. Goudie showed commendable understanding. First, the pilot was undoubtedly bored with his job. Secondly, because observers must expect to be thrown all over the sky in a scrap, such risks had to be taken.

The task of observing had originally been rated more important than piloting: one was merely the driver, the other the grand inquisitor and interpreter. In the German Air Force, too, initially, the observer was usually the captain, the pilot an NCO. But in time it was found that in most machines the pilot was better able to position himself correctly, whether for watching the fall of shot when working with the artillery, for the taking of photographs, or for the general exercise of aerial judgement. Thus over the years the observer in most types of machine became little more than a glorified look-out and gunner.

There was one other function that an observer might be called upon to perform, and that was to land the machine when the pilot was incapacitated. 'We always teach the observer something about flying,' wrote John Morris, of 49 Squadron, 'so that if the pilot is knocked out, they can save themselves and perhaps the pilot if he is only wounded.' In some machines there was a spare joystick and rudder control in the observer's cockpit, but this was not universal, and the contortions required to recover control of machines where the pilot had collapsed over the controls were often extreme. Yet there were many occasions when such contortions were successful.

Curiously enough, although more than one pilot was awarded the VC for getting a crippled machine back to the Allied lines and making his report, no such recognition was accorded an observer. No observer received the top award.

If observers came to reflect that it was a pilot's air force, they still had pride in their work and in the confidence placed in them. The tribute to their pluck by Leslie Horridge, paid during the Somme battle, was well deserved. Horridge's sympathies were aroused by the clumsiness of a fellow BE pilot. 'They have to go up with people like my friend of today, and if the machine crashes, they are the people who get it worst.'

Second-Lieutenant J.E.P. Howey, whose force-landing and capture have been related, said: 'I had a fight with two German aeroplanes at 10,000 feet . . . a shell burst very close to us . . . then the aeroplane started to come down head first, spinning all the time.' They were flying in a BE2c, and looking round from the front cockpit Howey saw his pilot, a boy named Claude Kelway Bamber, with a terrible wound in his head, 'quite dead', and realised that the only chance of saving his own life was to step over into Bamber's seat and sit on his lap, where he could reach the controls. 'I managed to get the machine out of that terrible death plunge, switch off the engine, and make a good landing . . . Poor Bamber, he was such a nice boy and only 19.' (According to records he was born in Bengal and was twenty.) Howey had badly damaged an ankle, and after fifteen months as a prisoner he was moved to Switzerland and subsequently repatriated.

Another captured observer who told his story later was Lieutenant W.O. Tudor-Hart, of 22 Squadron (FE2b's). His pilot, Captain G.W. Webb, was wounded when they were attacked by hostiles six miles on the German side of the line. Tudor-Hart was still firing when his pilot collapsed and the FE fell into a dive. He stood up, grabbed the joystick, and turned for home, but from his forward position in the cockpit he couldn't reach the rudder pedals. The machine settled into a steep turn and they lost height, but Tudor-Hart retained enough control to land without injuring himself or his pilot. Sadly Webb died of his wounds.

An unnamed pilot, in an appreciation of an observer named Brown, equally anonymous at first glance, wrote: 'A pilot never feels more lonely than when he is doing a difficult show, and he feels he cannot depend on the man in front of him to be cool and yet quick as a cat in the handling of his gun. One never worried about that sort of thing with Brown.' The Brown named so casually was Arthur Whitten Brown, later to navigate John Alcock across the Atlantic.

One of the most moving tributes was paid by Tommy Traill of an observer named Jones, 'an almost fearless man . . . I never knew his Christian name.' Traill knew absolutely nothing about Jones, where he came from, whether he had a family, what he did when they weren't flying. 'As far as we *did* know each other, we trusted each other completely.' Jones had a hot, potentially violent temper, no great sense of humour, and appeared to have no friends.

They were on a Bristol Fighter squadron, their job was to find and destroy German aircraft, and they never talked of anything but their fighting tactics and how to improve them. But their attachment was strong. 'Jones and I formed the habit, nothing said on either side, of shaking hands when we crossed the lines on the way home after a fight.'

Jones's preparations for a crash-landing in a severely damaged machine, obviously based on experience, involved a drill all his own. 'This was to unship his gun from its mounting and throw it overboard, so that it couldn't fly around and hit either of us. And then to sit down on his little seat facing aft, fold his arms, and relax. He really was a wonderful man.'

On their last flight together, Jones gave Traill the agreed emergency signal for hostile aircraft by tapping him on the top of the head. Traill kicked on left rudder, pushed the stick left and hard forward, and ducked. He heard a stuttering burst, felt a blow on his left shoulder, a bullet scorched past where his head had been a moment earlier, piercing his windscreen, and his controls were damaged. Jones shouted that he had 'got one of them', then suddenly it was over, and Traill coaxed the crippled Bristol back towards the lines. When he looked behind him, Jones was still sitting quietly on his little seat, his head resting on the butt of his gun. He hadn't unshipped it. 'I put my hand on his shoulder. I knew he was dead.'

Teamwork between pilot and observer or gunner was vital if either were to survive. Traill and Jones had lasted longer than most. Pilots soon rejected an observer in whom they had no confidence, but observers had no such choice. The contrast excited the sympathy, even the disgust, of 35-year-old Harold Wyllie, OBE (Military), a pilot who employed his skill as an artist (his father was the well-known marine artist W.L. Wyllie, RA), with the help of a carefully chosen observer, to map the German trenches from low altitude and circulate the results to the army. He got a frightful rocket from Trenchard, at the army's behest, for not going through 'the proper channels', but Trenchard added: 'That's the spirit! I'm too delighted for words!' Wyllie's euphoria was dulled soon afterwards when he watched a newcomer side-slip, stall, nose-dive, and crash, killing himself and his newly appointed observer, who happened to be a friend of Wyllie. Afterwards Wyllie wrote: 'He was a rotten pilot and should never have been allowed to carry a passenger.' And of the observer: 'He was one of the best fellows who ever lived and a valuable life thrown away by sheer bad flying.'

Being paired with a ham-fisted, timorous or over-confident pilot was a chance the average observer had to take. Many would find a congenial partner and be happy to live or die with him – or at least to survive until their own pilot's course came through. But a shocking number died as Wyllie's friend had died.

'It is generally admitted,' concluded a medical analysis of nervous instability in some 200 flyers, 'that an observer has a far greater strain placed upon him than a pilot...' Lack of confidence in a partner in the air was bad enough for a pilot: for the peace of mind of an observer it was paralysing. Another instance quoted was when a stricken machine was falling from height. Whereas the pilot was fully occupied in trying to recover control, the observer had nothing to do but sit there transfixed, anticipating the end. Even eventual escape might leave him devastated. 'Observers', it was contended, 'generally break down sooner and to a much greater degree than pilots.'

Supporting the theory that, because of their greater impotence, observers generally suffered the greater anguish, Gwilym Lewis

[129]

related how a pilot in a single-seater Morane had his controls shot away at altitude, spun 'for several minutes', survived the crash, but went out of his mind.

Again and again pilots returned with wounded or dead observers, often unmarked themselves. The Jamaican Berry King, for whom third time was to prove unlucky, was an example. The figures quoted earlier by Alan Dore bear striking testimony. At the end of the first week of April 1917 ('Bloody April'), of the original complement of eighteen pilots and eighteen observers assembled in France in mid-January to crew the 1½-strutters of 43 Squadron, eight pilots remained – but not one observer. They had all become casualties, for one reason or another.

Whether men were flying as qualified observers or as gunners, their vulnerability was much the same. They were volunteers, and there seems to have been no penalty attached to failure other than the blow to personal pride. What is remarkable is that so many of those who survived stuck it for so long.

McCUDDEN AND 56 SQUADRON: RHYS DAVIDS AND VOSS

WHEN Jimmy McCudden returned to France as B Flight
commander of 56 Squadron, his reception was wary. The
squadron's patrol area, opposite Richthofen's *Jagde-*
schwader, or hunting group, was one of the toughest on any front.
Yet in three months the squadron pilots had scored a hundred victories, a unique achievement, and many of them were established
aces. Some were ex-Sandhurst, many were ex-public-school, and
McCudden was an ex-ranker: there were adjustments to be made on
both sides.

A great deal depended on McCudden's first attempt at leading his
flight. Of the five pilots who constituted it, Barlow had especially
distinguished himself by his pioneering low-level machine-gunning
attack at Messines. Keith Muspratt, erstwhile instructor and future
test pilot, had learnt to fly at 16 in his holidays from Sherborne
School: one of his pupils had been the incomparable Arthur Rhys
Davids, also now in McCudden's flight. A few months earlier 'RD',
athlete and classical scholar, had been head boy at Eton: he had
gone into action almost straight from those legendary playing fields,
and had earned for himself, in the scrap when Ball was shot down,
the encomium from Blomfield that 'here is another Ball'. Completing
the flight, specially selected for their personal qualities, were Canadian Verschoyle Cronyn ('Versh'), and Englishman Maxwell Coote

— 'as splendid a lot of fellows', according to McCudden, 'as ever set foot in France.'

At 6 a.m. on 18 August they took off in their SE5A's to mount the early patrol. Almost at once they sighted a formation of four enemy reconnaissance machines, 6,000 feet below them, heading south. Soon they recognised the stubby silhouettes as Aviatik two-seaters.

McCudden gave the signal to attack, but then his guns jammed and he had to land to clear the stoppages. It was a wretched start. But his professionalism was equal to it. He cleared the stoppages and rejoined his flight in time to help Barlow shoot down one of the two-seaters before protecting him from eight avenging Albatros scouts, destroying one of them before leading Barlow back over the lines.

There were no rash heroics from McCudden. They had been hopelessly outnumbered. And he had a healthy regard for the Hun. 'The more I fight them the more I respect their fighting qualities.' But on the enhanced performance of the SE5A he was euphoric. 'It was very fine', he wrote, 'to be in a machine that was faster than the Huns, and to know that one could run away just as things got too hot.'

Breakfast that morning was an animated meal, with McCudden's swift return to the fray after his initial setback heartily endorsed. 'I hope', said one of his pilots, 'that your first Hun with 56 Squadron will be the first of 50.' McCudden, flying a really efficient fighting machine for the first time, did not dismiss this sentiment as fanciful.

He shot down a second Albatros on 19 August and a third on the 20th, though this one upset him strangely. He felt no sentiment for the enemy, but he had become so inured to the seeming invulnerability of enemy aircraft to the guns of two-seaters that he was caught off his guard when this third Albatros exuded a flicker of fire and then tilted earthwards in a candle of flame. With pulses throbbing and hands a-tremble, he thought he was going to be physically sick. All he could think of was the fellow human being in that holocaust. 'Poor devil,' he thought, 'Poor devil'. Such squeamishness was not typical of him, and he told himself it had to be eradicated. It was unprofessional.

In less than a week McCudden established himself as a flight commander of rare tactical ability, providing just the right mixture of caution and aggression, always mindful of his responsibility to the less experienced. Meanwhile in his spare time he was developing a talent for stalking enemy reconnaissance two-seaters, increasing the speed and ceiling of his machine by various modifications, biding his time, choosing his moment, often surprising his prey at 20,000 feet and beyond, where they thought they were safe. He planned these interceptions as meticulously as he organised the patrols of his flight. Studying the Hun's routine, he would announce: 'If there's nothing doing up the line I'm going after the 11.30.'

Curiously enough, within two days of McCudden's arrival at 56, Richthofen, too, returned to duty. But he had come back too soon. On 28 August he wrote: 'I have just made two patrols. They were successful, but after each one I was completely exhausted.' Dizziness and air-sickness assailed him, and early in September, after recording his sixty-first victory, he consented to taking convalescent leave. It was during this break that he completed his book, *The Red Air Fighter*. Efforts were made to stop him returning to duty, but he was adamant that he must do so. 'I should consider myself a despicable creature if, now that I am loaded with fame and decorations, I should consent to live on as a pensioner . . . while every poor fellow in the trenches, who is doing his duty as much as I am, has to stick it out.' This was strikingly similar to attitudes in the RFC. But he was not well enough to resume his role of Ringmaster until mid-November.

McCudden resembled Richthofen in that he always weighed up the situation carefully before attacking, although Rhys Davids noticed that once he was committed he fought brilliantly, with complete disregard for his own safety. His machine, though, was rarely hit, and he very rarely lost a man from his flight.

Whereas McCudden, like Richthofen, could be content to live to fight another day, Maybery and Rhys Davids would take on any odds. Of Maybery, in the squadron's early days, Blomfield wrote: 'He and Captain Ball and Lieutenant Rhys Davids did more harm to the morale of the German flying corps than any other fifteen pilots between them.' After one of Rhys Davids' more reckless forays he was urged to be more cautious, and he admitted, in a letter to his mother, Caroline Rhys Davids (D.Litt.), that he had taken 'four times the risks I ought to have done'. But his resolve to go more carefully collapsed when he got into a scrap. 'You are a different man. At least, you aren't a man at all . . . you are a devil incarnate . . .'

His friendship with Maybery had blossomed when they were transferred to England in June to meet the Gotha threat: he fell in love with Maybery's seventeen-year-old cousin. There were many sides to his nature. Brought up in orthodox fashion, he confessed to having religious doubts, 'but one simply does not get the time to think them out'. The only man in the squadron of a similar sensitivity was Cecil Lewis. 'Sometimes, returning from a patrol,' wrote Lewis, 'we would break off and chase each other round the clouds, zooming their summits, plunging down their precipitous flanks, darting like fishes through their shadowy crevasses and their secret caves; such pleasure lay in this that never did we seem more intimate . . .' After landing they would stroll to the Mess arm in arm, with no hint of self-consciousness in their friendship. 'Sometimes we used to walk at night down to the stream in the valley. He would quote some line of half-forgotten poetry. I would take it up . . . At such times the war was quite forgotten.' Could this quiet, contemplative boy, marvelled Lewis, really be a war hero?

There was no stronger contrast in temperament than that between Rhys Davids and McCudden. Yet they maintained a working relationship. McCudden treated Rhys Davids' volatile nature with a mixture of grudging admiration and stern reproof. RD 'would have chased the Huns over to the Russian front if I had let him,' wrote McCudden, and the younger man had cause to be grateful many times to his leader. But the gratitude was not one-sided. McCudden could still feel clumsy and inferior in company in the Mess, and any assumption of social superiority was swiftly checked by RD, who shamed his colleagues into accepting McCudden for what he was.

Many of the air aces, McCudden and Richthofen among them, built up their scores on two-seaters, but not RD, and by September he had won the MC and Bar and was famous as 'Eton's boy hero'. 'If one was ever over the salient in the autumn of 1917,' wrote

McCudden, 'and saw an SE fighting like hell amidst a heap of Huns, one would find nine times out of ten that the SE was flown by Rhys Davids.'

The weather for the remainder of August remained so unseasonable that only minor ground operations were attempted, the whole Ypres area having deteriorated into a quagmire. It was during this hiatus that Haig transferred the overall direction of the main advance to the Second Army under the more patient and methodical Plumer, with the Fifth Army under Gough in support. When the weather improved in September, and the ground began to dry out, the offensive was resumed, but with more limited objectives and on a narrower front.

Bombing by day and by night, contact and counter-attack patrols, low-flying attacks on enemy reinforcements, artillery observation, and air reconnaissance, aided by the use of parachute flares at night to illuminate enemy movements, all contributed materially to a run of comparative success in which twenty-six RFC squadrons were directly involved. And it was during the Battle of the Menin Road Ridge (20–25 September) that one of the greatest air battles was fought. Again, the principal participants on the British side were 56 Squadron.

In Richthofen's absence, his twenty-year-old pupil Werner Voss, flying one of the new Fokker Triplanes, had begun to challenge his supremacy. Richthofen called him 'my most redoubtable competitor'. The 'Krefeld Hussar', as he was known (he had joined the militia in 1914 and fought on the Russian front), had thirty-nine victories, and in the week Richthofen went on leave he added another eight. Unlike his master, but like Ball and Rhys Davids on the British side, Voss would attack whatever the odds. Indeed he believed it was easier to fight six machines than two: bigger numbers got in each other's way. The Fokker triplane, diminutive, light, sensitive, but not easy to fly, had a fantastic rate of climb and could turn on the proverbial sixpence in the right hands – and Voss's were undoubtedly the right ones. It was not particularly fast, but in designing it Anthony Fokker had sacrificed speed for manoeuvrability. Richthofen was not greatly enthused by it, but for Voss it became an obsession, an extension of his personality. The star of the Circus was no longer the Baron and his scarlet Albatros but Voss and his silver-blue *dreidecker*.

Air activity fell off in the next few days as the Allies prepared for the Menin Road attack, but it resumed with increasing intensity from 20 September. Voss was due to go on leave on the 23rd, but he took off that morning from his aerodrome at Heule, spotted a DH4 on a reconnaissance mission, and promptly shot it down. That was his forty-eighth. As the day advanced, opportunities increased, and Voss resolved to fly one more patrol before going on leave. He needed two more victories for fifty.

Taking off at 18.05, with wing-men on either side, each flying the sturdy Pfalz DIII fighter, he headed for the front. Climbing through a broken layer of cloud, they found themselves sandwiched in clear air between the lower cloud layer at 1,000 feet and an upper layer at 9,000. Horizontal visibility was good, and large numbers of aeroplanes were seen. Among them were two flights of SE5A's of 60 Squadron led by Captain K.L. 'Grid' Caldwell, returning from a patrol. (To Keith Caldwell, a New Zealander, every machine was a 'grid'.) Caldwell's formation had been broken up, and the rear flight now consisted of Captain Robert Chidlaw-Roberts and Lieutenant Harold Hamersley. Both were embryo aces. Hamersley was keeping an eye on a formation of Albatros scouts when he spotted a Fokker triplane, accompanied by a Pfalz. Avoiding the Pfalz, he put his nose down and dived on the triplane, opening fire as he did so. Chidlaw-Roberts followed.

They were treated to a sequence of manoeuvres by the triplane that astonished them both. Reversing the position in some miraculous way, the triplane pilot put a burst into Chidlaw-Roberts' rudder and drove him and Hamersley back towards the lines.

Grid Caldwell, setting off in pursuit, felt sure the man in the triplane must be Werner Voss. He then saw that two flights of SE5A's of 56 Squadron had taken up the challenge. Although their numbers had been reduced from eleven to seven by previous skirmishes (four had been forced to turn back), they comprised two flight commanders

(McCudden and Bowman), Maybery, Muspratt and Rhys Davids; and two 'ace' Canadians, Reg Hoidge (twenty victories) and Versh Cronyn.

Voss had lost height in chasing Chidlaw-Roberts and Hamersley, so that McCudden was able to build up to what he called a 'colossal speed' as he tore into the attack. He had no fear of the SE breaking up. Slightly to starboard of Voss, with Rhys Davids to port, he was aiming to box the triplane in. But Voss saw the danger, abandoned the chase of the two crippled SE's, whipped his tail-plane round sharply, like a goldfish in a bowl, and turned through 180 degrees to face his attackers, firing as he came. McCudden, with bursts from the triplane's twin Spandaus ripping through his wings, was left with a sense of bewilderment.

Zooming out of the dive, with Muspratt and Cronyn following, McCudden sought to line up a second time. But again the triplane flicked round, coming out on a reciprocal course. This time Muspratt's engine was shot up so badly he had to force-land, his machine a write-off.

The Pfalz pilots, too, had been unable to live with the triplane. 'That left Voss in the middle of six of us,' wrote Bowman later, 'which did not appear to deter him in the slightest.'

Cronyn too had been hit: falling oil pressure turned his attempt to zoom into a feeble climb. Voss saw this and whipped round as before. Attacking from abeam, he gave Cronyn a perfect silhouette of his new three-decker, wings stepped down from the top, with comic whiskered face painted on a black cowling. Then the bullets came. Three months earlier Cronyn might have attempted to run for it, but he was too old a hand now. He dived just enough to turn in under the triplane and prevent its getting on his tail. Soon one of the others would drive it off.

Cronyn lost count of the number of turns he did to keep under the triplane. Half the time, without knowing it, he was flying upside down. When Voss came in for the kill he put his machine into a vicious spin, and when he flattened off he saw with intense relief that Voss was busy with the others. Petrol was pouring from his left cylinder block and spraying into his face, his engine was missing badly, and he made for home. His machine too was a write-off.

Chidwell-Roberts, Hamersley, Muspratt, Cronyn, all experienced scout pilots, all forced down within minutes, with two machines written off. Voss had reached his fifty victories. How long could he keep it up?

The triplane was quite capable of outclimbing the five remaining SE's. Voss could escape whenever he wished. But he did not choose to do so. Plunging, hovering, climbing, corkscrewing, he was proving his theories by gaining protection from pilots cramped by the risk of collision, and of shooting each other down. But he was gradually being driven west, down to 2,000 feet, near the British lines.

A red-nosed Albatros appeared and began guarding the triplane's tail. McCudden counted eleven more enemy scouts high to the east, but six Spads and four Camels were daring them to interfere. Suddenly McCudden saw his chance; but no sooner had he fired than up came the triplane's nose towards him and he saw the red-yellow flashes of the parallel Spandaus. Hoidge saw the opportunity for a simultaneous attack but with a twist of the tail Voss evaded them both.

While the other SE pilots held the ring, Rhys Davids dived repeatedly at the triplane. Each time Voss skipped out of the way. Once, in dodging RD, he came up broadside on to Bowman. It was Bowman's first chance and he shoved his nose forward excitedly. But the German kicked on full rudder, skidded sideways, and got in a devastating burst at Bowman, who stared in amazement. He didn't think such manoeuvres were possible without buckling control surfaces or stalling and spinning. Yet he had one consolation. He had given Rhys Davids the chance to lock on to the triplane's tail.

RD would never have got there, thought Bowman, had Voss not been distracted. There was no doubt he was vulnerable now. RD was not quite able to straighten up behind the triplane, but it was good enough. He fired from a hundred yards range down to seventy, emptying an entire drum.

For once the triplane held its course. There could be only one explanation. The pilot was either unconscious or dead.

It is not surprising, after such convolutions, that discrepancies should exist between the German and British accounts. What is unique is the reverence in which Voss was held by the pilots who faced him that day. 'As long as I live,' wrote McCudden, 'I shall never forget my admiration for that German pilot, who single-handed fought seven of us for ten minutes.' (Bowman and Hoidge put it at twenty.) 'His flying was wonderful, his courage magnificent, and in my opinion he was the bravest German airman whom it has been my privilege to see fight.' Bowman wrote: 'It was not until later that we heard that it was actually Voss in the triplane. Our elation was not nearly so great as you might have imagined.'

The chivalry so often ascribed to World War I pilots scarcely extended to the heat of combat, but admiration for a fallen enemy did. It was Rhys Davids himself who expressed the general regret at the death of Werner Voss. '*Oh, if I could only have brought him down alive!*'

COMBAT – EXHAUSTING BUT EXHILARATING: SMART AND HIS 'CIRCUS'

THERE was a poignant postscript to the Voss fight: it marked the end of the career of Versh Cronyn. 'When I got out of the machine,' he recorded afterwards, 'the relief from tension was so great that I practically collapsed. For a minute or two everything went black ... I could hear someone asking, "Where has he been hit?" ... I wanted to laugh because I had managed to get down without crashing, but instead of laughing I started to sob ... Perhaps shell-shock would best describe my condition.' When he tried to relate what had happened he found himself stammering incoherently.

He asked for a fortnight's leave, thinking his depression would lift, but the medical officer grounded him and, feeling an outcast, he was posted home. Showing neither understanding nor sympathy, Major Blomfield said little more than 'Sorry I can't recommend you for promotion'. It was left to Major W.D.S. Sanday, the successor to Harvey-Kelly commanding 19 Squadron (Spads) on the same aerodrome, to catch up with him one day and take him by the arm in a most friendly manner. 'When you are better and return to France,' he said, 'I would be very glad to take you on my strength.' What a contrast, thought Cronyn. This man who went out regularly with his squadron and had the DSO and MC would be glad to have him, whereas Blomfield, who might take a machine up on test occasionally but never on patrol, and for whom he had flown thirty-four OP's in two-and-a-half months and been credited with seven or eight possible victories, could find nothing to say to him.

The effect of combat on the individual varied widely. Cronyn, joining No. 56, like Maybery, during its short sojourn at Bekesbourne, was given no instruction or advice on air combat or tactics. 'We will patrol the Menin–Roulers road area,' he was told by Bowman, his first flight commander. 'Don't take on what you can't finish and for God's sake keep a tight formation.' On his second patrol he found himself over the lines with four others surrounded by what seemed the entire German Air Force. In fact there were eighteen of them. 'After the first few moments it was born in on my consciousness that this was the real thing, that those vicious cracks were passing bullets aimed at me by the enemy, with everyone for himself, that the gun buttons on the control stick were there to be pressed, and to stay alive one must exert all possible skill in manoeuvring.' Somehow Bowman had extracted them from the mêlée without loss.

Later, in the Mess, animated and glass in hand, they might relive the action, and some discussion of tactics might follow. Cronyn never knew fear in the air because he was much too busy. 'The tense period was while waiting on the ground, or at night in bed thinking, when the fear shakes got me . . . These shakes are a strange thing. I was not conscious of fear but for no apparent reason I would just start trembling all over. We all had this condition at times . . .

'The toughest time for nervous strain was when called for the early bird flight. Little would be said, with no jokes, while we gulped a cup of coffee.' It was when the take-off was delayed, according to Cronyn, 'that their stomachs did queer things and we even got the shakes. One by one we would get up and walk away.' Cronyn wasn't actually sick, but others were. 'The tension was really beyond description. Yet once in the plane we felt we could cope . . .'

While few could stand the men who whistled unconcernedly while waiting for the order to take off, there were men like Ball and Maybery who seemed impervious to tension. 'It must be marvellous to have the sort of guts Ball had,' wrote Arthur Gould Lee, 'to be completely without fear, to attack regardless of the odds, not

[141]

giving a damn whether you're killed or not. Most of us like to try to go on living even when we have to risk our skins fighting Hun scouts far better than ours.' Yet when, on patrol with other 1½-strutters, he sighted eight Albatros scouts, 'I began to tremble with excitement, all tensed up for the coming scrap ... Swooping down on an enemy formation from a great height was a madly exhilarating feeling.'

Many others, like Lee, felt 'that tingle of excitement before action.' But of the action itself, 'things happen so fast I have only a hazy notion of what followed.' Of his first victim, Lee wrote: 'I came down closer and closer, holding my fire. My heart was pounding, and I was trembling uncontrollably, but my mind was calm and collected.' His coolness surprised him. 'You are scared before you start, but once in it you don't feel excitement or fear, you fight in a sort of daze. When it's over, and you find you're still alive, you feel both exhausted and exhilarated ... The thrill was felt later when celebrating in the Mess.'

Charles Kennedy Cochran-Patrick ('Pat'), DSO, MC, thought by Trenchard in July 1917 to be the equal of any pilot then at the front, and who later commanded 60 Squadron, recognised the blood-lust in his own reactions. 'The excitement of it all was in my blood ... I was at 7,000 feet, coming down in a giddy spiral, shouting at the top of my voice.' 'Pat' had a reputation for being phlegmatic – but he didn't feel cool when on another man's tail, and there was always the dread of the clack of machine-gun fire from behind. Of an imaginary but all too typical newcomer he wrote, with some feeling: 'He sees blood and goes blind and straight with all his attention on the machine appearing at his mercy. Then, God help him, there is another hostile machine about. He is attacked and shot down before he knows anything about it.'

Bert Harris wrote: 'I think most fighter pilots in France were troubled by sore necks, trying to look both ways at once, trying to keep an eye on your own tail in a scrap – if you didn't you'd had it ...' The trouble, he added, was that 'once you were in a dogfight you really saw very little except the fellow you were after.'

Werner Voss with his Triplane. 'His flying was wonderful, his courage magnificent.'

V.P. 'Versh' Cronyn. 'The relief from tension was so great that I nearly collapsed.'

A group of German Aces. From left to right: Sebastian Festner, Emil Schaefer, Manfred von Richthofen, Lothar von Richthofen, Kurt Wolff.

A Sopwith 1½-strutter of 43 Squadron, forced down beyond the lines with its crew during Bloody April.

Sopwith Pups of 46 Squadron about to return to the UK to repel the Gothas, July 1917. (Note, a Nieuport of 40 Squadron centre.)

An Armstrong-Whitworth FK8 of 82 Squadron. The sluggish 'Big Ack' required skilful handling.

P.N.M. 'Puggy' Shone and his pilot caused untold havoc amongst off-duty German pilots with their pranks.

J. 'Squibs' Sibley. 'The ~~tr~~ouble with this war is that ~~it'~~s so bloody dangerous.'

DH4 two-seaters of 217 Squadron lined up for action, some with 320 lb bombs ready for loading. By general consent 'the best day bomber of the war'.

A Sopwith Camel of 46 Squadron, showing flight commander's streamers and two Cooper (20 lb) bombs. *Below:* The F2B Bristol two-seater Fighter. Mistaken tactics did not long delay its effectiveness.

Jimmy Slater – a true professional (34 victories on DH5's and SE5A's).

C.M. 'Billy' Crowe (15 victories) followed Ball into cloud – but then lost him.

Arthur Gould Lee called Trenchard 'a leader after the hearts of Service pilots'.

Clive Collett, test and scout pilot, made the RFC's first parachute descent from an aeroplane, 13 January 1917.

'Alan would take on anything.' A 6'2", big-boned 18-year-old from Winnipeg, Alan McLeod won the RFC's last VC, but succumbed soon after to Spanish 'flu.

Arthur Hammond, a 23-year-old English observer with McLeod, los a leg but later emigrated . . . to Winnipeg.

John Todd
(18 victories)

Oscar Heron
(13 victories)

'My machine came back awfully damaged,' wrote
Paice in his diary. 'Todd all right.'

Caught at the work-
shop bench – Alec Paice.

Ewart Stock, the Camel pilot who kept an illustrated diary of the March 1918 Retreat. 'We had very few pilots left.'

Another Ewart, also a notable diarist – the Australian Ewart Garland, second from left, with members of his flight or DH9A bombers of the Independent Force, 1918.

'For many,' wrote Lee, 'it took a long time to realise that, whatever one's marksmanship, the only way to get your Hun in a dogfight was to get in really close before firing. The problem was to do it before someone did it to you.'

There were other apprehensions, even worse than the thought of the chap on your tail, which could cause Lee's goggles to mist up from the perspiration of fear. This was especially so in a dogfight. 'I levelled out, sweating from sheer funk. It's odd how the risk of collision frightens you more than the risk of bullets.'

Norman Macmillan was one of those to whom the tingle of antici-pation was familiar. 'The intensity of concentration was so great that the mental attitude became detached from all emotions.' Sometimes, when still hyped up after a patrol, he and his squadron colleague Ray Brownell, a Tasmanian who had won an MM as a soldier at Gallipoli, would go out again on a voluntary patrol in search of hostiles.

McCudden's squeamishness at seeing another human being, enemy or not, falling in flames, and his shock, when closing for the kill on what he thought of merely as an enemy machine, to realise that 'there's a man in it', were shared by Lee and many others. Once, as though in a reflection in a mirror, Lee saw practically his double, and it was borne in upon him that Hun pilots and observers were simply the reverse of the coin. 'Although we often get to very close quarters in our dogfights, our scrapping is impersonal. We don't hate each other.' And Ball had written, of an enemy 'flamer', 'poor old chap inside'. But some did seek revenge, often for the death of former colleagues, and a wild but diminutive Australian named 'Jerry' Pent-land (twenty-four victories), returning in a Spad of 19 Squadron from a kill, announced: 'I got the bastard stone cold.' Captain W.E. 'Moley' Molesworth (eighteen victories), wrote: 'Your first Hun in flames gives you a wonderful feeling of satisfaction.'

There were many who revelled in their role of scout pilot, anyway for a time. But for most, their nerve would fail them in the end. Even those with a natural flair for the job, the born scout pilots, if such existed, like Ball and Rhys Davids, soon tired of the slaughter. 'Oh, won't it be nice when all this beastly killing is over,' wrote Ball to

[143]

his girl friend. 'I hate this game, but it is the only thing one must do just now.' For Rhys Davids it was 'a tedious war' that had stymied his scholarship to Balliol. With youthful ambivalence, in a letter to his mother, he saw his work as 'an absolutely superb game' while at the same time 'hating the whole damn business'. He told Cecil Lewis: 'It's a job. We ought to try to do it well. But when peace comes we'll do better.'

Courage and skill as a scout pilot did not necessarily imply integrity or reliability, or the sensitivity of a Cecil Lewis. 'The worst bounders', wrote Tom Tillard of No. 3 Squadron, 'sometimes make the best flyers.'

It is difficult to imagine that the crews of the corps squadrons, the BE2's and the RE8's, can have taken much pleasure in combat. But the evidence is that some of them did. Since they had to expect it, may have been their attitude, they might as well enjoy it. The excitement of fighting for the ultimate prize, their lives, took hold of them. Yet there must have been many, like the actor Mervyn Johns, who admitted to carrying on for months in a state of blue funk – and are all the more to be respected for it.

'The shoot was going fairly well,' wrote Charles Smart of an artillery cooperation show in an RE8 on 12 August 1917, 'and we were well over the lines, and like fools both of us were gazing at the target, when suddenly there was a terrific burst of machine-gun fire and four Hun machines dropped through the clouds right on top of us. I at once put our machine into a vertical bank and fell like a stone about 500 feet, then I pulled her out straight again and we made a running fight of it back to our lines. The Huns were fairly out for blood and dived on us time after time. Short [Smart's observer] kept his head well and worked his gun like steam. The odds were all against us for each German machine is armed with two machine-guns firing through the prop so we had eight guns against our one.

'Bullets simply zipped all over the place and I never thought we could get clear. I did a series of very steep spirals and S-turns and managed to get back to our lines, where our Archie started. The shells came much nearer to us than to the Huns but it had the desired effect, for the Huns left us.' They then carried on with the shoot. 'It was a most exciting fight and I thoroughly enjoyed it while it was going on though I must say after the Huns had left us my knees felt a bit wobbly.' When they got down they found more than thirty bullet-holes in their machine, 'the nearest one went through about six inches below my seat.' Relief at his escape was overridden by annoyance. 'I would give half of what I am worth to have brought one of the beggars down.'

As it happened, such a sacrifice was unnecessary. 'The CO of the battery we were shooting with reported to the squadron that we shot a Hun machine down badly damaged. He says he saw it fall out of the fight and had not the least doubt but that it was in serious trouble.' A week later, on the eve of Smart's last flight with Short, who was going home to learn to fly, Smart noted: 'We have just heard that we are officially credited with bringing down a Hun machine during our fight on the 12th . . . Good!'

Such confirmation from the front line was not unusual. Recording a victory by a colleague in his diary, Smart wrote: 'The fight was seen by thousands of men in the trenches and the excitement was great. The machine that landed in our lines came down with a great crash and both man and machine were smashed into little bits. Smith, the pilot, managed to land his machine safely . . . from where he departed in an ambulance amidst cheers from the assembled multitude.' There was no squeamishness from the men in the trenches, who had little enough to cheer. Nor was the cheering any less jubilant on the German side when a British machine came down.

A week after converting to RE8's, Smart recorded how photographic sorties from No. 5 Squadron began to be accompanied by an escort from within the squadron. Of the five RE8 crews detailed, three were to take photos and two to act as escort. Smart was one of the latter: with him as gunner he had an air mechanic named Smith. They had reached the limit of their patrol, and photos were being taken, when 'twelve Hun scout machines came right through us and a real ding-dong scrap followed.

'A Hun dived at the machine I was guarding and I had to do something, so I pushed my nose down with the engine full on and dived at him, firing my gun like fury. At the same time a Hun dived at me and my gunner engaged him with the rear gun.' Glancing at his air speed indicator Smart noticed that the needle, which registered up to 140 m.p.h., was stuck against the maximum, 'so we must have been going some. Down we swirled for about 2,000 feet, both guns firing and making no end of noise at both ends. Anyhow my machine made it so hot for both Huns that they broke off the fight and cleared east.'

All the RE's were attacked, one by four Huns at a time, but 'the Huns got more than they expected'. The German pilots had probably mistaken the unfamiliar RE8 for their old Aunt Sally, the BE2: the silhouettes were not dissimilar. Anyway they withdrew and the photographic mission was completed. Smart wrote: 'It was a glorious fight. I have never been through anything quite so exciting, machines were whizzing about all over the place like mad swallows, the air resounded with the pop! pop! pop! of machine guns, and tracer bullets could be seen flying in all directions. No one in our crowd was hit but the machines were pretty well shot about. We now call ourselves the circus, and rightly so, for have not five RE8's engaged twelve Huns on their own pitch and licked them hollow? First-class Air Mechanic Smith behaved splendidly right through the show, he just sat on his seat like a block of wood and fired his gun like steam so long as there was anything to fire at.

'It is strange how little fear enters into one during a fight, I never thought of being hurt, my only desire was to kill a German and I feel sure I would have rammed a Hun machine if I could have got near enough to do it. As for handling a machine, one can do simply anything when there is a scrap on.

'You cannot compare fighting on the ground with fighting in the air. [Smart, of course, had experienced both]. The two are in about the same ratio as tiddlywinks and big game shooting for excitement. Perhaps I should not say this if I had been in a bayonet charge.'

Smart relished escort work, and two days later he was 'out with the circus again'. Herbert 'Jimmy' Larkin, his flight commander, an Australian, had been christened Captain Barnum, and Smart, as his second in command, was dubbed Mr Bailey. Larkin, after being wounded at Gallipoli, had transferred to the RFC and was later to make a reputation on Sopwith Dolphins as a 'cool, calculating killer'.

The crews rotated, taking the two jobs in turn, and Smart, who had earlier described photographic work as 'a poor game', highly dangerous and with no chance of cheating (since the photos told all), had become resigned to it. 'Photography is a good job when you don't get hurt.' It usually lasted no more than one and a half hours, as against the two and a half and more of artillery work, and there was an incentive for doing the job properly: provided they got their photos first time they were finished for the day.

Like the infantry, they rarely saw the scout squadrons that were supposed to be clearing the air for them. But on an artillery shoot that summer, on two enemy trench points, after Smart had had to transmit MQHA (cease fire, hostile aircraft) several times and retire to a safe distance, four Nieuports turned up and mixed it with the German formation. 'They disappeared into the clouds all fighting like Kilkenny cats.' Smart was able to continue the shoot.

Then it was back to escort work. 'In a fight the excitement is intense. It is only after you land that you realise the risks you run. When you are about two miles above the earth you never seem to think of the fact that if anything happens to you or the machine you have got those two miles to fall before you reach your natural element. And when you do reach it you will hardly be in a state to appreciate it.' Not once in his diary does he mention a parachute.

Was Smart's insouciance in battle typical? Were all the corps observers as cool under fire as Lieutenants Hendry, Short and Currie and Air Mechanics Tyndal and Smith? When Smart was drafted to Home Establishment after ten months on active service he wrote: 'Glad I am going home for I feel just about done in, but still I am more than sorry to leave all the good fellows out here. I am proud to have been a member of No. 5 Squadron RFC, which has done some great work while I have been with them. All the men in the squadron with perhaps two exceptions have been real men and worth knowing.'

A week after writing this, on 26 September 1917, Smart concluded his diary with the following lines:

Married to Helena May Irwin.
My word! This is a dangerous war.

SOME TRAGIC NEWCOMERS: NO NEWS OF RHYS DAVIDS

AIG's initial objective, to secure the ridge east of Ypres, still lay only partly realised, and after the successful Menin Road sub-battle he renewed the assault, on 26 September, in a second sub-battle at Polygon Wood. Overnight, the FE2b's of Nos 100 and 101 Squadrons, having concentrated earlier on German aerodromes and rail centres, dropped nearly five tons of bombs on villages where enemy troops were billeted, and on communications. Low cloud next morning hampered but did not prevent the work of the corps squadrons, and enemy counter-attacks were quickly detected from the air and repulsed. As a result of these sub-battles – there was a third, at Broodseinde on 4 October – Haig's Second Army now stood on the crest of the Ypres ridge.

For the RFC, the most notable features of these battles were first, the development of night bombing, and secondly, the increased employment of the fighting squadrons in harassing and sometimes scattering German infantry with light-weight bombs and machine-gun attacks, over and behind the battlefront. Night bombing, especially of aerodromes, was also practised by the Germans, but it did not amount in total to more than a seventh of the tonnage dropped by the British. And although the German Air Force was extremely active over the front in early September, it was forced back as the month advanced, the fighting squadrons keeping the skies clear for the corps machines, and the infantry free from undue harassment.

Meanwhile, in an effort to make good the disastrous losses of March–April–May, amounting to some 1,270 machines, the two aircraft parks, at St Omer and Candas, worked non-stop to feed over a thousand aeroplanes to the front-line squadrons in the month of September, enabling the flights of most squadrons to revert to eight machines each. For squadrons on artillery cooperation, each flight was able to maintain two machines in the air continuously from dawn to dusk. But the quality of the machines, standardised or reconstructed by the depots, was not always matched by the crews, expansion further diluting expertise. It was rare for pilot and observer to be of equal competence and fully familiar with the ground area: one or other was likely to be a novice. These novices often performed admirably, but their casualty rate was high.

John Worstenholme, a newcomer on No. 6 Squadron, was the pilot in one of a pair of RE8's on the morning of 21 September, the second day of the Menin Road battle, their mission to take photographs over Poperinghe. He was given an experienced observer named Frank McCreary, formerly of the South Lancashire Regiment, and they returned safely from what was his first mission. Afterwards, trying to relax, Worstenholme rehearsed what he felt had been 'some pretty tense experiences'. To begin with, he had lost the other RE8 in cloud. The sky had been stippled with machines, hostile as well as friendly, but neither this nor the fact that they were on their own had deterred them from trying to get their photographs. Worstenholme reflected, as he lay on his bed, that his experiences were probably commonplace and that pilots from his own squadron and every other squadron must get far more excitement daily, while scout pilots would already have forgotten about it. Yet every incident in the flight remained vivid in his memory and he couldn't sleep for thinking about them.

It wasn't that he was disturbed by the dangers that must have been present. He was insensible to them. 'I just lay there longing to be in the air again, and wanting to relive all those moments.'

That afternoon they were sent off again, to rendezvous over the same target with other RE8's to take more photographs. In extremely poor conditions he and McCreary managed to get their pictures, and 'I got a very good welcome from my CO, although I pranged his aircraft on landing.' His mind was still insulated from the more terrifying aspects of wartime flying.

Four days later, while on a contact patrol at 5,000 feet in cloudy conditions, Worstenholme's machine was attacked by a fighter out of the mist and he was knocked unconscious. McCreary was badly wounded in the hand, the machine started spiralling, and the enemy was following them down. McCreary had never flown an aeroplane before, but he *had* been shot down before, and as the RE8 nose-dived he brought it under control.

The RE8 was pointing towards the lines, but the enemy pilot attacked again, this time from astern, and McCreary had to relinquish control, face towards the tail, and open up with his rear gun. While he was doing this the RE8 fell into another dive, which he tried to control, but meanwhile he had driven the enemy off. Reasserting control, he found he had climbed to 6,000 feet.

Not knowing how to work the throttle, McCreary glided downhill until he was a mile from his aerodrome, but at about 200 feet he realised he was again losing control. The machine stalled and crashed, but it fell into an isolated clump of trees which cushioned the impact, and McCreary, seriously hurt but thankfully alive, was picked up by Australian troops and taken to hospital, where he 'gave a perfectly good reconnaissance report' to the General who visited him. His clear-headed display earned him an MC. But there were no more magic experiences to be relived for young John Worstenholme, whose wounds proved fatal.

The RFC was facing a familiar problem, that of preparing new pilots and observers for something for which there could never be adequate preparation. An extension of the training period would help, but perhaps no more than marginally: the moment of truth still had to be faced. More reprehensible was the continual drafting to squadrons in France of men who had not even completed the minimum of training laid down.

Jack Wightman was an 18-year-old from Coventry who had been rated the best pilot they had turned out at his training school, a distinction which may have cost him his life. Chosen to fly Bristol Fighters, he was unexpectedly sent to France to join No. 11 Squadron on 26 August 1917. 'He left England in a remarkably short time,' according to his brother, R.L. Wightman. 'I think he was sent out too quickly. He was not even sent to Scotland for a fortnight's gunnery course.' This was the kind of short cut that was still being taken, under pressure from France. Wightman was presumably selected as an outstanding pupil.

'The weather was atrocious for the first few days in France,' wrote the surviving brother, 'and no flying was possible. Then he was sent over the lines for an hour alone.' This would have been his familiarisation flight, when he would have been accompanied by an experienced observer, who evidently gave him a thorough indoctrination, as they were 'archied'. 'Next morning he went over again with three other planes under a captain.' This would have been his flight commander: the squadron was doing its best for him. 'They were met by a squadron of enemy planes. Jack went for one of them, but was soon outnumbered by about five to one, and his machine was last seen by another officer in flames.

'He had only been in France nine days and he was not quite 19 ... It is so terrible I can hardly write about it. I shall be joining a cadet school myself soon, but I shall not take the RFC if I can help it.' Lost with Wightman was Second Class Air Mechanic John Heedy: neither man has any known grave.

The grief of relatives was not a subject likely to influence the hierarchy, although squadron and flight commanders – and in special cases Trenchard himself – did their best to write letters of condolence and tribute. There were times, though, when they were overwhelmed, or when they themselves were casualties, or when little or nothing was known. Plaintive letters pleading for information about loved ones could draw a blank from a much-changed squadron personnel, leaving relatives even further distraught. Yet casualty lists seem only to have stimulated recruiting among the young, and few would-be RFC men needed the encouragement of women distributing white feathers – as they did – to any young man of military age not in uniform. Some, like Ronald Ivelaw-Chapman, a future air chief marshal but then aged 17, went down on their hands and knees and prayed that the war would last long enough for them to train and fight. 'We schoolboys', wrote Brian Sharwood-Smith, a Brisfit pilot on 48 Squadron by 1918, 'were fearful that the war would end.'

Night bombing, one of the features of RFC operations that autumn, developed so widely in 1917 that night flying in all types of machine came to be recognised as both feasible and desirable, forming a part of the repertoire of most squadrons. While the corps crews on the Ypres front were fully occupied in daylight, with no spare energy for night flying, corps and army crews elsewhere were given orders for night raids on targets where damage and harassment were judged to be helpful to the main offensive. Sopwith Pups of Gordon Taylor's squadron, No. 66, attacked German aerodromes at dusk, undeterred by the inevitable night landings. Brisfit crews on the Nieuport front did the same, Puggy Shone actually carrying a 16 lb bomb on his lap. 'If it got within ten miles of its target,' said Puggy, 'I'd be surprised.'

They were sometimes alerted to intercept German bombers returning from England. One morning Brian Baker emerged from his Nissen Hut in his pyjamas and announced, in his ebullient manner: 'I've got to go up!' He pulled on his flying kit over his pyjamas, took off, and was back within twenty minutes, shouting 'I got it!' Three others claimed a share in this victory, Baker's observer and the crew of another Brisfit. Four hours later Sibley and Shone, on an OP, saw parts of the wreckage still sticking out of the water, 50 yards off shore between Nieuport and Ostend.

The latest single-seater, the Sopwith Camel, hitherto regarded as unsuitable for night operations, was also employed, as the BE2's had been, for night interception. Camel pilots of a reserve squadron at home, and of the recently equipped 70 Squadron in France, climbed, unsuccessfully at first, to meet the challenge of the Gothas. Bombing raids on Gotha bases were also mounted by Martinsydes, DH4's, and FE2b's, and by the RNAS from Dunkirk, forcing moves to new aerodromes.

Most significant of all on the bombing front was the formation on 11 October of the Forty-First Wing, arising from the Gotha raids and the demand for reprisals. The forty long-range squadrons committed to the strategic bombing of German industrial targets, as originally mooted, were unlikely, as Trenchard knew, ever to materialise, but he had already chosen a suitable base at Ochey, near Nancy in north-eastern France, within range of Mannheim and other suitable targets. The two leading RFC bomber squadrons, Nos 55 (DH4's), and 100 (FE2b's) were transferred to the new wing, together with a naval squadron of Handley-Pages which had been operating at night from Coudequerke, inland from Dunkirk: each of these latter machines was capable of carrying fourteen 112 lb bombs, six times the load of a DH4. This was the beginning of the Independent Force, as it later came to be known. The 'Smuts Report' (Chapter 6) had meanwhile advocated the creation of an independent Air Ministry, and the amalgamation of the RFC and the RNAS into a single independent Service was soon to be accomplished.

The second feature of the succession of minor battles that autumn was the proliferation of low-level strikes on troops and other targets in and near the front line. Sometimes these attacks were substituted for operations farther afield that had been rendered impossible by the weather; but by the start of the Broodseinde sub-battle in October the single-seater fighters had become the fighting advance guard of the infantry.

All three Sopwith two-seater squadrons, the 1½-strutters, had meanwhile been rearmed with Camels, and it was in a Camel of 45 Squadron that Norman Macmillan, now a flight commander, 'rattled away at troops, transport, trenches, and, in the open, guns and gunners, anything that offered a target.' Pilots flew in pairs, they didn't carry bombs, just twin machine-guns, and for Macmillan, at least, 'these low-flying jobs were full of excitement', though many disliked them. 'You were shot at by friend and foe alike,' complained Fullard. Yet, hugging the contours, they were safe from aerial attack.

The exhilaration of seeing the ground rush beneath them, sighting some spontaneously selected target, perhaps a gun battery, splaying the whole emplacement with bullets, the gunners flattened and helpless, lent an illusion of invulnerability. 'Things flashed into view, were fired on, passed behind and were forgotten with the next target that loomed up.' Much of the time they would be flying through a tunnel of fire. Bullets spewed at them from all angles, the concussion of exploding shells threw their Camels about crazily, and although often unaware of it they were repeatedly hit. Simultaneously, in kaleidoscopic profusion, they caught glimpses of grey-clad troops hurling themselves into open shell-holes, trying to claw their way into the camouflaging mud. Terrified horses galloped into obscurity, dragging half-capsized wagons behind them, columns of marching troops broke ranks and disintegrated. No one liked it or looked forward to it, and it was fiendishly dangerous, as the casualties showed, but as an instant and visible contribution to the fighting it was unparalleled.

43 Squadron, under Alan Dore, one of the pioneers of trench strafing, was the last of the 1½-strutters to get Camels, and they continued with the old machine through most of September while they were converting, suffering further casualties. Yet their keenness to do the job was undiminished. 13 September, wrote Dore, was 'a sad day for us all'. To begin with, they were grounded by the weather. Then 'Rickards came to me and said he thought the weather was good enough for photos. He and Thompson went off.' Captain A.T. Rickards was one of Dore's flight commanders. They took their photos, but, as always with photographic work, their straight and level flying over-exposed them to Archie. 'Thompson was hit but got back; Rickards was seen to dive very steeply. Then his wings folded up and he fell for 8,000 feet ... Rickards fell out and was found 500 yards away from the machine.' His observer, too, was killed: 'Marshall-Lewis, one of my best observers, gone.' On the same day a second of Dore's senior pilots side-slipped while practising in a Camel and was very badly hurt. 'So I lose two flight commanders in one day.'

On 19 September, six machines were doing a line patrol when a raw Canadian, Second-Lieutenant M.G.M. Oxley, became separated, 'as is often the case with new pilots'. News that he and his observer were dead came from the pilot of a Hun scout shot down on the British side next day.

[155]

At last, on 25 September, they flew their final patrol in the Sopwith two-seater. 'Having accomplished much fine work,' wrote Dore, 'they are now the slowest thing on the line.' But the conversion to Camels did not eliminate casualties, included among them being some of the two-seater pilots who had been with the squadron six months. The death of Second-Lieutenant Charles H. Harriman, shot down on patrol, was described by Dore as 'one of the tragedies of the war'. That night Dore 'went up to trenches . . . to see if we could recover the body of Harriman'. The machine had come down in no man's land, not 50 yards from where they stood – 'a pitiful sight, upended in the moonlight'. If Dore entertained any hope that Harriman might be alive, it vanished now. 'It was impossible to get to him in that night of full moon.' Two stretcher-bearers later crawled to him and found him dead. Later, when Harriman's body had been recovered, Dore 'buried him at La Pugnoy, where so many of our lads lie'.[1]

A reminder that life was worse in the trenches came when Dore visited his old battalion, the 7th Worcesters, a few days later. 'At Ypres they lost 600 men and 28 officers. Hoare, one of the original 7th Battalion, was killed there. He died quite happy in the command of a company: all he desired in this war . . . The terrors of Ypres were told by the fireside. Running up to their armpits in mud. Messages so soaked that they tore apart and had to be pieced together. Men with the look in their eyes that borders on insanity.'

At least the 34-year-old Dore had an inkling of what all this meant. In his last days on 43 Squadron he had the satisfaction of shooting down a Hun, also the horror of cutting away the woodwork of a crashed Camel to release the mangled body of one of his pilots. 'How I loathe the war when these things happen.'[2]

* * *

1. Harriman had been feeling sick at heights for some time but had refused to give in. This probably cost him his life, as he was seen to come out of a cloud upside down and crash.
2. In 1930 Alan Sidney Whitehorn Dore raised and was the original commander of No. 604 (County of Middlesex) Squadron, Auxiliary Air Force. The squadron flew night-fighter Blenheims in the Battle of Britain.

The departure of Alan Dore coincided with the return to France of his former squadron commander, Sholto Douglas, recovered from his digression into horse-play and now in charge of a newly-formed SE5A squadron, No. 84. At this time the SE5A was probably superior to any other fighting machine at the front: indeed Douglas regarded it as the most successful of all the Allied single-seaters, inferior to the Camel numerically but otherwise superior. Douglas listed its qualities as:

Comfortable, with a good all-round view.
Retaining its performance and manoeuvrability at high level (unlike the Spad and the Camel).
Steady and quick to gather speed in the dive.
Capable of a very fine zoom.
Useful in both offence and defence.
Strong in design and construction.
Possessing a reliable engine, especially after the Wolseley Viper was fitted.

The squadron was granted a period of preliminary training before being committed to the battle. Meanwhile, in continuing bad weather, with the infantry floundering in the mud of Passchendaele, the RFC mounted bombing and machine-gun attacks from low level and all manner of patrols, often at near-prohibitive cost: fourteen pilots and observers were lost and five others wounded in one day alone. Even these losses were scarcely proportionate to those on the ground, and all hope of achieving the strategic aims of the campaign was abandoned. Yet Haig was still determined to secure the Passchendaele ridge. Although continuing the assault was against the advice of his subordinate commanders, success, he believed, would secure the British position for the winter months and make life uncomfortable for the Germans. And Haig did have other reasons. He wanted to divert attention from the French, who were planning an attack on the Aisne front, and from the surprise he himself was plotting for late in the year by attacking with a massed force of tanks near Cambrai. Thus the failure of the first attack on Passchendaele, begun on 12 October, did not deter him, and the attack was renewed a fortnight later. Only the soldier can tell of the horrors that followed, but Norman Macmillan was one of a great many airmen who 'looked down on the sodden mass of shell-pocked mud that was the swamp of Passchendaele'. And Garland wrote: 'I can never forget Passchendaele – a nightmare of mud and unmentionable visions.' At one point the advancing troops had to withdraw because their rifles were choked with mud.

When the weather improved on 27 October it was the turn of the British troops to be hounded by bombing and machine-gun attacks. Ten enemy machines were claimed as destroyed, but RFC casualties too were severe – one killed, nine wounded, and thirteen missing.

Four days earlier, McCudden had gone on leave, Rhys Davids taking over the flight in his absence. RD was one of only four of the squadron's original complement still alive and in France, and he too was due for home posting. He was the top scorer in his flight, with twenty-one victories. 'This officer', reported Blomfield, 'came out to France with 56 on April 7th 1917 and has abundantly proved his capabilities in the air and on the ground during the past six months. I strongly recommend him for transfer to Home Establishment as a flight commander.' But RD was looking forward to running the flight. 'I shall be really sorry when I have to come home,' he told his mother. 'With luck I may get another month or six weeks out here.' At this news Caroline, who had been looking forward anxiously to the end of the six-month period, was seriously alarmed; Arthur was surely tempting fate. On 14 October she heard from her son again. 'I shall be here now till the end of the month at least.' Four days later she received chilling news. 'I am now the only original flying officer left.'

Blomfield was doing his best to keep RD on the ground, but in McCudden's absence it was difficult. And McCudden's restraining influence had more than once been responsible for saving RD's life. For some days after McCudden's departure, the squadron was grounded by bad weather, but on 27 October, a day, as has been mentioned, of heavy losses, No. 56 resumed patrolling. When they returned, three pilots were missing. One of them was Maybery, another was RD. Soon it was known that Maybery had landed safely. But of RD there was no sign.

'It would take a damn good Hun', the pilots told themselves, 'to get RD,' and for a long time they refused to believe he was dead. So did his mother, who, starved of news, addressed letters to her son as a prisoner. It was two months before the Germans, evidently uncovering some scrap of identification, dropped a message to say he was dead.

Caroline Rhys Davids, her hopes shattered, wrote at once to the CO of 56 Squadron (Blomfield had been succeeded by New Zealander Rainsford Balcombe-Brown): 'We have received, since early November, *absolutely no news* save the CO's and the War Office's messages "missing October 27th" and the latter's letter of December 29th that German airmen had dropped apparently the baldest announcement of his death. No burial place, no relics.

'Not a soul of those who knew him and were on patrol with him that day have sent us a single word. I know that his best friends either preceded him on leave or have themselves become missing, but surely others must have seen something of him during that fatal flight?' She began to suspect that he must, in some way, 'after all his swiftly won fame, have disgraced the squadron in the end'.

Balcombe-Brown was able to set her mind at rest on that score. He could well have added that new pilots arriving on 56 Squadron were always reminded of the distinction conferred upon them. 'This is the squadron', they were told, 'of Ball, Maybery, Rhys Davids, and McCudden.'

Before the year was out, Maybery, too, had gone, killed on 19 December after recording his twenty-first victory, equalling RD.

The weather again restricted RFC cooperation in the last days of the Passchendaele battle, but on the ground the fighting was bitter, the ridge being gained but at terrible cost. On 8 November, according to the historian A.J.P. Taylor, Haig's chief of staff visited the fighting zone for the first time. 'Good God!' he exclaimed. 'Did we really send men to fight in that?' He was silenced by his companion's laconic reply. *'It's worse further up.'*

THE ALLIED OFFENSIVE FLOUNDERS: COUNTER-ATTACKED AT CAMBRAI

AFTER three and a half months of bitter fighting, causing some 250,000 casualties on each side, Haig's Flanders offensive had finally floundered in a morass of liquid mud at Passchendaele, leaving his armies with inadequate reserves for further adventures that winter. Yet, by mid-November, the pilots of III Brigade RFC under J.F.A. 'Josh' Higgins, one of the original flight commanders from August 1914, had reason to suspect that something unpleasant was brewing. First the brigade was being hastily reinforced, with two Camel squadrons, Nos 3 and 46, two new DH5 Squadrons, Nos 64 and 68 (Australian), two flights of a newly-arrived day-bombing squadron (DH4's), and the acquisition of Sholto Douglas's 84 Squadron (SE5A's). A pilot still serving in 46 squadron, converted from Pups, was Arthur Gould Lee. He thoroughly approved of the Camel, which he found lighter even on the controls than a Pup, and the 130 hp Clerget engine gave a wonderful surge of power. But why, he asked himself, were Camels appearing in such numbers in such a hurry? Why was his squadron being ordered to practise low-level bombing and low-level cross-country flying so assiduously? Every village in the back areas teemed with British troops, the cavalry were massing, and hundreds of tanks were assembling. Clearly a big push was imminent.

III Brigade now comprised the bulk of fifteen squadrons totalling nearly 300 aeroplanes, giving it an advantage on the Third Army front opposite Cambrai, of some three and a half to one. It was on this front, because of the rolling terrain that characterised it, that the Tank Corps commander, now disposing of 381 tanks, envisaged a major raid. Haig, with the Third Army commander, General Julian Byng, planned to expand and develop this raid into something more ambitious. Although seen as a limited offensive, it might be exploited if successful. German strength on southern sectors of the front had been denuded to bolster their resistance at Ypres; it would be a salutary reminder that they were vulnerable elsewhere.

There were wider implications. Soon, with the imminent collapse of Russia as an ally, large enemy forces would become available for the western front and for Italy, where the Italians were already in retreat after the Battle of Caporetto. By mounting an immediate diversion in France, an opportunity might be seized which might not recur, bringing relief to the hard-pressed Italians and making a significant breach in the German defences.

In order to achieve surprise, the standard pre-battle artillery bombardment, precursor of a likely assault, was dispensed with, and, on the morning of 20 November, in massed formation, the tanks rolled forward. Surprise was achieved, and the formidable Hindenburg Line and its main support line were overrun on a six-mile front to a depth of four miles. Meanwhile, from first light, despite low clouds and mist, army pilots began the strafing, practised earlier, of forward areas and aerodromes and other targets behind the enemy lines.

Pilots going into action for the first time were facing a tempestuous baptism. 'Many casualties occurred through pilots flying into the ground,' wrote Lee, 'but the majority were from ground fire.' Returning to the advanced landing ground several times to reload, Lee flew so low that he had to leap over the tanks when he glimpsed them labouring through the haze, drawing little groups of infantry in their wake, 'trudging forward', as he noted, 'with cigarettes alight'. He was dismayed to see flames belching from some of the tanks, not so much disabled as destroyed. Such was the confusion that to check his bearings he landed in a field, to find himself far to the east of

Cambrai, with marching German troops on a nearby road precipitating a panic take-off.

The commander of 64 Squadron (DH5's), Major Bernard Smythies, linguist and intellectual, formerly of 9 Squadron, realised from an early stage that he was ignorant of what was happening on the ground and was likely to remain so. This was typical of the army squadrons. They had their specific objectives and were fully occupied with those. Only the corps squadrons could normally hope to follow the course of the battle. The pilots of the DH5's, in their first taste of action, scattered troops with bombs and machine-gun fire, routed horse-drawn gun teams, silenced batteries, pounded dug-outs, blasted fortified shell-holes, and fired into trenches and gun emplacements. Those who escaped more or less unscathed rearmed and went again. But their single Vickers machine-guns, although synchronised to fire forward, and although supplemented by a bomb rack carrying four 20 lb bombs, combined with other inadequacies to make the DH5 a somewhat disappointing successor to the DH2. The change to a tractor configuration still gave a good forward view, but the rear view, where hostile attacks mostly originated, was obstructed by the wings. A poor performance above 10,000 feet did not matter for low-level strafing, but bombs could only be aimed in a dive. This was a particularly severe strain on the newer pilots, and casualties were heavy. On that first day alone the squadron had one man killed, one wounded, and two missing, a sobering introduction. Yet the squadron had within its ranks men of high calibre, and their performance drew a message of sympathy and commendation from Trenchard. 'Deeply regret your casualties today. Congratulations to all pilots on their splendid work under very difficult conditions.'

No. 64 Squadron was also notable for having three of the first pilots to be trained in Canada, under a scheme first examined by RFC veteran C.J. Burke ('Pregnant Percy'), and established in January 1917 by two more veterans in C.G. Hoare and Dermott Allen. To the 19-year-old Walter Daniel, who was one of the pupils, the early casualties imposed an additional strain: this was his first experience of life – and the loss of it – among the British. Previously, his countrymen had had plenty of time to adapt to the British while training in England, but Daniel, lacking this advantage, dubbed his flight commander 'a remote Englishman,' and thought he might have given him and other new pilots more encouragement. He was happier when the flight was taken over by Captain Philip Burge, who chose Daniel as his No. 2: 'I was very much encouraged by his personality and leadership.' Burge, from Potters Bar, had earned an MM in the trenches before transfer, and he later became an ace, with eleven victories and an MC to add to his MM. He was shot down in flames in a dogfight in July 1918.

Others who helped to restore the squadron's confidence included Captains Jimmy Slater (thirty-four victories) and E.R. Tempest (seventeen), although these victories were mostly gained after the DH5 was replaced by the SE5A. Meanwhile, during the battle for Bourlon Wood, Lieutenant J.A.V. Boddy had the misfortune to encounter not only the Richthofen *Jadgstaffeln*, swiftly transferred to this sector, but the Red Baron himself, returning after convalescence. Boddy was on a strafing mission when Richthofen intervened. But it was not quite the same old Richthofen. 'I am in wretched spirits after every aerial battle. That no doubt is an after-effect of my head wound.' But he was good enough to account for Boddy and his DH5 in what was his sixty-second victory, his first shots wounding Boddy in the head. Boddy was no stranger to being shot down, and he managed to glide in and crash-land in a corner of the wood.

He was not alone: moments earlier a squadron colleague, while strafing German troops retreating from the wood, had been brought down nearby. This was Captain Albert Morford, who extricated himself from his own pile-up in time to see Boddy's. Wounded himself, he managed to help Boddy out of his cockpit, and together they stumbled through the British forward positions to a dressing station. But both men had completed their task, earning the squadron another commendation for their work, this time from pioneer photographic pilot George Pretyman, now commanding the 13th (Corps) Wing under Higgins. 'Your people were simply magnificent today and probably created a record in showing what can be done in helping infantry with aeroplanes.'

These were deserved tributes to a squadron that had landed in

France less than a fortnight earlier and was facing a degree of exposure, in an inferior machine, which even hardened pilots cordially disliked. Perhaps this is why the beginners did so well. 'Trench strafing', wrote Lee, 'was all chance no matter how skilled you were.' It was a lottery, and it bore no comparison to air fighting, where experience, skill, tactics, good flying and accurate shooting gave the advantage, and luck, although essential for survival, was not the only factor. Strafing behind the lines Lee found less objectionable. Answering fire was nothing like so intense and the pilot could usually see the results of his attack, which was seldom feasible when trench-strafing. 'So much fire was directed at you that you felt every moment must be your last.'

Nevertheless Lee found releasing bombs at 100 feet before shooting up columns of lorries and other mechanical transport, seeing them swerve into ditches, and looking back on a scene of confusion, had its satisfactions, anyway in retrospect. 'I probably killed more Huns than in all my air fighting ... But I don't like it overmuch, in fact, I don't like it at all. Nor does anybody else on the squadron.'

How long could one's luck last? Sick at the prospect of diving yet again into those nests of machine-guns, he knew that he still had to do it. Superstitions, like touching wood before a flight, had long since been forgotten by Lee: all that was left was a numb indifference to his fate. This was preferable to the nightmares of some of his colleagues as they sweated and screamed in imaginary death-throes. He was sorry, too, for the horses.

The Germans were meanwhile bringing up reinforcements and resisting strongly. British reinforcements on a significant scale were simply not available, tank losses and tank failures mounted, and an important objective in the left-centre of the front remained untaken, partly through poor visibility hampering reconnaissance. Attempts to make the position on the Bourlon ridge secure were challenged, and on 27 November the Germans recaptured it. When the expected enemy counter-attack came on 30 November, the dependence of air operations on the weather was again underlined. Early morning mist clinging to the valleys obscured infantry movements from the prying eyes of the corps squadrons, surprise was achieved, and the British were compelled to withdraw.

It was now the turn of the British forces to be subjected to incessant attacks by low-flying aircraft, and for British commanders to complain of the casualties caused and their demoralising effect. The Germans had learned their lesson from the British, and they attached great importance to it. Hoist with their own petard, the British subsequently recorded: 'Our men did not seem to know what to do to minimise the moral effect of these low-flying machines.'

The RFC responded by strengthening formations and shifting their offensive patrols to the battle area, and a hotch-potch of some fifty machines from each side, writhing and cavorting above Bourlon Wood, was a familiar sight. But the low-flying aircraft got through. Forced to give ground at Bourlon, the British were in some peril as they extricated themselves but had successfully completed their withdrawal by 7 December. Neither side had been able to exploit its moments of gain.

If the Cambrai battle was a pointer to the end of trench warfare, it also revealed the mounting threat to infantry of low-flying aircraft. 'The object of the battle flights', said a German memorandum, 'is to shatter the enemy's nerve by repeated attacks in close formation and thus to obtain a decisive influence on the course of the fighting.' At Cambrai, as the British admitted, 'The moral effect of this was very great and no doubt tended to facilitate the enemy's success.'

Two factors militated against undue reliance on troop-strafing. One, as ever, was the weather. The other was the casualty rate. For each day at Cambrai on which this form of attack was employed by the British, losses averaged 30 per cent. If a similar loss rate could be inflicted on the Germans it would be equally prohibitive. It was a rate at which whole squadrons would need replacing every four days. Such losses, even more certainly than bad weather, would have brought the RFC's whole system of army support to a standstill.

By the end of the first week in December, many of the surviving pilots, too, had fought themselves to a standstill. Lee was one of them. Suffering himself now from nightmares, he was told he should have a rest before he cracked up, yet he continued to fly. One of the

five MC's awarded that week to 46 Squadron went to him, an excuse
for a party. 'There's nothing wrong with me,' insisted Lee, 'that a
good binge won't cure.' When he led a patrol next morning he was
still seeing double.

Fierce abdominal pain suggested that there was indeed something
wrong; by the end of the year he was living on brandy and milk.
The medicos, diagnosing appendicitis, took him off flying. He had
been longer on the squadron than anyone, half his colleagues were
strangers, he had done 222 hours actually over the lines, been
reported missing four times, had fifty-six combats and shot down
eleven Huns. Only the chance of his survival enabled his experiences
to be recorded, and his name to become known.

FIGHTER TACTICS: THE PEAK OF
McCUDDEN AND MANNOCK

THE rush to reinforce the Cambrai front had contrasting effects on the men drafted from England. The DH5's of 64 and 68 Squadrons, for all their deficiencies as fighting machines, were well led and well handled: the same could not be said of the two flights of DH4 bombers of 49 Squadron which had been adjudged ready for France. Despite past experience, and the long-term efforts of Smith-Barry and others, pilots, and even squadrons, or in this case parts of squadrons, were still being sent to the front in answer to emergency calls before they were operationally ready.

Lieutenant John Herbert Morris, although only just 19, had served with the Royal Horse Artillery in the Loos sector, on the Somme, and during the German retreat to the Hindenburg Line, and he was accustomed not only to the severities but also to the comforting presence of military discipline. He found it impossible to imagine anything more chaotic than the flight of 49 Squadron to join the BEF. Taking off on 11 November to cross the Channel, they ran into bad weather, circled in confusion, and eventually turned back. 'I never received one definite order from anyone,' complained the methodical Morris. He had given up hope of continuing that day when suddenly, at about three o'clock, they were told to hurry up and get off. They were to join the first formation they came across and take

up any position they liked. 'Can you imagine anything more indefi-
nite?' Each formation, contended Morris, should have been properly
detailed, with a leader and a deputy leader. Clearly the squadron
was totally unready for action. Engine trouble on the way – they
had been equipped with the Farnborough-built 200 hp 3a engine,
not the standard Rolls-Royce 'Eagle' – resulted in several forced-
landings, but somehow they all got through to their aerodrome at
Bellevue – a tribute more to their resourcefulness than their skill.

They were given a fortnight's familiarisation, during which they
had continual trouble with the new engines. Wondering whether the
servicing was at fault, Morris began to take his own mechanic up
with him on test, 'to make certain he takes an interest'. But the
mechanics were equally frustrated, and the teething troubles persisted. Eventually, on 26 November, all twelve machines took off on
their first bombing raid, with an escort of SE5A's to defend them
against the known depredations of Richthofen's Circus. According
to Morris, they failed to establish contact with their escort, and
although a further attempt was made later in the day it was foiled
by clouds.

Morris describes another raid soon afterwards when there should
have been nine of them present. This was reduced to seven by mechanical troubles, and at the rendezvous over the lines only four turned
up. Morris had meanwhile been appointed deputy flight commander
to a 22-year-old Londoner named William Chambers, formerly of
the Lincolnshire Regiment, whom he respected. Their target, a town,
was eight miles beyond the lines, and although monitored by hostiles
they had a height advantage and continued to the target. Morris
actually dropped his first bomb while there were five Hun machines
directly beneath him, vaguely hoping he might hit one on the way – a
somewhat bizarre notion. But he was well supported by his observer,
Second-Lieutenant W.H. Hasler. 'Hasler was carrying on a war of
his own, against a gentleman who had climbed a little higher than
the others and was shooting at us with tracer. Hasler gave him a
good burst and down he went.' At least two of their bombs hit the
town, after which they fought a rearguard action back to the lines,
some of the Hun pilots betraying a lack of persistence. Morris found

he could outmanoeuvre them easily at 15,000 feet and above, and this and the speed of the DH4's facilitated their escape. 'We all got back safely.'

Lack of persistence was not confined to the German side, and there were times when Morris did not mince his words. A disastrous bombing raid on 4 December when nearly everyone got lost and five machines were missing did not improve morale. Morris described the shelling as 'terrible': he was the rear man, and everything seemed to burst around him. 'Crump, crump, crump they went . . . What could I do? Ducking was useless. Hundreds of little black dots filled the sky around me . . . 14,000 feet to fall if one hit me.' He threw the machine about and somehow avoided most of the bursts. A hole near his seat, pointed out to him when he landed, made him shiver.

Next day there was news of some of their casualties. 'I hadn't been in an hour when someone came in and said they'd just come back from Whyte's and Coddington's funerals.[1] It is extraordinary. A fellow comes up on a stunt with you at nine o'clock one morning and at eleven o'clock next day he's dead and buried and another pilot has taken his place.'

For a time all shows were stopped. When they restarted, Morris's letters, addressed to his family in Blandford, Dorset, continued. 'On nearly all expeditions, eight or nine machines would be detailed but seldom more than three or four could get the height to get over, thanks to our rotten engines.' It may not always have been the engines. 'Some made a nuisance of themselves by continually turning back with a dud engine,' continued Morris, who strongly disapproved. 'I hated letting anyone else do a job which had been given to me.'

The harassed squadron commander, Major Basil Turner, a South African, was forced to rely on Morris more than was reasonable, and Morris complained that his CO was working him to death. 'The more you do for him the more he wants, whereas if you never do

1. Second-Lieutenants G.H. Whyte and C.E. Coddington, killed in action on 4 December 1917.

anything, like some of our people, who have never been over the line even once, he doesn't expect anything from them, and they never need to do anything.' Turner, like most squadron commanders, was under continual pressure to get results, and Morris, unlike some of his colleagues, generally got them. It was not a unique situation. There were shirkers on most squadrons, and the best men were generally entrusted with the vital tasks. Ewart Garland was a case in point. Even Charles Smart, on 5 Squadron, had acknowledged that there were exceptions to the general high standard. Advantage was inevitably taken of outstanding men.

Among the other newly-arrived squadrons, even No. 84 under Sholto Douglas started badly. Following its period of preliminary training, the squadron flew their first offensive patrols on the Passchendaele front. All through October they fought up and down the Menin-Roulers road, which ran north and south some six miles east of Ypres. Of the pilots, only the three flight commanders had experience in France, and at first there were many casualties, so much so that Douglas fell to analysing what was wrong. He came to believe that the policy of mounting OPs in single flights was mistaken. Three separate squadrons of SE5A's might each put up a single flight to patrol a single section of the front, but they would be operating independently, with no unified plan. 'Thus a single flight was often attacked and defeated before the other two were aware of it.' Douglas's preference would have been for all three flights of a single squadron to work together as a unit, but this did not get the blessing of his superiors until the spring of 1918.

Towards the end of October the squadron was transferred to the 13th Wing under George Pretyman, to strengthen the forces cooperating with the Fourth Army at Cambrai. Their task was to keep the sky clear not only for the corps squadrons but also for the low-flying strafers. But the fog, mists and drizzle that hindered reconnaissance forced Douglas to reduce rather than increase the size of his patrols and operate his machines in pairs and even singly. With the Germans also intent on giving protection to their low-flying and reconnaissance machines, the SE5A's succeeded in shooting down some half-a-dozen enemy scouts without loss. Douglas called this 'the fruits of our arduous apprenticeship on the Menin–Roulers road'.

The experience of 84 Squadron was that the most practicable fighting formation was not a flight of six machines, as often supposed, but a Vee-shaped formation of five, two machines stepped up behind the leader on either side. Another discovery was that losses occurred when a flight was attacking, rather than when it was being attacked. When under attack, the pilots stuck together for mutual protection; when attacking, they tended to break off in pursuit of individual targets, get separated from their colleagues, and be jumped on by superior numbers. The remedy, concluded Douglas, was for the flight leader to be regarded as paramount. When he dived to attack, the flight must dive with him. When he zoomed, they must zoom. This, during combat, was the only way to keep the flight together. Inevitably it meant that it was the flight leader who did most of the shooting. They learnt too, as McCudden had learnt, that they must always try to take the enemy at a disadvantage, and that it was often sensible, failing that, to refuse combat. In essence they were simply adopting the methods long favoured by Manfred von Richthofen.

Fortunate were the men posted to squadrons where strategy and tactics were so closely studied. Their chances of survival were dramatically improved. One of the luckiest was Ted Galley, whose vicissitudes as observer have been referred to. Joining up originally as a despatch rider, he had graduated from Sandhurst with a regular commission, and he had been serving on the Somme when he was attracted by the notice about transferring to the RFC as an observer, and he had soon found himself flying photo recces on FE2b's with 22 Squadron. Eventually his misfortunes with over-cautious drivers had got him home on a pilot's course. Told by his flight commander at CFS – it was Balcombe-Brown – that he'd never make a pilot, he had resolved to prove him wrong, promising that he would win the sweepstake for the quickest pupil on his course to go solo – and making good his boast. He was waiting at King's Cross for the train to Scotland to begin his combat training when an orderly accosted him. 'Report to Postings immediately.' There had been heavy casualties in France, there was a shortage of pilots, and he was to leave for France that night. It was a familiar story, though for Galley it was to have a fortunate outcome.

Balcombe-Brown, as already recorded, had meanwhile replaced Blomfield at 56 Squadron, and when he heard of Galley's arrival in France, soon after the loss of Rhys Davids, he sent for him. Galley then had the further good fortune to be assigned to McCudden's flight. Of McCudden and 56 he wrote: 'There were some dashing fellows there, but he and I saw eye to eye about things.' (If this seemed presumptuous in a newcomer, Galley, besides having had considerable experience as an observer, was, as we have seen, no shrinking violet.) 'He always got height before he attacked,' he wrote approvingly of McCudden. Strategy and tactics, as Galley soon saw, were McCudden's forte. 'He only lost one man [from his flight] the whole time I was with him.' It was the same with combat damage. 'I've only ever seen about three bullet holes through his machine.'

McCudden, indeed, was enjoying his finest period, building up to a remarkable sequence over Christmas 1917. Four enemy two-seaters fell to his guns on 23 December, and a hat trick five days later took his personal score to thirty-seven. A telegram from Trenchard ended with the words 'You are wonderful!' Despite Trenchard's dislike of publicity for so-called aces ('The British Army does not permit the names of its flying heroes to be published,' said an American news agency), anonymity could no longer be preserved. On 16 January 1918 the front page of the *Sunday Herald* was devoted to a picture gallery of the McCudden family – ex-Sergeant-Major W.H. McCudden, his wife Amelia McCudden, and their pilot sons, Willie (already killed, in 1915), Jimmy, and a third son, the impetuous Jack, who was making a name for himself on SE5A's with 84 Squadron (six victims in January–February). When Jimmy eventually went home on rest in March 1918 he had fulfilled the half-jocular toast that his initial victory with 56 Squadron should be the first of fifty: his score, the highest so far on the Allied side, was fifty-seven.

Mick Mannock, too, in the last weeks of 1917, was scoring victories almost daily. He was still with 40 Squadron under Leonard Tilney, but he was now flying SE5A's. His temperament, always volatile, had fluctuated wildly in previous months. Early in his career he had landed from a scrap with his knees shaking and his nervous system temporarily shattered; but there were others worse than him. 'Old Mackenzie goes on leave today,' he wrote. 'He is in need of it. If ever a lad was cracked up, Mac is. I wonder if I shall ever get like that?'

Mannock was befriended by a Scot named William MacLanachan, whom he dubbed McScotch, to distinguish him from another Mac on the squadron, Dubliner George McElroy, whom he called McIrish. It seemed to McScotch that the inner life that he was aware Mannock led was turning him into a loner. But he could do little about it. Emotional battles, he supposed, could only be fought alone. 'Feeling nervy and ill,' wrote Mannock. 'Afraid I am breaking up. Oh for a fortnight in the country at home.' Three days later the 22-year-old Tilney sent his 30-year-old flight commander home on leave. But there was no relaxation for Mannock in what was a broken home. His mother had become an alcoholic, and he sought sanctuary with friends. There he worked hard to crystallise his ideas about air fighting. Back in France the pace had hotted up and he was ready for it. 'Fights galore and thrilling escapes!' was all he had time to record.

After his award of the MC, and promotion to captain and flight commander, at first on probation, there was resentment at what some saw as his recklessness. In deliberate protest, Maclanachan left the patrol and continued alone. It was a salutary reminder to Mannock that his days as an individualist were over. As a flight commander he must think first of his flight. They did not know that Mannock, alone in his room, sometimes cried heartbrokenly when a colleague was lost.

From this point on he devoted his spare time to training his flight and to developing his talent for leadership. 'My nerves better lately,' he noted. And his violin-playing, which had stopped when a colleague who accompanied him at the piano was killed, was resumed. The tall, gaunt figure, standing in the shadows in a corner of the Mess, playing without accompaniment, displayed an emotional depth that proved spell-binding. Lest he reveal too much of himself, he would turn his face to the wall as he played.

He had been fighting continuously for eight months, and the strain was showing. His abiding horror of a flamer was becoming obsessive, and on 2 January 1918, with a bar to his MC, he was sent home again by Tilney; this time on rest.

'THEM AND US': THE GROUND CREWS

WHEN Arthur Gould Lee relinquished command of his flight in 46 Squadron, bound for Home Establishment, he put up three of his ground crew tradesmen for decorations for outstanding work – and was surprised and gratified when he heard they had been awarded. How many other squadron and flight commanders, he wondered, remembered the men who serviced their machines, the fitters and riggers and armourers on whose care and devotion their lives daily depended? 'We're cut off from them,' wrote Lee, 'we live in a separate world, simply because they don't fly and fight as we do.' (There was also the social gulf, widened rather than narrowed by the wearing of uniform.) Lee welcomed the chance, as he saw it, to cross the bridge between what he called 'them and us.'

Here the RFC was at a basic disadvantage compared with the front line troops, where officers and men were all in it together. Yet this dichotomy, felt Lee, should not obscure recognition of exceptional effort behind the lines.

It does seem that standards in the RFC were above average. Whereas, back in 1911, the first officer recruits to the original Air Battalion could be selected from any regular branch of the army, other ranks could be recruited only from the Corps of Royal Engineers, lending a sense of exclusivity from the start. Later, with the expansion that followed the creation of the RFC and the outbreak of war, the favourable terms offered for ground tradesmen made attracting the best men possible. Alan Dore, after transfer from the Worcestershire Regiment, expressed his amazement at the wealth of talent around him. He wrote that, in his squadron alone, 'we have the best mechanics in England, the best wireless operators, the best instrument makers, and the most highly-skilled armourers.' Many of these men took the opportunity to fly.

The negative reaction of one engine fitter ('No fear!') to the extra two shillings a day blood money paid to air gunners ('They get all the dirty long-distance bombing jobs'), emphasises the spirit of the men who took up the challenge. Of those who did, the number who lost their lives runs into hundreds, many were taken prisoner, and some were decorated. But it was of the ground tradesman dedicated to his job that Trenchard had declaimed: 'These men are the backbone of all our efforts.'

An average squadron might include as many as 200 other ranks of various trades, but it was usually the men working directly with the machines and the pilots who volunteered for flying. Not all such volunteers could be accepted: the ranks of expert tradesmen would have been seriously denuded had this been so. One engine fitter, who later graduated to senior NCO and then engineer officer, applied for pilot training but was told: 'We can recruit fit young men and train them as pilots in three months: we can't do that for engine fitters.' Another mechanic, after volunteering, was ordered to cease pilot training and revert to his ground trade.

Squadron commanders were fully aware of their dependence on their ground tradesmen. 'Josh' Higgins once told a pilot whose careless flying with a mechanic as passenger had alarmed and enraged him: 'If you want to kill yourself you can, but don't kill one of my men.'

During the March 1918 retreat, Trenchard put a harsher complexion on the responsibilities of the ground crews. 'You men must guard these machines with your lives. Without these machines the army is blind ... And if it's between you and the machine, the machine comes first.' Few aerodromes were more than perfunctorily guarded.

[177]

The relationship between pilot and ground tradesman was on a level of trust, not always absolute. John Morris, of 49 Squadron, has been mentioned as one who encouraged responsibility by insisting that his mechanic accompany him on air test. Charles Smart wrote: 'Took the engine sergeant up to prove to him that the engine was dud.' It was in test flights like these that adventurous air mechanics got the bug for flying.

Machines that ran well on the ground sometimes under-performed in the air, but the pilot who continually blamed his engine when he failed to reach his target was soon rumbled, while the careless mechanic was disciplined. More often than not, though, an attachment grew.

Bert Harris, in speaking of this three-cornered team, listed his machine, his observer, and himself; but he then made special mention of 'your own favourite mechanic, who looked after your machine. You felt you were just a team together.' The mechanics, too, shared this team spirit, never more poignantly than when, gazing eastwards, they waited in vain for man and machine to return, knowing that something in their lives which they valued had gone.

The rapid arrival of replacement pilots, and the intensive work involved in keeping the aircraft flying, checked morbidity. Some of the most genuine mourners were batmen, who got to know the officers they looked after, their idiosyncrasies and their weaknesses, better than most. 'Lost two more nice gentlemen,' was one sad comment.

Hugh Walmsley – later Air Marshal Sir Hugh – had a fitter named Laidlaw and a rigger named Taylor who before the war had both worked at Avro's in Manchester. 'They looked after my aeroplane', said Walmsley, 'as though it were their own child.' There was no such thing as working hours. 'If there was anything to do they did it, they used to work like blazes night and day.' Only years later did Walmsley realise how close he had been to these men, the perception coming when he discovered that his mother had been sending them food parcels throughout.

Such contacts were based on mutual regard. Each knew the other's worth. 'We respected them,' wrote Walmsley, 'and they respected us because of the high casualty rate; they knew that compared with us they had a cushy job.' Air mechanic Callender put it more humorously – and humour was a vital ingredient. 'Our relationship with the officers was very good indeed. We kept our place and we kept them in theirs.' They were asked to do things, he says, but never ordered. As for discipline, on a front-line squadron, rough justice was inevitable, and the men accepted it.

Ewart Garland believed that ground crews understood the gulf that was bound to exist between flyer and non-flyer, quite apart from any question of rank. One incident he never forgot was when, after a particularly rough day in the air, pilots and observers, on taking their seats in a hangar for a concert, were applauded by the men.

Signing himself 'Your faithful mechanic', Leslie P. Tupling wrote from France in April 1917 of his pride in having had Garland's 'valuable life in my keeping' over a period of ten months. Respect, as in this case, was frequently tinged with affection. 'I am absolutely fed up now and have been ever since you left good old 10th Squadron.' He consoled himself with the thought of what Garland's fate would inevitably have been had he stayed any longer. 'Every time I saw you take wing my thoughts were far from happy until you returned.'

Men who had transferred to the RFC from the army appreciated the contrast and were eternally grateful. Walter Cobb, a photographer, wrote: 'What a relief from the infantry! We never had enough to eat in the line as there were too many pickings on the way up, but in the squadron [No. 59] we were never short.' Life was much more bearable in other ways. 'NCO's were not drill-and-yapping experts but men with some trade who knew what they were doing and worked with others more as a team. They got the best out of us by cooperation and help.' Sport and entertainment were other fields of contact.

It was not that ground tradesmen were immune from danger. When aerodromes were bombed, as they increasingly were, other ranks suffered in proportion to their numbers. Battery wireless operators were special targets of enemy action. 'Conspicuous Gallantry' was the verdict on an operator named H.V. Howlett, of 52 Squadron, who left his dug-out three times to re-rig a damaged aerial under heavy shell-fire. The citation for his Military Medal stressed how the accurate shooting of the artillery depended on operators maintaining contact with pilots and observers, thus saving the lives of thousands of troops.

In the course of the war, casualties among Battery wireless operators ran into hundreds. One who had a lucky escape was Stanley Gorringe, of 21 Squadron. Dissatisfied with the trade of Stoker offered him by the RNAS, he transferred to the RFC via the Wireless School at Aldershot, but must surely have regretted it when his dug-out was hit. His diary and log-book were pierced by shell-splinters and splashed with the blood of a comrade, but he himself escaped. 'I was on the scene in about half an hour,' wrote his CO to his parents, 'and found your son badly shaken but quite unwounded. He has a mild dose of shell-shock.'

Willie Read, as already mentioned, invited his batman to join him in the air, knowing that he was eager to do so. 'He would always come aboard with a packet of sandwiches and a Thermos . . . During a raid he would come aft and serve me with sandwiches, as if he were waiting at table.' This was in a Handley Page bomber. Read's reputation for looking after his men was very properly accompanied by a habit of looking after himself.

It was mostly the older men who kept diaries. Among pilots, Read by this time was 33, so was Smart, and Dore was 34. Among mechanics, diarist Alexander Paice, originally of No. 34 Squadron under John Chamier and Eric Routh, was 33 and married, with a small son. A cabinet-maker by trade, working for a family firm in Gloucestershire which designed and built folding furniture for the top London hotels and stores, he heard of the RFC's desperate need for tradesmen and was quickly signed on as an air mechanic (flight rigger). Despite a crisp shorthand style his diary confirms a greater-than-average maturity. At Christmas 1916, for instance, he was a sober witness of festivities that left 'nearly everyone in the billet drunk . . . What a Christmas'.

In 1917 he moved to 70 Squadron, where he teamed up with an engine fitter of equal conscientiousness named Tom Webb. The most dangerous job on the squadron appears to have been Pay Parade: three times Paice tells of officers who had paid them that morning and who were casualties virtually within the hour. One of his pilots was New Zealander Clive Collett, the test pilot and guinea-pig parachutist; he records with pride Collett's eighth Hun on 18 August.[1] But early in 1918 he and Webb got a new pilot, Lieutenant John Todd, formerly a student at Edinburgh University: Todd had been punished as an infantryman, wrote Paice, for 'shooting himself in the foot'. Whether this was true physically or metaphorically Paice did not elaborate; no doubt Todd kept it a secret. But it was to prove a rewarding partnership. In recording Todd's exploits, Paice basked in reflected glory, and his pride in 'his pilot' grew.

'*19th January – New pilot, Lieutenant Todd. 20th January – Lieutenant Todd gave me five francs.*' (Presumably Webb was treated the same. There were 25 francs to the pound.)

'*22nd January – Lieutenant Todd brought his first Hun down.*' It was an Albatros DV: within three days, Todd had achieved something that took most men weeks and even months.

'*24th January – Todd nearly brought a Nieuport down in a fight with an Albatros.*' The older but vastly junior man was becoming the father confessor: Todd, as before, appears to have kept his escapade to himself.

On 28 and 29 January Todd made claims, anyway to Paice, but only the first was confirmed. It was a Fokker Triplane. Then:-

'*9th February – Up early for special flying. Lieutenant Todd volunteered to go over the lines at daybreak to catch a Hun which comes over bombing every morning. But weather wet and rough.*' The attempt was repeated a few days later, when Todd brought down an Albatros DV.

1. Collett later returned to test flying with twelve victories, but was killed in December 1917 testing a captured Albatros scout over the Firth of Forth.

'24th – My machine came back awfully damaged. Todd all right, only dazed. There were pieces of shrapnel sticking to his flying coat. The Major had it photographed.'

On 5 March Paice is made acting corporal. On the 11th, with the great German March offensive imminent, Todd takes delivery of a new Camel, and next day he shoots down another Hun, his fourth. But the new machine, with a longeron perforated, has to go away to be rebuilt. Meanwhile Todd is promoted to captain, and Paice, for the first time, is appointed to take charge of the Guard.

A move by road to Marieux on 15 March, one of many in the ensuing weeks, brings out Paice's aesthetic appreciation. *'Best aerodrome I've been to, on the edge of a large wood. The daffodils, primroses, and cowslips are in lovely bloom.'* He also evinces an impartial appreciation of man-made things. *'A captured Albatros brought to Marieux, a splendidly-built machine.'*

There was appreciation, too, perhaps less aesthetic, from Todd. *'19th March – Captain Todd gave me fifty francs for looking after his machine.'* (£2, more than a week's wages; again one can perhaps assume that Tom Webb got the same.) On the 21st, Ludendorff launched the offensive that was to win the war before the Americans could intervene. *'Worked day and night,'* recorded Paice.

On the 22nd, as the Allies retreated: *'Busy erecting hangars, German POWs helping. Todd got two Huns, squadron got ten. Fritz was over again tonight.'* German night bombing was becoming severe.

On the night of 23 March, as recorded earlier, Paice worked right through until 5 a.m., and then for another eight hours until midnight on the 24th. *'Terrible fighting just in front of us. May have to leave any time.'* Todd's new machine was damaged but Paice repaired it, and 70 Squadron never let up, bombing and strafing all day. This was the day when Paice's flight broke all records by getting thirty-six hours' flying out of their machines. Next day they began digging trenches.

'Terrible raid on our aerodrome. Many of our chaps wounded and five killed.' Continually forced to retreat to fresh aerodromes, bombed and machine-gunned as they went, their conditions

worsened. '*No bread, only biscuits. Fatal crashes almost daily, mid-air collisions frequent.*'

So it continued for Todd and for Paice, and for countless others, throughout the retreat and on into May, June and the first half of July, moving from one aerodrome to another, hounded out at first and subsequently advancing, but bombed continually, with many casualties. Pilots and machines went missing or were shot down in flames, or collided or broke up in mid-air, or crashed fatally on landing, to be faithfully diarised by Paice. But Paice himself survived, and so too did Todd. Promoted to flight commander in May, and awarded the new Royal Air Force decoration, the Distinguished Flying Cross, in July, John Todd went home next day after six months at the Front with eighteen confirmed victories – and with no more wounds in the foot. A modest enough ace by comparison, he was a hero of heroes to Paice, as Paice was to him.

For Paice the war went on. Soon he was involved with another hero, Oscar Heron: of Heron's thirteen victories before the armistice, all in a Camel serviced by Webb and Paice, ten were the formidable Fokker DVII. No doubt Heron was equally appreciative of his mechanics, but his generosity may not have matched John Todd's: anyway there is no mention in Paice's diary of francs changing hands.[1]

---

1. Alexander Paice returned to the family business in 1919. When the new Dorchester Hotel was being furnished in 1931, the firm were asked to build a simple but attractive folding trunk-stand in Swedish birch for each of its 283 rooms. When Queen Mary visited the hotel she was so taken with these trunk-stands that she said she would like some at Buckingham Palace. They were duly made, in solid walnut, leading to further orders. Paice died in 1946.

1918

FACING THE GERMAN OFFENSIVE: THE RFC IN DEFENCE

THE reputation of General Smuts as a visionary was confirmed and enhanced when he presented his report to the War Cabinet on 17 August 1917. He looked ahead to a time when air power, because of its potential for the 'devastation of enemy lands and the destruction of industrial and populous centres on a vast scale', might actually take precedence over those naval and military operations to which it was then subordinate and ancillary. In pursuit of his vision, he recommended the amalgamation of the two air services into a unified command, spelling an end to duplication and to the competing and often conflicting demands that had exacerbated the supply problem. With surprising alacrity the War Cabinet approved; Smuts was appointed to chair a committee to work out the details; and one of his principal advisers throughout remained David Henderson, the RFC's first commander in the field.

Trenchard, so often called the Father of the Air Force, ahead of Henderson, resisted rather than sought an amalgamation. The RFC, he felt, had only just settled down after the changes and uncertainties of previous years. Why disturb the present set-up? He feared that a separate air force, uncontrolled by the Navy or the Army, would be drawn towards the spectacular, at the expense of the job of work it was doing. How were the duties of the new force to be allocated? Competition between the Navy and Army for existing resources was fierce: wouldn't they simply be introducing a third competitor? He feared, too, that such a major reorganisation would have an adverse effect on production. Then there was the personnel side. Operational pilots soon wore themselves out. What would happen to them? At present, where appropriate, they could be absorbed back into their relevant service or regiment. Finally, Trenchard expressed a personal wish to remain in the job he was doing, where he felt he was being employed most fittingly, rather than be tied, as suggested, to an office and staff work, to which he felt he was unsuited. But the decision was made.

On 29 November the Air Force Bill duly received the Royal Assent, and an Air Ministry, on a par with the Admiralty and the War Office, was formed on 2 January 1918. Lord Rothermere, the newspaper baron, was appointed Air Minister, and Trenchard, who was knighted, was designated Chief of a newly established Air Staff. An Air Council, with executive powers, assumed the functions of the old non-executive Air Board, and Jack Salmond succeeded Trenchard in command of the RFC in France. The new service, to be named the Royal Air Force, was to come into being on 1 April 1918.

For the Royal Flying Corps, as for the Royal Naval Air Service, the year 1918 thus began with intimations of mortality. Jealousies and friction in Whitehall had sometimes been reflected at squadron level, and a distaste for the merger was general. The RNAS, having been part of the senior service, felt superior, 'and they acted it', according to Lieutenant H.R. Puncher, who flew alongside them on what had been a naval squadron. The RFC, in the front line of the ground fighting for so long, could not accept inferiority. Both services were proud of their origins and achievements and had developed loyalties almost as fierce as those of a regiment. They were lukewarm, if not hostile, to the change, which, as typically understated by Bryan Sharwood-Smith, was 'greeted with no great enthusiasm'. Tommy Traill wrote more frankly: 'We were proud of the RFC and of ourselves, and we wanted none of this new thing.' Yet the ugliness was often in the eye of the beholder. 'I can only say that as a squadron officer,' wrote Lieutenant-Commander R.M. Bailey, RN, of the alleged animosity, 'I never experienced it at all in France.'

The greatest achievement of the RNAS up to this point lay in its contribution to the anti-U-boat war, specifically in the Channel and the North Sea, an area of 4,000 square miles which they systematically combed in spider's-web fashion from coastal bases in Britain and France. In 1917 alone they made 175 U-boat sightings and 107 attacks, and although their claims of sinkings were modest they greatly assisted the surface forces besides acting as a deterrent. They had also undertaken most of the strategic bombing that had been attempted thus far. For the RFC, however, in what were to prove its climactic months of existence, its greatest challenge still lay ahead.

During the winter of 1917–18 the pendulum between attack and defence had swung drastically away from Haig and towards Ludendorff. The Bolsheviks, following the October revolution, were negotiating a separate peace, and an armistice between Russia and Germany was signed on 15 December, removing, for Ludendorff, the bane of war on two fronts. Furthermore, vast quantities of manpower and material were thereby released for transfer to the western front. Yet although these welcome accessions would eclipse any immediate infusion of American strength, they would be a diminishing and irreplaceable asset, which American strength was not. The Austrian breakthrough at Caporetto had been arrested (with the help of eleven divisions from the British and French) by a determined stand on the natural barrier of the river Piave, stabilising the front; but the Austrian army remained in a strong position, unlikely to need early reinforcement. And whereas the U-boat campaign, as a means of securing a negotiated peace, had disappointed, the Allied blockade was beginning to bite. Clearly, in Ludendorff's mind, the time to strike was now, before American manpower and industrial output tipped the scales.

On the Allied side, the French were still consolidating with an eye to the American build-up, while disillusion with Haig as a commander-in-chief, after the exhausting campaigns of 1917, had led to a reluctance by the British War Cabinet to back him wholeheartedly, for fear that resources might be squandered. Indeed there was a move afoot to replace him, to Trenchard's disgust, though it came to nothing. Meanwhile the armies in the field were smarting under the experience of Cambrai, which had begun so well and ended in stalemate after a thoroughly daunting reverse.

It was the daunting reverse that exercised the minds of the General Staff. British troops had taken part in a more open engagement than the trench warfare to which they had become accustomed, and the Germans had adapted the more readily. The German principle involved the use, as a spearhead, of specially trained *sturmtruppen* who by infiltrating their adversary's forward positions caused confusion and panic. As an antidote, the British adapted a German method of defence which relied on a thinly-held front line or Forward Zone, with a Battle Zone a mile or two behind it, supported by strong-points in depth, and a Rear Zone, four to eight miles behind the Battle Zone, on which the defence could fall back if necessary. But anything approaching mobile warfare was subject to the same imponderable as air support, namely, the weather.

While the tactics of elastic defence were being overhauled and practised by the army, in preparation for the imminent German offensive foreshadowed by Intelligence reports and by aerial reconnaissance, Trenchard, as his last contribution before leaving France, fell to considering how the RFC should best be employed in a ground campaign based on defence. Obviously the first and foremost duties would lie in reconnaissance, watching for signs of possible attack and helping army commanders to determine whence and in what strength such attacks might come. Secondly, once preparations for an attack were established, would come the routine work of (a) artillery cooperation, (b) bombing aimed at hindering the enemy's preparations and harassing his troops, and (c) an energetic offensive against the enemy's air force to facilitate (a) and (b).

Once an attack started, the primary duty would lie, as always, with the corps squadrons, 'to render our artillery fire effective.' If this object could be attained, thought Trenchard, 'it will be the most material help which can be rendered to the infantry although it may be invisible to them.' Trenchard had always insisted that the RFC should work as an integral part of the army, and he was anxious to reassure Haig, who feared, with the introduction of a separate air service, a conflict of interests. He had argued logically and lucidly against the practicality and moral advisability of Smuts's theories, without effect. He was fortunate in having, in Trenchard, a man devoted to the army, for whom nothing must detract from the RFC's primary duty.

Trenchard also saw a secondary duty: the violent low-level strafing of enemy reinforcements behind the lines, of his communications, and of his advance troops, in close cooperation with the infantry. He specifically stressed the moral effect. And it was in low-level strafing, when the battle started, that pilots and observers of the RFC were to take perhaps the greatest personal risks of any of the combatants in their endeavours to halt the German advance.

Trenchard's homily on 'The Employment of the Royal Flying Corps in Defence' did not end without a reminder of the basic philosophy on which he had always insisted, and always would. Success was only possible through gaining and maintaining an overall ascendancy. This could be achieved only by attacking and defeating the enemy's air forces. Even when the Army was forced temporarily on the defensive, as now, the action of the RFC must always remain essentially offensive. In this he had no more fervent a disciple than Jack Salmond.

The agitation in the UK, in the summer of 1917, for the formation of an Air Ministry, and the news that Winston Churchill, who had long since argued for an Air Ministry, had been appointed Minister of Munitions, seemed to the Germans to portend a substantial growth in British air strength, and in response they formulated and hastened a programme of expansion which gave priority to their air service. The result was that enemy aircraft production was more than doubled, from 8,100 in 1916 to 19,400 in 1917. The British, too, were expanding, and their assessments of where the blow might fall were based on hard-won evidence, but as defenders they were bound to spread their strength, which must inevitably give the attackers a numerical advantage wherever they struck. Haig had good reasons for keeping the Second and First Armies in the northern sector, fearing a drive for the Channel ports, but he also had to be prepared for an attack somewhere in the centre, in the area Arras–Cambrai–St Quentin–La Fére, aimed at separating the British armies from each other, and perhaps from the French farther south. Thirdly was the fear of a drive southwards for Paris. To increase the problems of prediction, Ludendorff seems to have planned tactically rather than strategically, the intention being to strike hard at what he considered the weakest points in the line and be ready to exploit any success achieved.

German efforts to keep the Allies guessing as to the precise direction of their attack were less successful than their masking of its scale. In the centre, where the indications remained strongest that the main assault would come, the British Third and Fifth Armies, of fourteen and twelve divisions respectively, faced three German armies totalling twice that number, a disparity that was soon to become distressingly evident.

In this period of nervous apprehension, waiting for the attack that everyone knew must come, the work of surveillance was paramount. But the corps squadrons, under the protection of offensive patrolling, and with minimum interference, did not neglect the artillery, while bombing, by day and by night, mostly of aerodromes and communications – to which the Corps squadrons contributed – attracted few casualties. An example was a major raid on 9 March, when fifty-three machines of various types, with strong fighter protection, took off to bomb a clutch of German aerodromes from low level. Eighty-eight bombs were dropped, direct hits were recorded on hangars and buildings, and all machines returned safely. But only a fortnight earlier, the General Staff had declared that 'spasmodic bombing is wasteful', and the principle of concentration in time and space had yet to be learned. The profusion of targets listed by the General Staff was in direct contradiction to their declaration, and the raid of 9 March might have been more effective had all the bombs been aimed at a single target. Another recommendation, that a succession of attacks on the same target multiplied the effect, did not register immediately.

Inevitably the winter weather brought a lull in air activity, although the RFC, true to Trenchard's dictum, were much more active than their adversaries, continually probing for signs of unusual movement and, where appropriate, bombing what they found. The accent in the German Air Force was on consolidation, and it was difficult to bring them to battle, even Richthofen going for several weeks without a victory. But the Circus, like many of the RFC's fighter squadrons, was based in the central sector, and by early February there were some spectacular clashes. One of these involved a 19-year-old Camel pilot named A.D.G. 'Grey' Alderson of No. 3 Squadron, whose CO's policy was to allow his pilots forty-eight hours' grace before they went on leave and another forty-eight hours' on their return 'to get over it', subject always to the 'exigencies'. And it was the exigencies that forced Alderson into a patrol late in January, on the morning he was due to go on leave.

He soon appreciated the CO's point: he had never known so much Archie, the sky was full of it, and he fancied it was all directed at him. He admitted to having 'the breeze vertical', and he feared he would never live to go on leave.

As compensation the CO arranged for him to fly a Spad back to England, instead of going by sea, and he was lucky, too, after a fortnight in his native Yorkshire, to find a reinforcement DH4 to fly back. Next day he took his Camel up on test, but again the promised interval was denied him: that afternoon he and three others were sitting by the fire in the Mess when they were called to the squadron office. The Circus was out, it was a chance not to be missed, wing headquarters were calling for an offensive patrol, and they were the only pilots immediately available. They ran to the hangars, pulled on their flying kits, and were airborne within minutes.

Before they reached the lines, one of the four turned back with engine trouble, a serious loss in view of what faced them. Soon they sighted six Albatros single-seaters at 13,500 feet and noted their vivid colours and squadron markings: the Circus, for sure. When the firing started the flight commander sheered off at once with a damaged tailplane, which left only two to cope with six.

How long the fight lasted Alderson never knew, but an Archie gunner who witnessed it wrote: 'One Hun was sent down in flames by the remaining two Camels, shortly followed by a second. Then one of our two went down, shot out of control, and the remaining machine went down in flames. It was a fight against impossible odds.'

There was no chance for the chap in the flamer, but Alderson was in the Camel going down out of control. No chance, it seemed, for him either. An explosive bullet had hit the rudder bar, shattering his right leg, and as he saw the second Albatros burst into flames he passed out. From two and a half miles up his Camel dived, zoomed, somersaulted and spun under its own volition, engine full on, with Alderson still in it, unconscious.

He had often wondered what a man felt like in those last despairing moments, and he had convinced himself that a pilot would be so engrossed in the task of trying to lessen the force of the crash that he would have no time to think of anything else. But once, in a formation that was diving steeply on a Hun battery, he had seen the wings of one of the Camels suddenly fold back, the machine plunging like a meteor and bursting into flames on impact. He had conceded that when a machine broke up in the air like that, the pilot's anguish might be prolonged. But as it was, he was aware of none of these things. A week elapsed before he recovered even a proportion of his senses, and then, suffering from a fractured skull and delirium, he imagined he was in a London hospital, surrounded by exotic blossoms and no less exotic nurses. In reality he lay in a small, bare, dimly-lit room, and a German sentry stood guard at the foot of his bed. It was then that he wrote the postcard which, as related earlier, so outraged the German general.

The day-bomber squadron on the Third Army front, opposite Cambrai, was No. 49, and throughout February it was engaged on high-level reconnaissance. A 260 hp Fiat engine was being tested in some of the DH4's, replacing the disappointing Farnborough 3a, and John Morris, the man who had been so overworked the previous year, wrote that 'it went rippingly'. But he was deafened by the noise it made. With the engine 'bang in front of my head', and with 'practically no exhaust pipe to quieten it', it was 'like a motor-bike without a silencer'. He was becoming aware, too, of the problems of high altitude. One pilot, on a height test, reached 18,000 feet in thirty-three minutes, but anoxia at these heights was causing drowsiness for some and physical debility for others. Some suffered from headaches, others found themselves fighting for breath. A pilot named G. Fox-Rule, 'really only a boy,' said Morris, 'he looks like a kid of about fifteen', was taking photographs over the line when he felt faint. He managed to get back to the aerodrome and land before collapsing, but it was several minutes before he could be revived – with the oxygen that should surely have been fitted in his machine. He seems to have suffered no ill-effects, as he was later credited with seven victories, a high score for a bomber pilot, and the best on 49 Squadron.

Medical studies into what was known as 'mountain sickness' were begun. The Germans were already one step ahead, as with parachutes: they had already begun to fit oxygen into some of their high-flying machines.

Morris was certainly no malcontent, but the tenacity of some of his colleagues could still not be relied upon, and he was sickened by the continuing tendency of some of them to abort. Of ten crews detailed on one bombing show, only eight started – and even that, felt Morris, rightly as it turned out, was too good to be true. 'Sure enough one by one they departed with engine trouble.' The smallest formation of DH4's allowed to cross the lines was four, and Morris had climbed to 13,500 feet with three others when another crew dropped out and back they all had to go. On a similar occasion, again on a bombing show, Morris couldn't bear to take his bombs back, and seeing no Huns about he went on and bombed the target alone.

Although Morris took great care of his engine, he too had problems. Descending from the heights at which they operated was a long process and needed patience and care, lest the engine, throttled back, went cold. Wise pilots throttled down only just enough to lose height. Morris was far over the lines late one afternoon when his engine started playing up. It was getting dark, and captivity beckoned, but he just managed to get clear of the lines before being forced down, breaking his propeller. The nervous tension had been such that 'I sat there for a few minutes without attempting to get out'.

No. 49 Squadron continued for some time to operate with only two flights, and the CO, recognising Morris as a future flight commander, borrowed him on one occasion from A Flight to go as deputy leader with B Flight. Morris was 'a bit put out about this, as both flights are equally denuded', but he recognised it as a compliment. They were on a photographic job, but again Morris found something to criticise: the flight leader failed to keep them together. Morris had now done more shows than anyone in either flight except Chambers, his flight commander and the man he most admired.

The discerning Morris always gave credit where it was due. 'We always teach the observer something about flying, so that if the pilot is knocked out, they can save themselves and perhaps the pilot, if he is only wounded.' He spent a whole day flying around with a new observer named Cuttle, familiarising him with the machine and the countryside, then took him up again for an hour and a half in the evening, showing him the lines. 'Cuttle put up a good show when he once got started, and after a few more shots he should be able to get down at any rate without killing himself.'[1] But with another youth he was less patient: he was 'too slow and thick-witted', and he was returned to his unit.

These and similar contretemps and imperfections did not feature in RFC communiqués, but they were the stuff of squadron life, revealing yet again how, in the average squadron, fortitude depended on the few. These were the men the RFC relied on to eliminate faults and foibles before the offensive broke, and to lead the way when it did.

In early March No. 49 Squadron was switched from long-range photo reconnaissance to the bombing of villages where enemy troops were billeted, and of ammunition dumps. It was on one of these raids, on 6 March 1918, that the squadron suffered a loss it could

1. Lieutenant G.R. Cuttle, from Victoria, Australia. He had won the MC on the Somme, but was killed in air combat as an observer in No. 49 Squadron on 9 May 1918.

ill afford. The estimable John Morris, whose letters from the front to his family in Blandford, Dorset had numbered two a week over a four-month period, and whose name, like so many, does not appear in any list of awards, was killed in action. He was still only 19. Flight-commander Chambers did not long survive him.

Among the fighters cooperating with the Fifth Army under General Gough were the SE5A's of Sholto Douglas's 84 Squadron, and they used the hiatus between January and March to work out their most efficient fighting formations and to plot how best to tempt or trap their adversaries into action, in pursuit of the ascendancy Trenchard had demanded. Lieutenant-Colonel F.V. Holt, DSO, commanding the Wing, was an advocate of strong offensive patrols, even at the expense of leaving parts of the line thinly protected, and Douglas, by trial and error, arrived at what he regarded as the ideal squadron formation. Of his three flights, the lowest led the squadron, normally at about 15,000 feet. Five hundred feet above it, and a mile distant, behind and to the flank, flew the second flight, whose absolute duty was to conform to the movements of the leading flight. The third flight formed a covering force, 3,000 feet above the leading flight, some two to three miles behind it and on the other flank. This flight only came to the assistance of the other flights in extreme emergency: its very presence often acted as a deterrent. When working as a complete squadron, this was the formation arrived at.

There were attempts, in this period, to operate three squadrons together, in one large formation at different heights, Camels at 15,000 feet, SE5A's at 16–17,000, Brisfits at 18–19,000 – but this only frightened the enemy off. More subtlety was needed, and the alternative tried was for three squadrons, flying independently, to meet at a prearranged point – say over an enemy aerodrome – then return westwards together, enfolding any enemy patrols between them and the lines into their net. For whatever reason, on the three occasions when this manoeuvre was tried, the enemy responded with vigour, and tremendous dogfights developed. Unfortunately these did not always end with advantage to the RFC, victories being gained at sobering cost. 'As the fighting took place fifteen or twenty miles east of the lines,' wrote Douglas, 'our casualties were fairly severe.' Pilots tended to lose formation in the mêlée and often had to return independently, with perhaps a damaged machine or a failing engine, all too liable to be picked off. Nevertheless Douglas was convinced that this was the best method of carrying out multi-squadron offensive patrols, assuming the need for them, giving the best chance of surprising a small number of enemy machines with a large concentration of fighters.

Not everyone was happy with these attempts at enticing the enemy into combat, and Gwilym Lewis, of 40 Squadron, also flying SE5A's, thought the Huns, by using the winter months to rest and re-equip their scouts, as they were obviously doing, were 'showing twice as much common sense as we were'. His squadron existed, or so he believed, to protect the corps machines, indirectly more than directly, but most of their work that winter lay in seeking out the enemy's reconnaissance two-seaters at various levels, up to 20,000 feet, and escorting bombers in daylight. He confessed to having moments over the lines when he was so paralysed with fright that he longed to turn back, and sometimes did, but he already had five hostiles to his credit, had been promoted to flight commander, and had a reputation as a disciplinarian. Yet he did not compare himself with the top scout pilots, men like George McElroy, Mannock's 'McIrish', who 'has been going absolutely full out. He is quite mad and seldom returns without having brought something down'.

The man Lewis admired most of all was Mannock himself. 'He strafes about on his own – he is an excellent fellow.' Yet, paradoxically, while Lewis, who looked up to Trenchard and admired his ascetic way of life, could see no merit in the policy of maintaining the offensive at all costs, and wrote of the work of escorting DH4's in raids on German aerodromes that winter as 'stupid daylight bombing stunts', the socialist Mannock, who associated Trenchard with the top-brass, upper-class mentality and wrote that he 'talked bilge, don't like him', exerted himself in support of that policy to an exceptional degree. 'Our expert', wrote Lewis of Mannock in January 1918, 'has recently been sent home, very much against his will. He has been out here about eight or ten months, and has 18 Huns to his credit . . . He even went up on the morning he was due to leave.'

Lewis's opinion of Trenchard had improved on acquaintance. Having disliked him at first on principle, he now believed him to be an exceptional man. He had built up the RFC in France with immense pertinacity, yet there was nothing of the regular soldier about him. 'He doesn't smoke, I have never seen him drink anything but water, and one stares at a general who lives like that. Very strong minded and independent. Our present position out here is largely the result of his efforts.' He added: 'He thinks nothing of Sykes.' This was Major-General Frederick H. Sykes, who had gone to France in August 1914 as chief staff officer and deputy to David Henderson, a big blow at the time to Trenchard, who had had to be content with being left in charge at Farnborough. But when Henderson returned to the War Office in August 1915, he was succeeded not by Sykes but by Trenchard.

Trenchard's straightforward manner contrasted and frequently clashed with that of the more politically astute Sykes, of whom it was said that he was hampered by a personality which 'strongly engendered mistrust'. But he remained a powerful rival.

Trenchard went home on 18 January to take over as the new Chief of the Air staff, only to find, in the next few weeks, the machinations of Rothermere intolerable. Eventually he resigned, making way for none other than Sykes. This brought a second resignation, that of Henderson, who was no happier than Trenchard with Sykes.

The day after Trenchard's return to the UK, the RFC lost its youngest and best-loved brigadier-general, Gordon Shephard, one of the early flight leaders and by then commanding No. I Brigade at Bruay. In addition to taking every opportunity to fly reconnaissance sorties himself, Shephard visited the squadrons under his command almost daily in his Nieuport scout, making a point of getting to know all his pilots and observers personally, and taking a special interest in newcomers. He was about to land at Auchel aerodrome when he spun in and was killed. Trenchard rated him with pioneers Don Lewis

[199]

and Bron James as one of the begetters of aerial reconnaissance. He was 32.

Flying of all kinds still held its hazards, even for so experienced a veteran as Gordon Shephard. His reputation as an operational pilot had been 'bold, but safe', yet he made what seems to have been a simple error, stalling in the turn and spinning in. Others to lose their lives in non-operational flying that winter included two of McCudden's original flight in 56 Squadron, Keith Muspratt and Leonard Barlow: both were killed while test-flying at Martlesham Heath. Of McCudden's famous flight on No. 56, only Rhys Davids actually died in combat. Coote and Cronyn survived the war.

German reticence in the air, as Ludendorff completed his preparations for the offensive, became less pronounced, and it was not long before Richthofen himself was leading his Circus again. The rest had done him good. But much of the old conceit had evaporated. His book, *The Red Air Fighter*, had meanwhile been published, and he blushed when he read it, it was so brash and immature. 'I no longer possess such an insolent spirit.' He was now leading thirty machines and more into battle, and on 12 March his Fokker triplanes and Albatris shot down four out of a formation of nine Bristol Fighters for the loss of half that number, Richthofen scoring his sixty-fourth victory. He seems at last to have been back to his best, and the Brisfit pilot he shot down, who like his observer was captured, later paid a warm tribute to Richthofen's skill and marksmanship. Richthofen, for his part, did not forget the courtesies between opposing airmen that still informed the air war. 'During my second day in hospital,' wrote the observer, 'a German officer came in and said he had come from Baron von Richthofen, who wished me to accept half a dozen cigars with his compliments. I did, with thanks.'

Next day Richthofen shot down a Camel, but in an ensuing dogfight his brother Lothar was wounded, needing several weeks in hospital to recover. From this point on, Manfred seems to have acquired or inherited some of his brother's panache, revising his earlier tactics of caution and stealth. He had taken part that winter in discussions on military strategy, and was aware that the war situation was 'very grim'. Of his destruction of another Camel soon afterwards, one of his pilots demurred. 'We all saw you fly so close to him that a collision seemed inevitable.'

The RFC was still bidding for the ascendancy, and a favourite ploy remained trying to trap the enemy at a disadvantage. The Circus was caught out on 17 March when five DH4's mounted a bombing attack with the sole purpose of luring them into an ambush, and in the resultant dogfight three single-seaters were destroyed by SE5A's without loss. But an attempt to repeat the ruse next day was answered by some fifty of the latest German fighters in a ferocious mêlée in which the British came off decidedly the worse, losing five Camels, two SE5A's and a DH4, against a bag of four Germans. The morale of the German Air Force, powerfully reinforced as it had been, remained high.

The RFC, too, was approaching a peak, equipped with the machines with which it would be obliged – and tolerably happy – to fight the rest of the war. On the western front the basic corps machine, finally replacing the BE2c, was the RE8, of which there were sixteen squadrons, complemented by five squadrons of Armstrong Whitworth FK8 two-seaters – 'Big Acks'. Another machine that had disappeared, its passing unmourned, was the Martinsyde Elephant – largely peculiar to 27 Squadron – which had been succeeded by the DH4. This machine was now equipping six bomber squadrons and was confirmed as the best day bomber of the war. Ten Sopwith Camel, ten SE5A, five Bristol Fighter and two Sopwith Dolphin squadrons – the last-named widely used on escort duties – formed the bulk of the so-called fighting or army machines. The four FE2b squadrons that remained in service were mostly employed on night bombing.

In the Third and Fifth Army areas the RFC had mustered a total of 579 serviceable aircraft, of which 261 were single-seater fighters. Ranged against them the Germans could bring to bear a total of 730 machines, of which 326 were single-seater fighters. So although the Germans could no longer claim any technical advantage, numeri-

[201]

cal superiority, which the RFC had hitherto enjoyed, had passed to them.

The readiness of the Circus to mix it with the RFC on 17 and 18 March was only one of many indications that the great German spring offensive was about to begin.

THE MARCH RETREAT: LOW-LEVEL STRAFING AIMS TO STEM THE TIDE

'... into our minds had crept for the first time the secret, incredible fear
that we might lose the war.'

VERA BRITTAIN, *Testament of Youth*.

SOON after 4.30 on the morning of 21 March, the pilots of the
three army squadrons based at the aerodrome at Flez, nine
miles west of German-held St Quentin, were awakened by a
tumultuous roar. The German spring offensive, as confidently predicted by aerial observation, the interrogation of prisoners, and other
forms of Intelligence, had begun.

Sleep became impossible, the whistling of shells overhead provided
a strident descant, and the pilots, pulling warm clothes over their
pyjamas, stood in half-dazed groups outside their huts, gas masks at
the ready. This was it: soon they would be called into action. But for
all the chill apprehensions of early morning, their minds, saturated by
the barrage, still registered fellow-feeling for the less fortunate.
'*Thank God we're not in the trenches.*'

The tasks allotted to the RFC to assist in repelling the coming
onslaught were well rehearsed and well known. Of the two brigades
immediately involved, both commanded by men who had led
elements of the original Channel crossing three and a half years
earlier, No. III, under Josh Higgins, was attached to the Third Army.
It comprised four RE8 squadrons for gun-spotting and photography,

three Camel squadrons to protect the corps machines, three SE5 squadrons for engaging enemy fighters, a Brisfit squadron for low-level strafing, and two bomber squadrons, one day and one night. No. V Brigade, under Lionel Charlton, had five corps squadrons (three Armstrong-Whitworth and two RE8), and, in fighters, one Camel, two SE5, one Brisfit and one Spad squadron, and again two bomber squadrons, one day and one night. Although outnumbered by the enemy – because of his ability to concentrate his forces – they were at least his equal in quality, well able to make him pay a heavy price for his aggression. Every pilot knew his specific duties and the targets and tasks to which he was assigned. But as they groped around in the candlelight that morning, at Flez and at a dozen other bases, to prepare for the dawn patrols that were ordered, the din of bombardment, accompanied by the whining of terrified pets, continued to assail their ears despite a curious muffling of sound. Not until dawn came at 06.30 was the blanket of mist that clung like an adhesive to the earth belatedly revealed. Sound, however attenuated, might penetrate it, but not aeroplanes. The multiple tasks allotted to the RFC could not be discharged because they could not even get airborne.

Massed along more than fifty miles of front were fifty-six German divisions, with twelve more in reserve. In all they had assembled close-on a million men. When, an hour or so later, they began to move forward, staggering their times between sectors, the British, although forewarned, knew nothing until enemy troops suddenly swarmed out of the fog, penetrating and infiltrating their positions before they were properly aware of it. Plans for enfilading fire that would devastate advancing *sturmtruppen* were aborted, and for vital hours no one knew what was happening. Many of the forward troops, already overwhelmed by the bombardment, were annihilated, and by noon the enemy assault troops had reached the battle zone. Although the timing of the assault had been predicted to the minute, the scale of it, and the unparalleled concentration of firepower, with a gas attack for good measure, came as a cataclysm.

For the RFC it was a case of *déjà vu*, of seeing the picture round again. This was where they came in. In the retreat from Mons they had contributed decisively by spotting first the threatened isolation of the BEF, then the great wheeling movement which left von Kluck's army vulnerable to counter-attack. Now British armies were in head-long retreat again, disastrously, or so it seemed. Could they contribute decisively now?

The Germans were advancing along the entire Somme front, facing Arras and the Third Army in the north, down to St Quentin and La Fére, where the Fifth Army joined the French, in the south. The initial thrust seemed to threaten the junction between the Third and Fifth Armies, but no one could be sure where the major blow might fall.

The only successful attempts at reconnaissance that morning were made in the north, where visibility was clearer. The RE8 crews of 59 Squadron did best, reporting with precision on a bulge in the line along seven miles of front south of Arras. Some of the early wireless calls to batteries were dealt with expeditiously, one call for fire on groups of advancing German infantry being answered – so it was recorded – 'with devastating effect': but all too often the batteries themselves were enacting or contemplating retreat and had not erected their aerials, so that countless such calls went unheeded. The first low-flying attacks were also mounted on this front, six Camel pilots of 46 Squadron bombing and machine-gunning active German batteries north of Bourlon Wood.

When visibility in the south improved, the three army squadrons at Flez, Nos 48 (Bristols), 54 (Camels), and 84 (SE5A's) lined up their machines in front of the hangars in readiness. Meanwhile the bombardment continued with undiminished fury, and four miles to the north, at Mons-en-Chaussées, the DH4's of No. 5 (Naval) Squadron were driven out by the shelling, moving south-west to Champien, fifteen miles south of Flez, near the town of Roye, and burning their buildings and hangars before they left.

The first reports from the corps squadrons in this sector brought alarming news: south of St Quentin, in an area thought to be impregnable, the enemy had broken through. Among the first of the army pilots to take off from Flez were Lieutenants Stock and Drysdale. Their CO, George Maxwell, was on leave and had been temporarily replaced by Captain Francis Kitto, commanding C Flight. This left 19-year-old Ewart Stock, Kitto's deputy, to take over the flight. A few months earlier he had been opening the batting – and had been adjudged the best fielder – at Caterham School. Now he was opening for C Flight, 54 Squadron. He had given up a place at Hertford College, Oxford to join up.

Stock and Drysdale left at 11.30 on a low-level reconnaissance of a section of the St Quentin canal. They found the mist still clinging to the contours, giving them some protection. As they neared the lines the glutinous fog was penetrated by bursts of flame as gun after gun exploded; they could also see groups of British infantry returning the enemy fire. Flying at 500 feet towards the canal, they passed column after column of grey uniforms on the roads beneath them, heading west.

. Stock estimated that there were many thousands on these roads, with not a single shell bursting amongst them. They passed over the canal, and still the roads were crammed with troops and transport, splendid targets if their role had been troop-strafing. But their job was to glean as much information as they could on the strength of the enemy in this area. They continued east until they were beyond the enemy's observation balloons, then headed back for Flez, engines full out until they were clear of the battle zone. As they approached Flez they could see British artillery in hurried retreat, with every cross-roads behind the lines so jam-packed as to be impassable. Stock was surprised on landing when his mechanic pointed to a rash of bullet-holes in his machine.

In the afternoon and early evening, contact patrols, in improving weather, clarified the situation – generally for the worse – on the Fifth Army front. Efforts by the DH4 squadrons to fulfil the bombing programme were neutralised not only by the weather but also by an outdated order, not yet rescinded, that they must not bomb from lower than 15,000 feet. Against the kind of opportunity targets that presented themselves, this condemned them to failure. As an instance, two hundred 25 lb bombs were dropped on bridges over the St Quentin canal but they all survived more or less intact.

Despite protective patrols at low level along the Fifth Army front, the corps squadrons all suffered casualties. More successful were the SE5A's of 56 and 64 squadrons farther north, who clashed with a formation of twenty-six hostiles over Bourlon Wood, shooting down four. But the German Air Force, intent on supporting the advance, mostly avoided combat.

The one major success scored by the RFC on that first day was the low-level strafing of enemy infantry. Some pilots were familiar with this form of attack, others were not, but all responded in spirited fashion. 'After lunch,' noted Stock, 'I was ordered to head a formation along the St Quentin/Estrees-en-Chaussée road and bomb and fire at enemy infantry and transport. We had never undertaken this sort of job before.' Leading his flight of six Camels, he covered the four miles north to the road and then followed it eastwards, diving to 500 feet and peering ahead for a target. Each machine was carrying two 20 lb bombs and 800 rounds of ammunition. 'Enemy infantry everywhere,' noted Stock, 'advancing in the open and in large columns on the road.' The first necessity was to get rid of the handicap of the bombs, and he gave the sign to drop when he recognised grey uniforms directly ahead, accoutred with large helmets and long bayonets. His bombs 'must have hit the road squarely in the centre. I could hear the explosions.'

The others followed, scattering the enemy columns. Stock then led them west and dived on the troops in the open. 'At one time I must have been at the level of their heads: they lay down on the ground when they saw us coming.' The Camels repeated this until their ammunition was exhausted, when Stock led them home. They lost one machine but heard later that the pilot had escaped to the Fifth Army lines.

Returning for afternoon tea at 16.30, Stock went out again in what was now a glorious evening, paired, as in the morning, with Drysdale. They spotted an RE8 being chased by a hostile and dived to its aid, forcing the German pilot to head east, his observer slumped over his gun.

On the ground the enemy was still advancing, with shells bursting incessantly in the British lines, and they returned to report what they'd seen. 'We retired that night at an early hour as another day's work, equally strenuous, lay before us.' The Third and Fifth Armies were in universal retreat, and the enemy had made formidable inroads along the whole length of the line.

As pilots and crews adapted to the changed pattern of air operations, all played their part in the bombing and machine-gunning. Most of the RFC casualties were caused by small arms fire from the ground. Sensing that their most treasured possessions were exposed to the greatest danger, pilots sat on flattened steel helmets for protection.

The biggest disappointment continued to be the breakdown of communications between pilots and battery commanders, and in an effort to correct this failure the commander of No. 8 Squadron (Armstrong-Whitworths, Major Trafford Leigh-Mallory), supporting the Fifth Army, sent his wireless officer to locate the batteries with which he was trying to cooperate, only to find that most of them had discarded their wireless equipment. 'As soon as the retreat started,' complained Leigh-Mallory, 'all idea of cooperating with aeroplanes seems to have been abandoned.'

The overall situation was critical, if not desperate, the immediate danger being that a gap would be driven between the Third and Fifth Armies. Plans for repelling the assault had been totally distorted by the fog, both on the ground and in the air. For many vital hours the RFC had been grounded, and they had been deprived, in the panic and confusion of the retreat, of their long-practised liaison with the artillery. This was the function on which Trenchard had set the greatest store. Yet in their frustration and impotence they had turned to the alternative of low-level strafing and bombing of enemy troops and transport with outstanding success.

Again and again the battered German regiments reported with understandable vexation – but with ungrudging admiration – on how, when visibility improved, the British airmen flew 'in the most daring manner very low over the ground and threw bombs causing us considerable losses'. Concentrations were spotted and bombs were rained upon them. In a raid south of St Quentin, 'the signal officer, the excellent Weisz, was killed instantly. The regimental staff was decimated.' At Honnecourt, behind the German lines south of

Cambrai, an artillery unit had 'sixty horses killed by a British airman who caught them on the march'. Another regiment which had halted temporarily in a hollow was so heavily bombarded from the air that they were ordered to fall back. Also on the Third Army front: 'About a dozen English low-flying battle aeroplanes whizzed up, and from an incredibly low height bombed our advancing troops. This caused great confusion.' These were the Camels of 46 Squadron. And again, 'The English got valuable support from their aircraft, which attacked regardless of the consequences . . . Our own airmen were absent.'

The greatest damage was still done on the rare occasions when aeroplane and artillery were able to cooperate; but when this was denied them, the RFC found a way of helping directly to slow the German advance. It was a form of attack that the enemy, despite their much-vaunted battle flights, seemed unable to mount in comparable violence; it was a form which their troops were to dislike even more intensely than the pilots who mounted it.

CAMEL PILOTS EWART STOCK AND ROY CROWDEN

'We are again at a crisis of the War'
DOUGLAS HAIG

FOR the British, the first day of Ludendorff's offensive had been one of the most disastrous of the war, with casualties estimated, in round figures, at 7,500 killed, 10,000 wounded, and 21,000 taken prisoner – losses exceeded only by the slaughter on the first day on the Somme. The number of guns lost was unprecedented – 382 by the Fifth Army, 150 by the Third, about one-fifth of the whole. Retreat was universal over the entire 50-mile front, to a depth, at its farthest point, of nearly ten miles. Yet although British losses mounted daily, and the retreat continued, the Germans suffered even more severely as the two defending armies, far from collapsing, continued to inflict heavy losses on their pursuers. The moment of crisis, though, was yet to come.

On the second morning, 22 March, the fog was thicker than ever, but when it cleared, at about eleven o'clock, corps and army machines went into action again. In the south, the enemy were now clear of Holman Wood and well on their way to Mons-Estree, on the St Quentin–Amiens road. Pilots from Flez, on strafing missions both morning and afternoon, reported masses of the enemy still advancing, pushing the defenders back by their sheer weight. But the thin line of infantry that confronted them was still making them pay for their gains. Ewart Stock had dramatic evidence of this in the afternoon when firing on troops in the open. 'I saw what seemed to be a long wall of sandbags. I could not understand for a moment why I had not seen it before, until diving at the enemy behind it I noticed that it was a wall of dead bodies heaped one upon the other. The enemy were on the east side of it, so I was able to sweep this wall with machine-gun fire until there must have been a hundred or so German soldiers to add to their human wall.'

By this time Stock's former companion Drysdale, replacing a casualty, was leading A Flight; but that afternoon he too was wounded, and he left the squadron that evening. Casualties were getting unacceptably high, and Stock revealed in his diary a dissatisfaction with the squadron's tactics so far. Formations of six machines, he judged, were too cumbersome for ground-strafing; they got in each other's way, risking collision. The decision taken for the future was to work in pairs, a method that other squadrons either copied or were already practising.

No. 84 Squadron's activity was equally unceasing, and they too were working in pairs. But their actual style of attack, according to Hugh Saunders, a South African, differed from the converging method of the Camels of No. 54: each pilot dived separately, firing from 500 feet down to 50 before zooming away in a climbing turn. Whether this was as effective as the converging attack is impossible to gauge, but it eliminated the risk of collision, and Sholto Douglas was also able to claim that it was safer, not one of his pilots being lost to ground fire in the March retreat. Saunders added that it was a method made possible by the robustness of the SE5A, the dive and steep pull-out being made without fear of structural failure.

In paying tribute to Douglas as their inspiration, 'Dingbat' Saunders, as he was known, described him as 'a very stern CO'. Although he himself was a future air chief marshal, Saunders admitted to being 'quite frightened of him'.

Such was the weight of the German attack that they were still pouring through the gap opposite St Quentin, and low-flying attacks by squadron after squadron could not dislodge them, despite losses of some thirty machines on both sides. Yet German accounts testify to the awe in which the RFC pilots were held and the confusion and

[211]

casualties they caused. All told, 730 25-pounders were dropped by a variety of squadrons, causing extreme pessimism in one regiment: 'Under the heavy artillery and machine-gun fire and frequent attacks by air squadrons the attack cannot go on.'

Air fighting that day was again of a desultory nature, the German air force, for all its concentration in numbers, seeming to operate to no coherent plan. Against this, the RFC pounded away at the same railway junctions they had bombed the previous day, while that night the FE2b's, on roving commissions, aimed their bombs wherever they saw evidence of activity. More than that, they spotted fresh masses of troops moving in darkness towards the fragile Fifth Army line, in time for General Gough to reverse his earlier resolve to offer battle east of the Somme. Instead, a gradual withdrawal west of the river was ordered, almost certainly saving the Fifth Army from a defeat that would have opened the approaches to Amiens. This was where the RFC had first landed on French soil three and a half years earlier, and it was a communications pivot that had to be held if a retreat to the coast was to be averted.

Relentless German pressure continued along the entire battlefront on 23 March, and the RFC were called upon to redouble their low-level strikes. Every machine not otherwise gainfully employed was switched to harassing the enemy troops. The withdrawal of the Fifth Army obliged the Third Army to adjust to the same line, and for a time the two armies actually lost touch. All this was reported in lucid detail by contact patrol observers who, although frequently attacked, were granted a panoramic view by improved visibility. With batteries in retreat still unable to erect wireless aerials for reception, or lay out ground strips, the corps crews themselves, flying below 1,000 feet, bombed any targets they saw.

Crews were flying several patrols daily, assessing whether or not bridges had been destroyed, bombing and firing at advancing infantry, and sending urgent signals for specific masses of troops to be blasted by all available batteries. One such report, by Lieutenants W.E. Joseph and G.W. Owen of 35 Squadron, concluded: 'Attacked by seven enemy aircraft (Scouts) at 300 feet and followed as far as Foucaucourt.' Yet the enemy pilots, strangely irresolute, pursued them no farther. Within half an hour of landing, Joseph and Owen were airborne again on another patrol.

The enemy were now so close to Flez aerodrome that the rattle of machine-gun fire, three miles to the north, disturbed the pilots at breakfast. Targets that morning again lay along the St Quentin–Amiens road, and 'after a hasty lunch', with the aerodrome about to be overrun, they took off for the Ham area, a town eleven miles south-west of St Quentin. There they attacked transport on the Ham–La Fére road before joining No. 5 (Naval) Squadron at Champien. What upset them most was that the Hun was now in possession of their old aerodrome, 'where we had lived in peace for several months', though ground crews had burnt the Mess and the hangars before leaving. Again there were parallels with the Mons retreat as they dined in a hotel in Noyon and slept the night in a chateau. Other squadrons, too, were forced to move, one of the FE2b night bombing squadrons suffering a temporary pause in operations for that reason.

The fourth day of the retreat, Sunday 24 March, was no day to return from leave, let alone find oneself in command of a squadron for the first time, but this was the fate of Gwilym Lewis of 40 Squadron at Bruay, nominally attached to the First Army farther north but now working with the Third. Leonard Tilney had been killed leading the squadron on 9 March, and with the imminent merger of the two air services, the new commander was to be the RNAS Australian ace Roderick Dallas – but not until 1 April. It seemed to Lewis that from this point on he lived in the air. Five squadrons were crammed into Bruay, instead of the usual two, and they were all feverishly bombarding the German infantry.

The SE5A pilots carried four 20 lb bombs, and Lewis found a macabre humour in 'laying nice little eggs' on what he described as 'rows of fat Huns' (Lewis's sense of humour – and of propriety – demanded that every Hun should be 'fat'). The eggs were the curtain-raiser, preliminary to the main entertainment of shooting them up and 'seeing them run in all directions'. But it was not so

[213]

funny when one was being Archied and hosed point-blank with small-arms fire. It was good for a laugh afterwards, perhaps, but 'everything is spoiled at the time by being so frightened'. Life became so hectic that more than once he nearly fell asleep in the cockpit.

On high-level patrol, Lewis got numbed and frozen at 17–19,000 feet. Coming down to refuel, he had barely thawed out when he was off again. But, as with low-level strafing, he could recall little of what happened, one patrol running like damp colours into another. 'Sometimes we get Huns and sometimes we don't.' But thirty-nine German machines were claimed as destroyed on this day, for only five British losses, although twenty-eight more, as squadrons were chased out of one aerodrome into another, were wrecked. Enemy casualties included Ludendorff's son, buried unnamed by the British. Later Ludendorff was to have the task of identifying him.

For the British the news on that Sunday morning was grave. The German thrust in the centre, as confirmed by air observation, was continuing, and a critical situation was developing between Peronne and the Bapaume–Cambrai road, where the wedge between the two British armies had been widened to nearly three miles. '*We are again at a crisis of the war*,' warned Haig in a special order of the day. He reminded his forces that the enemy was aiming at nothing less than the destruction of the British Army, which they must do their utmost to prevent. Clery, near Peronne, had fallen, and the retreat was continuing under extreme difficulty. Yet the RFC reacted so ferociously throughout the day that several German regiments were forced to pause, one admitting that 'very active fighting and bombing squadrons of the enemy in the clear air imposed a very cautious advance on us'. Another regiment, aiming to cross the Bapaume–Peronne road, was delayed by 'hostile airmen, flying low', their weapons machine-guns and bombs.

South of Peronne, too, where German troops were assembling after crossing the Somme, low-level strafing was ordered. One German account told of the sudden appearance of twenty or more British aeroplanes diving until they were virtually scraping the earth. 'My company commander, Lieutenant Nocke, had to fling himself flat on the ground, but for all that he was struck on the back by the wheels of one machine, thus being literally run over.' Typically of the dive-bombed, the writer imagined himself under personal attack. 'At the last moment I was able to spring clear as the machine whizzed past me.' This madcap, trigger-happy low flying and bombing created havoc wherever it occurred, but not without cost. The German account went on to describe how one attacking machine was brought down, with four others destroyed in the same area.

Farther south, facing the thrust from St Quentin, Camel pilots Ewart Stock and Roy Crowden, who were rooming together, were called at 6 a.m.; they walked to their heavily-patched machines and headed for Ham with the usual load – two bombs and 800 rounds of ammunition. Approaching the Somme they noted that their com-patriots were digging trenches on the west bank, where they were preparing to make a stand. Flying low on the east side of the river, they spotted Hun cavalry advancing through Matigny, four miles north-west of Ham. Here was an ideal target.

After climbing to 2,000 feet and scanning the sky to make sure there were no Huns about, they flew flat out towards Matigny. The bulk of the cavalry were on a straight road running east of the village, and, with Crowden following, Stock released his bombs. Simultaneously his Camel was hit, severing a landing wire, a piece of which just missed his goggles, but he was able to turn in time to see the results of his strike. 'I had never seen such confusion amongst horses as I saw then. They were darting all over the field, knocking men down who were trying to catch them.'

Seeing another squad of about twenty horses galloping across a field, he tried to line them up, but his wheels struck the ground with such force that his Camel leapt into the air before he could shoot. He dived a second time and got in a lengthy burst, then, as he was pulling out, he saw a group of four mounted officers on the road, with a fifth squatting nearby. 'I distinctly saw one firing with a revolver at Crowden.' This was enough, and he dived on them and fired about a hundred rounds. 'Two of them fell off their horses and one galloped off along the road. He was a tall man and was wearing the spiked Hun helmet.' Stock hit either him or his horse and they crashed together into a hedge. Then a machine-gun opened up at him and

[215]

he could not shake it off. He had lost touch with Crowden and did not see him again till after he landed. Stock's wings were riddled, two flying wires were severed and there was a bullet through his rev counter, but he was off again that evening in a different machine, this time leading a formation of five to bomb enemy transport at Athies, close to their old aerodrome at Flez. With Champien also becoming untenable, they were to retreat afterwards as far as Bertangles, four miles north of Amiens.

With gaggles of retreating artillery, transport and French peasant carts hurrying west below them, they followed the Somme until they were in sight of Flez. Looking round to check that the formation was with him, Stock saw a clutch of six Huns flying 2,000 feet higher and about a mile on the far side of the river. He immediately turned and climbed towards the sun. As they were all carrying bombs the climb was sluggish, but 'before we got far the Huns went east, thus showing their usual spirit of avoiding a scrap unless the advantage is with them'. The German Air Force, in turn, was paying the price for too-rapid expansion.

At Athies they descended to 500 feet and bombed a large convoy parked on the east side of a wood. Then they made for Bertangles. No transport had arrived for them, but they borrowed a car from another squadron, dined in Amiens – 'I never wanted a hot bath and a big meal and bed as I did then' – and found another chateau to sleep in. Good news was that the CO was back and that Captain Kitto had shot down two Albatros DV's, the fifth and sixth victories of his career. As always there was bad news too. 'We had very few pilots left of the old squadron by this time, about six were missing and at least five had been wounded. This meant more work for those that were left, so we were up early again next morning for another day's work.'

At Marieux, seventeen miles west of Bapaume, mechanics worked all night on the Camels of 70 Squadron, finishing at five o'clock, starting again at tea-time, and working until midnight. On 22 March the squadron had shot down ten hostiles, but they had suffered for it. 'Own aircraft badly shot about,' noted John Todd's mechanic Alexander Paice, 'rather stirring times. Fritz dropped six bombs not far away.' This was when he commented: 'Terrible fighting just in front of us. May have to leave any time.' And on the 24th his flight broke all records for flying hours in one day.

The most spectacular achievement of 24 March, however, belonged to a flight commander on 43 Squadron (Camels) named John Trollope. Like Kitto he was a veteran of 1½-strutters. Already credited with seven victories, he actually scored six more in the course of two patrols that day, morning and afternoon, five two-seaters and an Albatros DV. He was still scrapping on the afternoon patrol when he ran out of ammunition. Forty-two German aircraft were shot down during the day, but the British losses exceeded these – eleven missing, eight burnt or abandoned, forty-six wrecked.

A new crisis emerged on 25 March when an RE8 crew of 59 Squadron reported a powerful enemy thrust against the Third Army in the north. On the Cambrai front the enemy had been reinforced by nine fresh divisions, Bapaume had fallen, and masses of infantry were concentrating east of the town. Meanwhile, in the south, a great bulge towards Roye, where the Fifth Army was contiguous with the French, produced a second wedge which aimed at capturing Montdidier and cutting the lateral railway link that served the whole front. The Fifth Army, outflanked on both sides, with the French on their right tempted to fall back on Paris, and the Third Army on their left protecting the Channel ports, was threatened with extinction. Soon after eleven o'clock, with the line crumbling, Salmond ordered every available machine on to a designated line west of Bapaume. *'These squadrons will bomb and shoot up everything they can see on the enemy side of this line. Very low flying is essential. All risks to be taken. Urgent.'*

[217]

FOCH TAKES OVER: 'MANY GALLANT DEEDS WERE DONE'

E ARLY on the morning of 25 March, some hours before
Salmond issued his order, squadrons at Bertangles and
elsewhere were alerted to the crisis. Among the first to be
called, at five o'clock, were Stock and Crowden, who were ordered
to harass the enemy as much as possible on the Bapaume–Albert
road. All pilots were aware that the fateful hour had come. 'The
situation is apparently very serious,' noted Stock. The Hun was now
in Peronne and Bapaume and was likely to be in Albert at any
moment.

'It was a glorious morning when we set out for the lines,' wrote
Stock. 'As far as I could see we were the only machines in the air
around Albert when we reached it.' Albert was in ruins, but the
church, crowned by its statue of the Virgin, still stood. 'The area
over which we flew was the old Somme battleground of 1916, one
mass of trenches and shellholes and a stump of a tree here and there.'
A thin haze covered the ground and there was cloud at 2,000 feet,
perfect conditions for ground strafing. They worked the entire day
on this front, going out twice before breakfast and five times in all,
'dropping twenty Cooper bombs and firing 4,000 rounds of ammunition each before dark appeared and we went to bed.' Compared
with some squadrons, 54 were lucky in that no one was missing
from the day's strikes. Even the pilots who were wounded managed

to get back to Bertangles, to be whisked away by Red Cross car to hospital, 'envied by those who remained whole'.

With the maximum possible effort diverted to low-flying attacks in the north, following Salmond's order, the influence of the RFC on the day's fighting was indisputable, as German accounts confirm. In the hutted camps east of Bapaume, life was 'not very pleasant because airmen bombed us causing heavy losses', while west of Bapaume the advancing troops were given no respite. 'After only twenty minutes' marching the first hostile airmen flying low appear and seek to delay the advance with machine-gun fire. There were about twenty-five airmen over the regiment. There is very little cover.' And again: 'This afternoon the hostile airmen are present in crowds. We count more than thirty above us at the same time.'

Expanding his emergency order, Salmond called that evening for every available machine to be concentrated in the same area next morning, and, of a total of sixty squadrons on the western front, no fewer than thirty-seven directly intervened on the right of the Third Army. At Pozières, little more than three miles north-east of Albert, Camels of 54 Squadron and SE5A's of 84 flew up and down the road continuously from early morning attacking troops, while DH4 bombers caused extensive damage at Bapaume, Peronne, and also at Pozières, where they set fire to trains containing ammunition and supplies, and where 'continual heavy explosions could be heard which destroyed one wagon after another'. On the Bapaume area alone, 117 heavy bombs and 1300 25-pounders were dropped, and more than a quarter of a million rounds were discharged at advancing troops. With this crucial assistance, the situation north of Albert was eventually stabilised by Commonwealth forces.

No sooner had the crisis on the Third Army front been relieved, if only temporarily, than an escalation of the enemy's threat to separate the British from the French in the south seemed imminent. Ludendorff was keeping his options open. Massive German forces, as seen and reported from the air, were concentrating in an arc around Roye, where a gap had been forced. Fifth Army squadrons that had been cooperating in the Bapaume area were quickly redeployed, testing the resilience of pilots almost to destruction. Called early for breakfast, pilots could face nothing more than a cup of tea and a slice of bread. Food had lost its attraction; the strain of low-level strafing quelled appetite. The only thing Stock, for one, looked forward to now was a cigarette at the end of a flight.

Early on the morning of 26 March, 'with a Gold Flake between our lips', as Stock recorded, he and Crowden strapped their helmets on, wound scarves round their necks against the cold, adjusted their goggles, and walked to the hangars, where the faithful flight sergeant awaited them. All he ever said was 'Good morning, sir,' as they arrived, and 'Good luck, sir,' as they prepared to take off. Once airborne, Crowden followed Stock in his usual position, slightly behind and to the right. 'We had flown together so many times now that we were able to keep together in the thick of machine-gun fire from the ground.'

Heading south-east for Roye along the road from Amiens, they had the familiar experience of seeing clusters of British troops, hampered by peasant carts, hurrying in the opposite direction. A pall of smoke lay over Roye, and with the French evidently still fighting in the town they concentrated their fire on enemy infantry battalions debussing from the north-east. As the day advanced a thick mist reduced air activity, and indeed little was seen of the Hun air force all day. 'There are many British but no German flying men up,' complained one enemy account.

Most of the pilots at Bertangles went into Amiens that night for dinner at the Savoy. 'One would have thought that we had had enough excitement during the last few days,' wrote Stock, but not so. Energies miraculously restored, they homed on Charlie's Bar 'like needles to a magnet', holding animated discussions on the latest snippets of news. They returned before midnight to be greeted with congratulations on their work during the past week from a visiting general, who emphasised, with the aid of a pocket flashlight and a map, that Amiens itself was still in grave danger and that they were to do all they could next morning to harass the enemy on the Bray–Corbie road, another approach road to Amiens.

Strategically, the best news on 26 March was the appointment of General Ferdinand Foch to coordinate the Allied armies on the western front – a measure, long overdue, now forced on the hitherto reluctant generals by events. Haig's plan to assemble the First and Second Armies near Arras for a counter-attack had met with a cautious response from Pétain, who seemed more concerned with covering Paris, threatening a catastrophic split. At a conference at Doullens attended by the French Prime Minister Georges Clemenceau (an ardent disciple of total Allied victory), Lord Milner, Secretary of State for War and a campaigner for closer Anglo-French military accord, and Generals Haig, Foch, Weygand, Pétain and Wilson, Chief of the Imperial General Staff, Foch was appointed to coordinate all Allied Armies on the western front. He became, in effect, Supreme Allied Commander; his first task would be to save Amiens.

Bombing on the night of 26 March reached a new intensity, stimulated by an RFC Headquarters message that 'It is hoped that a record number of bombs will be dropped'. Beginning with an assault on Ham, the FE2b's were soon switched to the north, where air reconnaissance reported abnormal train movements southwards from Lille and the arrival of reinforcements at Cambrai. 'It is of the utmost importance', continued the message, 'to delay enemy reinforcements coming up at this crisis . . .' The target for J.C.F. Hopkins, a pilot on 83 Squadron at Auchel, was the Bapaume–Albert road, which showed up incredibly white in the frosty moonlight. From 1,500 feet he picked out individual vehicles, then a long black blob of marching troops, perfect targets for his anti-personnel bombs. He did two shows that night, as did many others. Two Handley Page squadrons (Naval), carrying 250- and 112-pounders, joined in the bombardment.

From dawn on the 27th onwards, low-level strikes were resumed in unremitting sequence. At last the DH4's were freed from height limitations, and, in bombing and strafing generally, the RFC reached a peak on this day. 'Our efforts were of course entirely directed to the assistance of our hard-pressed infantry,' wrote Sholto Douglas. 'All machines and pilots were concentrated on low-flying attacks against the advancing enemy.' He felt afterwards that the value of much of this work was obscured by the rush of events. 'Many very gallant deeds were done by our low-flying aircraft of which only the

[221]

scantiest records were kept: we had little time for writing up our achievements.' Lack of documentary evidence later militated against a full appreciation of what was done.

Douglas also dilated on the difficulties of having to move almost daily from one aerodrome to another. 'It was impossible to carry out any but the smallest repairs to machines and engines; our machines stood out in the rain for days at a time. But both pilots and mechanics, inspired by the importance of the occasion, worked themselves to a standstill . . . One felt that one was directly helping to stop the enemy's victorious advance.'

Losses varied widely from squadron to squadron, illustrating how opposition differed between sectors; but the discrepancy in skill and experience between pilot and pilot was also a factor. Whereas 84 Squadron escaped lightly, casualties in 70 Squadron, where Jock Andrews was a flight commander, were high. New pilots were arriving with as much as forty hours' solo experience, but there was no time to give them squadron training, and almost at once they were sent to the line. They were exposed, too, to some atrocious weather, which contributed to many crashes, due to the inability of newcomers to cope.

Andrews' own flight disappeared completely, as eventually did Stock's, but in neither case could the fault be pinned on the leadership. Andrews realised he was fortunate in knowing every inch of the country; whereas he could hug the ground at 50 feet, pilots without his knowledge had to climb occasionally to locate themselves, thus exposing themselves to sharpshooters. Yet even Andrews found the strain too much, and after seven days of the retreat he was given a break.

Australia's toughest and highest-scoring air ace, 24-year-old Arthur Cobby, of No. 4 Squadron Australian Flying Corps, who was to become renowned, despite many indisciplined escapades, as a good shot and a brilliant tactician, got his first two confirmed victims during the retreat, both Albatros DVs. But he confessed that once he got involved in troop-strafing he could no longer eat, because of overstrain, nervousness, and a mixture of fear and hypertension. He lived on champagne and brandy and the occasional biscuit. Yet air combat (in which he eventually achieved a score of twenty-nine), never worried him.

Another squadron fully committed was 64, much happier since their DH5's had been swapped for the SE5A. Like most squadrons they had their stars. Flight commander Jimmy Slater, already mentioned, got two Albatros DVs and a half-share of a Fokker triplane on the day the retreat started. A true professional, still only 22, Slater had graduated through regimental service as a private, five months as a commissioned observer, nine months on Nieuport Scouts, and a spell as an instructor. A more junior member of the squadron, Walter Daniel, the Canadian who had begun by finding the English aloof, wrote: 'We were really in the thick of it, flying and sleeping and flying again . . . The turbulence from passing shells and bursts on the ground and in the air made me more airsick than I have ever been before.' He was passing over an ammunition dump when it blew up. 'I went up over a thousand feet with the blast and debris before I righted the plane and found it to be all in one piece.'

Many squadrons received attention from German bombers in this period, and 64 was no exception. Daniel was blasted from his hut one night to find a huge crater outside, with a visiting chaplain lying face down peering into it, evidently looking for victims to rescue. Whether or not this influenced Daniel, he served with the RCAF as a chaplain in World War II.

Meanwhile the corps squadrons, too, were playing their part in the bombing and strafing, all too often unsung. There was rarely a story to tell when a crew were shot down. But there were exceptions. An exuberant young Canadian from Winnipeg named Alan McLeod, 6' 2", raw, big-boned, and chubby-cheeked, still only 18, was briefed to fly with five other Armstrong-Whitworth FK8's of No. 2 Squadron, their mission to strike at German infantry and artillery massing at Bray-sur-Somme, near Albert. With McLeod as observer was a 23-year-old Englishman named Arthur Hammond. McLeod liked Hammond for his directness, but most of all because he could shoot. Experience had taught 'Babe' McLeod, as he came to be known, that, in the sluggish Big Ack, skilful handling needed to be allied to deadly shooting.

[223]

After two bombing trips the previous night, McLeod and Hammond were in bed when they were called for the attack on Bray-sur-Somme. They had scarcely got airborne when down came the fog. After two hours of trying to find a pinpoint, McLeod turned west to look for an Allied airfield to refuel. He found one, but in landing on a strange airfield with a full load of bombs he touched down heavily and cracked his tail skid. While a replacement was being sent for, he and Hammond had lunch with 43 Squadron (Camels), on whose aerodrome they had landed.

At one o'clock the Camel pilots took off, but within minutes they were back, reporting that conditions were hopeless. Yet McLeod and Hammond, remembering the importance attached to their mission, decided, when their repair was completed, to make an effort. The Germans had now taken Albert, and a hot reception at Bray-sur-Somme seemed certain, especially as their approach coincided with a lifting of the cloud base.

Casualties for the strafers had mostly come from ground fire, but the German scout squadrons, forced back on the defensive, still had to be reckoned with. Richthofen alone claimed three victims on this day. Hammond, although preoccupied with the bombing run, spotted the approach of a Fokker triplane just in time, tapped McLeod on the shoulder, and pointed down. McLeod immediately executed a tight turn to port, increasing height marginally, and held the turn, describing a perpetual circle. It made the Fokker pilot's twin Spandaus difficult to bring to bear, while allowing Hammond, swinging his Lewis on its swivel mounting, to fire almost at will.

Many German scout pilots would sheer away from a well-handled two-seater: but not this one. He was a member of Richthofen's Circus. Hammond's aim, though, was deadly, and the Fokker fell into a spin from which it never recovered. Waving excitedly to each other, McLeod and Hammond resumed their bombing run. But as they did so, the clouds above them parted to reveal bright sunshine, out of which another triplane was diving at them. Six more were tagging along behind.

Running away from a fight was against McLeod's instincts, but he was no hothead. If he couldn't plant his bombs where they were wanted right now, he would live to drop them later. But he judged that flight would be even more certain to bring destruction than fight. He would stay to do battle.

'Alan would take on anything,' a previous crew-mate had averred. 'He would turn round to me and laugh out loud.' But seven Fokkers were no laughing matter. One pilot, losing patience, dived to close range, McLeod pulled abruptly to port, and Hammond fired, so destructively that the triplane broke in half, ejecting the pilot. But the Germans, aware now that they were up against a worthy adversary, and led by 21-year-old Leutnant Hans Kirchstein of *Jasta 10*, reformed for the kill. Both McLeod and Hammond were wounded, yet a second triplane exploded and broke up when Hammond's bullets punctured its fuel tank.

It was Kirchstein who, in an attack from astern and below, ruptured the Big Ack's fuel tank in turn. The petrol immediately ignited, the flames blowing back under the cockpit seats. Fanned by the slipstream, they burned through the wooden floor, scorching McLeod's flying boots and setting fire to his wicker chair. His response was to throttle back, set the rudder pedals to neutral, ease the stick forward, and climb out of the burning chair, stepping on to the lower port wing and manoeuvring the joystick from there, in a crabbing side-slip that kept him clear of the flames.

Satisfied that plane and crew were doomed, Kirchstein and others went off to look for alternative prey. But one pilot determined to finish them off. Hammond had perched himself on the cockpit coaming, and as he struggled to manipulate his gun the floor of his cockpit gave way, carrying with it the revolving stool on which he had planted his feet. Grabbing the half-circular gun-ring aft of his cockpit and straddling the fuselage, facing aft, he was wounded again as the Fokker closed. Grappling with the Lewis, he fired a burst that drove the triplane off.

Still manoeuvring so as to direct the flames away from himself and Hammond, McLeod was preparing to land. As soon as he flattened off he was choked by smoke and flames and the fabric around him caught fire. Hammond, forced to abandon the cockpit area, dragged himself up until he was standing on the cockpit coaming, steadying

[225]

himself by clutching the trailing edge of the upper wing. One last effort from McLeod and the machine ploughed into the earth and slithered to the edge of a mud-filled crater. They had landed in the morass of no man's land and were under ground fire.

There were eight bombs still strapped to the FK8, and about a thousand rounds of ammunition in Hammond's cockpit. McLeod had been thrown clear, but Hammond was lying close to the burning mainplane, half-buried in the surrounding quagmire, unconscious.

Wounded in five places, his burnt flying clothing hanging in shreds, with bullets already exploding like firecrackers, and with the bombs about to go off, McLeod returned to the burning wreck and dragged Hammond clear.

For weeks McLeod's life hung by a thread; but Hammond, after having a leg amputated, made good progress. McLeod was recommended for a DSO, Hammond for a Bar to the MC he already had. Hammond got his Bar, but McLeod's DSO was upgraded to a VC.

Alan McLeod recovered sufficiently to return to Canada to a rapturous welcome, only to succumb in his weakened state to a plague of Spanish influenza. Arthur Hammond, after emigrating to Canada, chose to settle in Winnipeg, where he lived another forty-one years. McLeod's was the RFC's last VC.

Although the enemy advance north of the Somme had been halted, withdrawal from Bray-sur-Somme had exposed the left flank of the Fifth Army, and at 08.30 that morning, 27 March, Ludendorff began an attack south of the Somme on the Fifth Army, and farther south still on the French.

Determined to protect Amiens, the Fifth Army fought hard to hold on, greatly assisted by the transfer of low-level air attack to the Somme. Despite an inevitable weariness, little ground was given, but the weight of the attack on the French was such that they were forced to cede Montdidier.

Some of the squadrons at Bertangles were cheered that morning to find themselves warned for an old-style offensive patrol at altitude, ground strafing being postponed till the afternoon. The enemy were so fully occupied in trying to check the peppering of their own troops that they had largely deserted the upper air, but their scouts were known to be out in strength that morning.

With the return of George Maxwell, commanding 54 Squadron, Francis Kitto had resumed the task of running C flight. They took off at 10.30 in a formation of six, with Stock as deputy leader, and after following the twistings and turnings of the Somme they spotted a formation of eight enemy scouts over Peronne. Kitto had the advantage of height and he went straight into a dive, the rest following. Then Stock, whose job it was to protect the rear, was surprised to see a second Hun formation, some way above them, beginning to nosedive in turn. With Kitto intent on attack, Stock fired a burst over his top plane to attract his attention, then turned to face their attackers.

The nearest Hun was now about to fire and Stock met him head on. He could sense the German pilot's hesitation, and he zoomed up over him and turned sharply round to get on his tail, at the same time trying to keep Kitto in sight; but the German turned too. 'Thus we turned round and round, each trying to make a sharper turn than his adversary . . . But the Hun did the wrong thing . . . He changed or attempted to change from a left-hand to a right-hand circuit, thus giving me my opportunity, and I let him have it . . . he went down in a steep nosedive and burst into flames . . . A glorious sight at the time, since one does not realise that a human being like oneself is within, for after all as far as war is concerned it is merely a mechanical bird.'

In Stock's experience, the scene after landing from an offensive patrol was always the same. First, from the flight commander:

'What luck, old man?'
'One. And you?'
'Two, one near Athies and the other near St Quentin.'
'You've been to hell and gone over, then?'
'Yes, didn't realise where I was until the scrap was over. Got a gasper?'
Up walks the major. 'What luck, Kitto?'

[227]

'Three so far, sir. The rest are not back yet.'
Maxwell: 'Good old C Flight. Go and make the report, Kitto. Oh, by the way, Russell's wounded.'
Stock: 'Is he sir? Where?'
'In the leg.'
Kitto (under his breath): 'Lucky devil.'

After lunch on 27 March it was pairs again, a low reconnaissance in the Noyon area, during which Stock and Crowden for once got separated, and Stock, having penetrated much farther than he had intended, noted large enemy groups moving westward and a variety of transport. He memorised the different roads and the direction the troops were taking, ready to report back at Bertangles. His was one of the scores of reports that afternoon that enabled army dispositions to be adjusted.

After dark, bombing was again aimed at stifling the enemy's reinforcement routes, and 840 lbs of bombs were dropped and over 18,000 rounds of ammunition fired by the four FE2b squadrons. Unconfirmed though the results were, the crews reported many hits on columns of transport and on encampments and dumps. More convincing perhaps were the widespread reports of confusion and delay culled later from enemy documents.

THE CLIMACTIC DAY

NEXT morning, 28 March, after a brief but intense bombardment, Ludendorff launched another series of attacks, beginning north of the Somme towards Arras. Here the British resistance was at its strongest and the attack was repulsed, with Camels, SE5A's and DH4's causing panic and stampedes. By the end of the day the main battle north of the Somme was virtually at an end, but south of the Somme, where the exhausted and outnumbered Fifth Army remained under pressure, German troops had infiltrated across the river during the night, reaching the Amiens–St Quentin road. The battle for Amiens was boiling up, and a further assault on the Fifth Army front and on the French was simmering. At this point Ludendorff, confident of success, did not perhaps realise the extent of his own troops' exhaustion and demoralisation.

In front of Amiens the Fifth Army were withdrawing to a defensive line on a north–south axis, from the Somme in the north through Hamel and Ignaucourt to Mezières, at the junction with the French in the south. The withdrawal was conducted in good order, as confirmed by contact patrols. The Fifth Army, supported by its air component, was still defending grimly despite all its handicaps, and indeed General Gough, although aware of the crisis, felt that the challenge was being repulsed. It was at this moment, following political intervention, that Gough and his staff were relieved of their duties, being replaced in command of the British troops south of the Somme by General Rawlinson and the staff of the Fourth Army, which had hitherto been held in reserve.

Whatever the justification for this, for the RFC it changed nothing: maximum effort was still demanded. Records kept remained scant, and even some that were kept were subsequently lost; but Stock was still keeping notes from which, when time allowed, he made up his diary. His first reaction, on waking up on the morning of the 28th, was one of intense relief: rain at last! Crowden was still asleep. At 07.30 their batman Neville appeared with two large cups of tea. 'Dud, sir,' he whispered.

Stock could not resist passing the good news on. 'Crowden!' 'Go to hell.' 'Look at it!'

Crowden was sceptical; he had had his leg pulled by Stock before, and he threatened to throw his cup at him. 'Neville,' called Stock. 'Open the door.' The aperture revealed low cloud clinging to distant hills and sheets of rain falling on hutment roofs. 'Does that satisfy you?'

Crowden brightened. 'Neville,' he said, 'go over to the Mess and order me breakfast for eleven o'clock.' Both men dropped off to sleep again instantly, but within minutes the door opened again and another voice, recognised at once as that of authority, penetrated their slumber. 'Get into flying kit at once.' They sat up and stared in amazement: it was Major Maxwell. 'Can't help it,' they heard him say, 'Wing orders.' As Maxwell left, Stock swore that he heard him mutter: 'Damned shame.'

'Hell!' said Crowden. 'Things must be getting critical.' Stock agreed. To send them up in driving rain was unheard of.

The mechanics were waiting for them at the hangars, and despite the rain they were already starting engines. All remaining fit pilots had been called. With the clouds at 200 feet they were compelled to fly underneath them, and when Stock glanced over the side to try to pick up a landmark the rain blinded him and slashed his face. He lost sight of Crowden, and the first warning he got that he was near the lines was a staccato thud underneath him which bumped his machine crazily. He was down to 100 feet, and there was a battery of 60-pounders directly below him, firing frenziedly towards the river.

He could see that the Hun was attacking across the river at two points, at Maricourt and Cerisy-Gailly, apparently trying to outflank the British troops defending the Amiens road four miles to the south. 'Everywhere was a mass of smoke and flame, of 60-pounders and heavies of all kinds, all firing at Mericourt and Cerisy.' On reaching these riverside villages he was greeted by a bombardment such as he had never experienced before. His outer struts were immediately splintered, and he throttled down and twisted and turned as much as he could – 'to fly straight would be fatal' – then saw what all the noise was about. The large stone bridge over the river at Cerisy was covered by a mass of Hun troops edging across, under fire from the British artillery south of the river.

The Germans had lined the river-bank with field guns and were also bringing up machine-guns. A determined effort was being made to cross the river and outflank Villiers-Bretonneux, the last village before Amiens. Stock resolved on an equally determined attempt to stop them.

He was unlikely to destroy the bridge itself with a couple of 25-pounders. Flying through a blizzard of fire towards the bridge, he decided to drop his bombs on the mass of troops who were approaching the bridge, then to machine-gun from low level the men who were actually endeavouring to cross. How well he succeeded may best be judged from the citation for his subsequent award of a Military Cross, the incident having been watched by hundreds of British artillerymen. First, he 'caused great confusion' with his bombs among the men approaching the bridge. Then,

> diving on several parties of the enemy who remained on the bridge in a state of indecision, he almost completely annihilated them. His action undoubtedly hampered the enemy by making the bridge impassable for half an hour . . . On numerous other occasions he disorganised and hindered the enemy's advance by his attacks on troops and transport. He has destroyed three hostile machines, and has always set an excellent example of courage and enterprise.

Owing to the dense smoke caused by his bombs and by bursting shrapnel, Stock himself was unable to evaluate his attack, nor could he locate the precise position of the British artillery or assess the strength of the enemy forces. Crowden had meanwhile bombed the bridge (he too got an MC later), and they joined up and headed back to Bertangles.

Many other fighting squadrons, together with the DH4 day-bombers, were diverted that day south of the Somme, ground targets southwards of Cerisy-Gailly attracting special attention. The corps squadrons, too, when patrol work allowed, made a maximum low-strafing effort. 'It was on this day,' said one report, 'that an extraordinary number of enemy troops were reported and our machines had a field day attacking columns in fours. Heavy casualties were inflicted . . .' The bridge at Cerisy-Gailly was attacked again, this time with 112-pounders, and a party attempting to repair it was slaughtered. At Hamel, west of Cerisy, much of the German artillery was brought forward successfully, but, according to a German account, 'the replenishment of ammunition broke down owing to bombardment by the enemy's aeroplanes', and the attack was beaten off.

There was little fighting in the upper air that day, the enemy doing their best to avoid combat, although seven of their machines were shot down. More surprising was the failure of the German battle squadrons to persist with the low-level assault they had planned on the retreating army and its communications. Heavy losses in the first few days, and preoccupation with defence against the aggression of the RFC, contributed to this. For the RFC, too, casualties were high, nearly all from ground fire. 'March 28th,' wrote Stock 'was perhaps worse as far as we were concerned than all the others during the push. We lost more on our squadron than on any other single day. I feel certain that if it had not been for the splendid example shown by our CO we could never have carried on . . . We came back from the firing line several times utterly done, and caring naught for anything or anyone, to find the CO awaiting us or perhaps about to take off on his own and trench-strafe.'

By nightfall their machines were in an appalling state, cobbled together like patchwork but still showing bullet-holes everywhere. 'Some poor fellows', wrote Stock, 'came back with half an arm or leg, and others not at all.' Stock had a special word for Roy Crowden. 'He looked upon these gruesome sights with perfect calm. In fact it was partly through his cheerfulness that we managed to carry on together when nearly everyone was either wounded or missing.' Experience was similar in squadron after squadron, RFC losses that day amounting to seventeen machines missing with twenty-five crew, thirty-five machines wrecked, and six more burnt out or abandoned, not to mention the wounded. But on the ground, the day had gone well.

In retrospect, 28 March can be seen as climactic, and when German pressure continued on the morning of the 29th, the British line south of the Somme was dominated by the relieving Fourth Army. The French were driven from Mezières, at the junction with the British, and were forced back towards Moreuil, twelve miles south-east of Amiens, but they recaptured Montdidier. Night bombing of distant targets was attempted when the weather allowed, and vigorous offensive action on ground targets was continued on the 30th.

Already the dense enemy columns approaching Moreuil had suffered from the V Brigade squadrons and those that had reinforced them, and further low-flying attacks on the 30th drew bitter complaint. 'The French and British flying men circle over Moreuil Wood and join in the battle, attacking with bombs and machine-gun fire . . .' Disappointment was voiced when a pair of British aviators, after almost destroying themselves by hitting the ground, just avoided the tree-tops. 'They have dropped their bombs and used their machine-guns, and now, flying at the speed of arrows, attack our batteries . . . one bomb dropped from a negligible height places the whole staff of the 1st Battalion *hors de combat*. Moreuil Wood is hell.' It would be hard to find more convincing evidence of the influence of the air on the battle.

The one disappointment remained the loss of reliable contact with the artillery, belying Trenchard's contention that it would be through rendering artillery fire effective that the RFC would make its greatest contribution. The blame for this, if blame there was, could certainly not be attached to the RFC. But by this time the enemy battle flights, baffled by lack of liaison with their army commands, and deprived by the stricken landscape of suitable aerodromes near the front, were again showing signs of returning to the upper air, and for a time the RFC fighting squadrons were switched from ground targets to high-level patrolling. This order was reversed when Foch, in an effort to co-ordinate the British and French air services in the battle area, ordered, for the bombers, the concentration of every resource on a few vital railway junctions, rather than dissipation over a wide area, and, for fighting aircraft, the primary duty of assisting the troops on the ground by incessant low-level attacks.

Meanwhile, on 1 April, the Royal Flying Corps was absorbed, with the Royal Naval Air Service, into the Royal Air Force. On the same day, Ewart Stock was wounded in yet another low-level attack and invalided home. Soon he was back at Hertford College, Oxford, where, in 1920, he matriculated. Lucky devil, he must surely have said.

Under Trenchard's leadership the RFC had espoused the doctrine of the offensive, the forcing of the enemy air service on the defensive and the establishing of a degree of superiority in the air, whatever the cost. From this all blessings would flow. That this was repeated during the March retreat, in spite of the enemy's numerical concentrations, is unarguable, in view of the torments of the German ground forces in comparison with the British. A German document on the employment of their battle flights dated 20 February 1918 makes it clear that the General Staff fully understood what was required. 'The object of the *battle flights* is to shatter the enemy's nerve by repeated attacks in close formation and thus to obtain a decisive influence on the course of the fighting.' But it was the RFC that exerted this influence. That the enemy did not achieve it was because they were not allowed to, through the offensive posture adopted by the RFC, not just during the retreat but over the years. It was a posture foreign to the German pilots, who in any case were thrown on the defensive almost from the start. This was in accordance with Trenchard's predication that the only effective way to counter a more aggressive stance by the enemy, if it were ever adopted, was to pursue a still more aggressive policy oneself.

There was plenty of room in the RFC, as has been shown, for qualities of doggedness, perseverance, and staying power, but it was the 'sporting audacity' – as General von Hoeppner had described it – of the scout pilot which won air superiority, and incidentally won fame, perhaps at the expense of a full understanding of the more direct but humdrum, routine, cumulative contribution, with only the occasional highspot, of the corps squadrons, still underestimated by history.

If it is true that the British tend to glorify retreats, according them an almost mythical quality, then the part played by the RFC in the March 1918 retreat has been monstrously neglected by the myth-makers. No less a military historian than B.H. Liddell Hart paid tribute to the low-flying form of attack perfected by the RFC in this battle, calling it 'an important factor in stemming the German onrush, and one that has been inadequately recognised by historians'. It is paradoxical, for a force that prided itself above all on its ethos of attack and aggression, that the RFC should have first earned respect in one retreat, and reached the zenith of its achievement in another.

Perhaps some nations really are at their best in retreats. Both sides were fighting in conditions bordering on the chaotic. The most serious problem for the British was to keep the squadrons flying, to find them new aerodromes when they were chased or shelled out of the old ones, to keep them supplied with essentials, and to replace losses in aircraft, arms, and personnel. Due to the foresight of Jack Salmond, a substantial increase in transport had been agreed and provided just in time. The Deputy Assistant Quartermaster-General at RFC Headquarters, Brigadier H.R.M. Brooke-Popham, had done the job once before, admittedly on an infinitely smaller scale, in the retreat from Mons, and he initiated emergency schemes for rushing convoys from the supply depots and parks to the squadrons, which kept them up to strength as the enemy's re-supply problems mounted.

Thanks to the expansion schemes that bore fruit that winter, the supply of new aeroplanes to make good the losses was never a problem, and the pilots required to replace casualties, now better trained, flew them where they were wanted. All this was achieved while the supply depots were themselves on the move, and when fall-back arrangements included such precautions as the planning of new routes for reinforcements from England in case the Channel ports were lost.

Against this, the comparative ineffectiveness of the German air service in this period stands out. Their opportunities for the intensive bombing and strafing of British columns in retreat, along roads often blocked by refugees, must have been unequalled. 'Congestion behind our Third Army was extraordinary,' wrote one airman who witnessed it, with peasants fleeing westward, blocking the roads with their carts and barrows, while relief battalions struggled against the tide to reinforce the front-line. The British troops were certainly not unmolested from the air, but the enemy pilots, after the losses of the first few days, were never able to approach the carnage wrought by the RFC. General von Hoeppner himself admitted that the operations of his forces had not been coordinated with the march of events on the ground. 'It therefore happened that the infantry were deprived, at the decisive times and places, of the help of the fighting pilots.' The supply problems of the advance, for the German air force, were not foreseen: they had no Brooke-Popham. The supply problems of the retreat, for the RFC, were brilliantly resolved.

It may be, too, that when the initial impetus of the attack had abated, and success seemed assured, there was not the inspired resolve on the German side that stems from forces at bay. The enemy pilots had no such rallying call to respond to as Salmond's '*Very low flying is essential. All risks to be taken. Urgent.*'

The RFC's concentration on low-flying attacks in moments of crisis, as against spotting for the artillery, which Trenchard had seen as the best way of helping the infantry, aroused controversy, but it argued a new flexibility, and it was justified by the impossibility of keeping track of battery positions in the fluidity of mobile warfare. Captured enemy documents fully confirmed the RFC's impact on the land battle. The German air service was not technically inferior, and they were ahead in such matters as providing parachutes and oxygen for their pilots, but the quality of these pilots was not maintained. The *Jastas* still fought magnificently, but their overall tactics were haphazard, while the Royal Flying Corps had become a fully-fledged Air Force, in fact as well as in name.

GROWTH OF THE RAF:
MEMORABILIA, RFC

I N the seven and a half months that were to elapse before final victory, the Royal Air Force grew to a size and potency unimagined six years earlier when the RFC was formed. From a force of 146 RFC officers in August 1914, the RAF worldwide in November 1918 had more than 27,000 officers. Other ranks swelled the total to over 290,000. A force of less than 100 machines in a handful of squadrons in 1914 had grown to an estimated 22,677 by November 1918, spread over 188 squadrons. Over half of these were in France.

The number of air actions in support of the army in those final months was vastly greater than anything that had gone before, and many new reputations were deservedly made; but they are not a part of this story. It remains to follow, in brief, the fortunes of some of the RFC men who had survived this far, men who had helped to set the example, to lay the foundations on which the independent air force was built.

Even before the end of the March Retreat, Ludendorff's Somme offensive was beginning to falter. Despite having made advances of up to forty miles in places, by far the deepest penetrations in any campaign since 1914, no decisive results were achieved. Resistance, whether on the ground or from the air, was undiminished. The vital communications centre of Amiens lay only ten miles distant, but it remained tantalisingly inviolate, and a final attempt to break through on 4 April failed. 'Our strength is exhausted,' admitted Hindenburg, and Ludendorff wrote: 'The enemy's resistance was beyond our powers.' Next day, 5 April, he abandoned the offensive against Amiens, at least for the moment, electing to try elsewhere.

His second attempt was not long delayed. Switching to the north, he attacked on 9 April in Flanders, at a point where the River Lys separated the British First and Second Armies. The immediate objective was the communications centre of Hazebrouck, the ultimate a new threat to the Channel ports. The Army general staff, refusing to believe that the offensive in the south, which had come so close to success, would be abandoned, were sceptical of air reports which offered clear evidence of Ludendorff's intentions, and his preparations went ahead unhampered. Then, when Ludendorff struck, bad weather restricted flying and contributed to a situation of extreme gravity until, on 12 April, Haig issued his famous 'backs to the wall' order, enjoining that 'each one of us must fight to the end.'

The RAF's answer, as visibility cleared, was to fly more hours, drop more bombs, and take more photographs than on any other day in the war so far. 'Throughout the whole of this vital day of the battle,' says the Official History, 'the advancing German divisions were subjected to relentless attacks by the British air squadrons . . . every squadron was used unsparingly from dawn to dusk.' Observers in kite balloons enjoyed panoramic views in the crystalline atmosphere, while incessant contact patrols made the progress of the battle 'clear as had never been made clear before'.

There was no break either in the air fighting. Anxious to redeem themselves for their failure to protect their troops in the Amiens débâcle, German low-flying machines, supported at altitude, disputed the RAF's ascendancy – and were sharply rebuffed. On 12 April, forty-nine hostiles were brought down and another twenty-five driven down out of control. One squadron alone recorded thirteen victories: this was No. 43 (Camels), where the extrovert H.W. 'Willie' Woollett, already credited with thirteen victories and two balloons from RFC days, and acknowledged by colleagues as having an uncanny flair for air fighting, destroyed six machines, three in the morning and three in the afternoon, thus equalling the record set by John Trollope, also of 43 Squadron, three weeks earlier. Trollope had meanwhile been shot down and taken prisoner, with wounds that resulted in the amputation of a hand – and much later, of the arm itself. Woollett eventually raised his score to thirty-five.

Another man with a reputation from RFC days who scored that day – two single-seaters – was Mick Mannock. Sent home on rest by Tilney on 1 January, he had talked his way back as a flight commander on 74 Squadron. These were his seventeenth and eighteenth victories, and they began a remarkable sequence of success, both for him and his new squadron commander, 'Grid' Caldwell, who also scored that day.

By 18 April, with the help of French reinforcements, the German advance had been halted. The main weight of the RAF effort, although restricted by the weather, was again directed at stemming the advance, and by 29 April Ludendorff's second great offensive had been held. German casualties since 21 March amounted to some 350,000, while Allied casualties, most of them British, exceeded 300,000. The wastage in aircraft was proportionately high: over the same period, of 1,232 machines on the strength of the RFC in France on 21 March, all but 200 had been lost or wrecked beyond repair. But again, the aircraft supply and repair depots, and the rail and road organisation, had coped.

The same could not be said on the German side, where early superiority was again rapidly checked and reversed. Whereas the Allies could fall back on undamaged aerodromes, fresh landing grounds remained impossible for the Germans to find in the devastated battle areas, leaving their bases out of touch. There were complaints from the troops, as before, that they were inadequately protected from strafing.

These and other battles that summer were different in one major respect from those to which the RFC had become accustomed: mobile warfare had superseded static. But it was a change to which the RFC had already adjusted, and the new service adapted similarly. Speed became a vital factor, the fighting coming in bursts, two or three days of rapid movement being followed by a lull of perhaps a week, during which artillery moved forward or back, new positions were registered by air reconnaissance, and photographs to a depth of four miles behind the lines were taken and circulated. The work was done under intense pressure, with the German Air Force active although sometimes non-aggressive.

As new stars appeared in the firmament, some of the old ones shone less brilliantly, or were extinguished. An old opponent, so much a part of the RFC story, was Manfred von Richthofen, and he did not long survive the amalgamation. Can it be said that the RAF achieved what the RFC could not? That remains a matter of debate to this day.

The pilot credited with shooting down the Red Baron, on 21 April 1918, in the middle of the Lys offensive, was not even ex-RFC. His name was Captain Roy Brown, a Canadian, and before amalgamation he had been in the RNAS. But there were other claimants, namely a group of machine-gunners from the Australian Field Artillery, who fired at Richthofen's Fokker DVII more or less simultaneously with Brown's attack. The impact of the crash was not lethal, and the gunners ran excitedly towards the damaged machine, intent on capturing the pilot. But the man in the cockpit, head pitched forward, was dead.

They lifted the body from the cockpit and riffled through what papers they could find, casually at first, then with mounting incredulity. '*My God! We've got the bloody Baron!*'

Studies of the probable trajectory of the single bullet that killed Richthofen were contradictory. But whatever the truth, Richthofen was dead.

Hundreds of soldiers and airmen filed past his body next morning as it lay in state, like that of a deceased monarch, on a dais in a hangar at Bertangles. That afternoon, eleven days short of his 26th birthday, he was buried with full military honours, mourned, perversely enough, by friend and foe alike. His score of eighty victories, involving 123 pilots or crewmen killed or captured, was compiled almost exclusively against British and Commonwealth airmen. It remained unequalled.

A special floral tribute came from survivors who had flown against him, with the inscription: 'To Captain von Richthofen, our valiant and worthy foe.' But lest too much emphasis be placed on sentiments not perhaps universally shared, Mannock's reaction, when asked to drink a toast to the dead Baron, may be quoted. '*I won't drink to that bastard.*'

Ludendorff's policy now became to weaken Allied reserves with a succession of minor attacks at selected points, meanwhile preparing for an offensive on a grand scale. The responsibility for guarding against surprise when the major attack came rested squarely on the reconnaissance crews. And although, on the Aisne river (27 May–2 June), and further south against the French between Montdidier and Noyon (9–13 June), Ludendorff kept up the pressure, his early successes were again neutralised.

Ludendorff's last great gamble was to be in Flanders, but first, on 15 July, as a diversion, he attacked in strength on the Marne. Driven back by the French, he then had to face an Allied counter-attack which caused the postponement, and finally, after 8 August (Ludendorff's 'black day for the German Army'), the abandonment, of any further major German offensive action. There were still three months of desperate fighting ahead, but from this point on the German army was battling for its very existence, the RAF, despite enormous losses, was achieving something approaching mastery of the air, and Germany had nothing to hope for but what might be rescued from an armistice.

When Jimmy McCudden left 56 Squadron for Home Establishment on 5 March he resumed his role of fighting instructor, this time at Ayr. But first he enjoyed a brief spell of leave with his younger brother Jack, now flying with 84 Squadron and boasting eight victories and an MC. Whatever Jimmy may have said to try to curb Jack's impetuosity was of no avail, as Jack got into a scrap with the Richthofen Circus on the day he got back and was killed. This left Jimmy and a sister the only survivors of the McCudden brood. Eleven days later Jimmy's career may be said to have peaked when he was awarded the VC, the citation stressing his responsible leadership as well as his personal triumphs. Meanwhile he was completing the manuscript of a book, as Richthofen had done.

McCudden stood out, with Albert Ball, as the most highly decorated and most charismatic of British scout pilots, his theories on air fighting being widely respected and copied. By combining superb leadership of his flight with a flair for the lone stalking of potential victims he had established himself as a unique all-rounder, at the pinnacle of his profession. Yet there were others threatening to challenge his supremacy.

Billy Bishop, after recording forty-seven victories with 60 Squadron, had returned to Canada briefly to help with a recruiting drive, and to marry. He too wrote a book at this stage. Then, over a brief period from 27 May to 19 June, while commanding 85 Squadron (SE5A's), and before being recalled again to Canada, he scored another twenty-five victories in twenty-four days, passing McCudden's record of fifty-seven in the process and ending with a total claimed of seventy-two. Since so many of his victories were scored on lone patrols, unsubstantiated by colleagues, and have often been queried, it is noteworthy that his total claims were approved at this point by Wing Headquarters.

Whereas Bishop, as an individualist, was not unduly concerned with welding his squadron into a team, Mannock, who replaced him as commander of 85 Squadron, 'planned every manoeuvre like a chess player', according to one of his pilots. In three months as a flight commander on 74 Squadron (also SE5A's), from mid-April to mid-June, he added another thirty-six victories to his sixteen with 40 Squadron, taking his score to fifty-two. He had become an outstanding tactician and leader, nursing newcomers, shedding those he deemed not up to standard, and inspiring a respect and affection in his pilots approaching idolatry. But many others were increasing their scores dramatically in this period, among them Mannock's old friend from 40 Squadron days, the Irishman George McElroy.

In the following month McCudden, after pleading for a quicker return to action than the authorities were planning, was posted back to France to command another famous fighting squadron, No. 60. The threat to his supremacy, it seemed, was not to go unchallenged.

He was on his way back in an SE5A on 9 July when he landed by mistake at an aerodrome close to his destination. Checking his bearings, he took off, circled the field, and, according to an eye-witness, carried out the conventional dive-and-zoom salutation that courtesy demanded. At the top of the zoom his motor cut out and he had no chance to recover. A wrongly-fitted carburettor has been blamed.

Accounts which record McCudden as making the novice's mistake of attempting to turn back towards the airfield when his engine failed on take-off seem less plausible – or perhaps too painful to contemplate. All three McCudden brothers were gone.

Neither Mannock nor McElroy was to survive McCudden for long. At a farewell party on 18 July for Gwilym Lewis, going home, so he said, 'a physical wreck', the two aces upbraided each other for taking unnecessary risks in pursuit of the enemy at low level. Eight days later, machine-gun fire from the ground was to prove Mannock's undoing. He had meanwhile raised his score to sixty-one. Another five days and McElroy (forty-six victories), fell in similar fashion.

The Germans dropped a note about McElroy; such courtesies were still being observed. As for Mannock, the area where he had crashed in flames, as he had always predicted he would, was blasted soon afterwards by artillery. The Germans just had time to take possession of documents, which were later returned to the family, and to bury the body. Attempts to locate the grave still persist.

To his colleagues Mick Mannock was incomparable, the ace of aces, and it was only through their sense of dismay and injustice, expressed by no one better than Captain Ira 'Taffy' Jones, one of Mannock's flight commanders and himself an ace with thirty-seven victories, that his achievement was properly recognised. Mannock, his colleagues knew, had allowed many of his victories to be credited to others, and an investigation, at the Air Ministry itself, amended his official tally to seventy-three. That this reassessment made him top-scorer on the Allied side, one more than Billy Bishop, inevitably raised eyebrows, and it is probable that both totals should be scaled down. However, to quote the Official History on Mannock, 'there are grounds for the claim . . . that he was the greatest fighting pilot of the war'. Eventually, nearly a year after his death, and with the backing of the then Air Minister, Winston Churchill, he was awarded a posthumous VC.

There was no shortage of newcomers to fill the empty chairs still tragically vacated, an inevitable diminution in the quality of candidates from Great Britain being redeemed by the influx from the schools established in Canada. 'All the Canadians', Garland had written, when he was instructing at Andover, 'are very quick and seem adapted to the air.'

In support of Ludendorff's offensives, a night bombing campaign against selected military targets behind the Western Front was waged by the Gothas, reaching a culmination in May, when huge losses were inflicted on congested ordnance depots and dumps. But the Gotha units lacked the capacity to keep up a simultaneous campaign against southern England, where their losses had anyway been prohibitive, and this enabled a squadron to be formed from Home Defence units for service in France. Major C.J. Quintin-Brand, a South African, many years later to command No. 10 Group in the Battle of Britain, was promoted from flight commander of a home-based squadron to command a new squadron of Camels specially adapted for night fighting, No. 151. Quintin-Brand's previous record included seven victories in Nieuports while a member of No. 1 Squadron in France, and the rare distinction of shooting down a Gotha bomber over Kent: most of the sixty-one lost in raiding England fell to anti-aircraft guns and to accidents.

Among the pilots transferred with Quintin-Brand was Captain A.B. Yuille, and it was Yuille who claimed the first Gotha victim for No. 151, on 23 July. Searchlights and guns assembled at strategic points assisted the night flyers, and Yuille was successful again when he destroyed a five-engined Giant on 10 August, shot down in flames with its nine-man crew.

Most successful of the night-fighters was Quintin-Brand himself, with four, but the squadron accounted for twenty-six Gothas of various types, often in spectacular fashion when unreleased bombs exploded in mid-air, or when bombers broke up while illuminated by searchlights. Eventually the pilots took to intercepting the Gothas over their own aerodromes as they attempted to land. So great was the effect on morale that by the time the ground forces had reached the Hindenburg Line in early September, having recovered all the ground lost in the March Retreat, night bombing by the Gothas had virtually ceased.

Another major development, in the final months of the war, was the expansion of the 41st (Bomber) Wing into the so-called Independent Force. Inheriting the bombing policy stimulated by the Gotha raids on London ('to carry the war into Germany by attacking her industry, commerce and population'), and originally intended to function as an Inter-Allied force, it was restricted, at its inception on 6 June 1918, to five RAF squadrons, three day and two night. Later four more squadrons were added. Commanding the force, after refusing several other possible appointments following his resignation as CAS, was Trenchard himself.

At least two of the pioneers who had crossed the Channel four years previously, on 13 August 1914, were still flying operationally in the final months: one of these was the pertinacious Jimmy Read, now 33. His stubborn refusal to take no for an answer had eventually overcome an equally stubborn Trenchard. 'If I *did* take you back,' warned Boom, 'it would be as a lieutenant, and you'd go to England as an instructor.'

Read accepted this, convinced that if he committed some minor breach of discipline he'd be posted back overseas, as was the fashion. But he would have to make sure it came to the notice of the authorities. He chose a fine day, saddled a Sopwith Pup from his training school, headed for London, and flew provocatively under Tower Bridge, then back under it again as an encore. He was lucky to escape unscathed – he had forgotten about the pigeons. Nothing happened for a fortnight – and then came a posting to command No. 216 Handley Page bomber squadron of the Independent Force under

Trenchard. Had Boom heard about the Tower Bridge incident? Anyway he must have relented.

No. 216 Squadron had formerly been 16 (Naval), and Read found a residue of animosity between old RFC and RNAS men which needed prompt action. To complicate matters, he was the first non-Naval man to command the unit. There was one consolation. 'There was no silly order about squadron commanders not being allowed to fly over the lines.' This gave him an idea. When he landed back from his first night raid on industrial Germany he reloaded and went again, an innovation that he hoped might encourage *esprit de corps*. In the morning there was a congratulatory signal from Boom; and the squadron responded. 'Read soon became a popular CO,' wrote one member, 'and made many operational flights as pilot during the latter weeks of the war.' With his batman, of course, manning the front gun and providing the comforts.

Despite heavy casualties, Read seems to have been perfectly content to be running a squadron again under Trenchard. Earlier that summer he had submitted a plan to the Air Ministry for the bombing of Germany by the new four-engined Handley Page V/1500's, staging at Prague, and he was hoping 216 would be chosen. (A Wing to undertake this project was indeed formed but was overtaken by the armistice.) Of Boom himself, Read wrote: 'Trenchard was always practical. We didn't think he had a great brain, but he had a great personality and strength of character and ability for getting things done.'

Among other pioneers still active operationally was Louis Strange. Ever the innovator, as a lieutenant-colonel commanding an all-purpose wing – fighters, bombers and reconnaissance machines, under brigade commander Ludlow-Hewitt – he conceived and developed the low-level tactical strike, involving massed assaults on German airfields and communications. Many of these strikes, designated 'Voluntary Offensive Patrols,' were virtually impromptu, involving aerial combat, attacks on airfields, and the disruption of enemy supply columns far behind the lines, often with devastating effect. Strange flew on these strikes himself, tucked in behind the Australian Arthur Cobby, whom he appointed leader; but it was

Strange's 'high influence and unexampled leadership' which characterised these operations. They excited Ludlow-Hewitt, who planned them, and provided many tactical lessons.

Air superiority had become essential for success in all operations over the battlefield, coordination reaching a stage at which aircraft were cooperating directly with tanks. It was in this period, according to Vincent Orange, biographer of Arthur Coningham (better known as Maori or 'Mary'), that Coningham, then commanding an SE5A squadron under Strange, learnt the tactical lessons 'which he would apply with excellent effect in the Western Desert' in a later war.

The Germans defended desperately, and inevitably there were losses, but Strange survived and was awarded the DSO. To the end there was no let-up in the scale of the air fighting: as late as 30 October the enemy lost sixty-seven machines on the British front alone and the British forty-one, their casualties including three killed, eight wounded and twenty-six missing.

The crews of the Independent Force, beset by mechanical troubles, confronted by strengthened defences, and hampered by foul weather, rated their chances of survival even lower. One young observer, Lieutenant Roy Shillinglaw, on arrival at Nancy, was taken aback at the sums of money that changed hands amongst the card players in the Mess. Cheques for £50, £100, even for £250, a huge sum for the time, were, as he put it, 'flying around'. 'What does it matter?' he was asked. 'We shall all be dead in a week – we're being swatted like flies.'

Trenchard's attitude to casualties was the same as it had always been: if their efforts could shorten the war by a single day, and thus relieve the men fighting the ground battle, losses must be accepted. This was soon obvious to another former RFC man whose impatience for action had been blunted by a belated appreciation of social life and female company while stationed in England on rest. Depression and foreboding, normally quite foreign to him, were activated by a posting as senior flight commander to 104 Squadron

(DH9's), about whose crippling losses he had just been reading in the newspapers. This was the Australian Ewart Garland.

Garland had served with the squadron's CO, John Quinnell, twice before, on 10 Squadron in France, and again, after he had been ordered home in September 1917, on a reserve squadron at Andover. The months at Andover had been traumatic, the leadership (not Quinnell's) brutal. 'Crashes are so usual now I don't think of mentioning them,' he noted in his diary. 'Things are worse than ever as regards the Col. He asks the most impossible things and then strafes the heart out of you for not doing what is humanly impossible.' The 'Col.', promoted after running 40 Squadron efficiently – but by all accounts ruthlessly – before Laurence Tilney took over, was Bobbie Loraine, DSO, MC. 'He was a holy terror as a CO,' wrote Garland, 'but I found him good company off duty.'

Others at Andover more senior than Garland, led by John Quinnell, combined to get rid of Loraine. By what Garland called 'a dirty trick', they got him court-martialled for being drunk on duty. Garland was in hospital at the time after an appendectomy and was glad to be out of it. Loraine was acquitted but was demoted to major after pleading, in his indignation, to be sent back to France. There for the next two months he was attached to a night bomber squadron, until a gunshot wound in the left knee-joint ended his operational career. He had gone to France as an observer almost at the beginning, and had still been flying in France almost at the end. Garland acknowledged him, for all his faults, as 'a brave flying man'. The 'Actor-Airman', as the Press called him, returned to the theatre.

It was soon after this that Garland arrived at No. 104. 'This is the very squadron which the newspapers reported as losing seven machines out of nine on one raid . . . The casualties are enormous . . . The squadron consists almost all of new pilots and observers, as so many were wiped out recently.' The squadron had already been closed down twice for rehabilitation, casualties amounting to 250 per cent overall.

At first Garland's nerve almost failed him. 'Damn me for a frightened fool! But not a coward – it's one thing to be in a funk and yet do your job and another to shirk because you are frightened.' In

September he was ordered, in a hushed, sepulchral tone, to lead a raid on Mannheim: it was on Mannheim a few weeks earlier, on 22 August, that forty enemy fighters had attacked the DH9's and shot down seven. '*Mannheim! It's like being under sentence of death.*' But perhaps his luck would hold. 'I will trust in God and all that, but at the same time I'll take with me spare socks, a cheque book, and my vest-pocket Shakespeare.'

Next day his mood was almost euphoric. 'Hurrah! We have bombed Mannheim and only lost three machines.' Two of them were from his flight – but they were seen to go down under control. This was followed by many other raids, often led by Garland, generally with losses, reducing the squadron to impotence. But the news on the western front was of the breaking and then the capture of the Hindenburg Line. Right through October Garland pronounced the news good almost everywhere. 'Bulgaria surrenders, Cambrai fallen,' and so on.

Then at last: '*Germany has agreed to peace terms!*' Yet the war staggered on. Quinnell went on leave, others, wounded, languished in hospital, still more were dead or had been sent home. 'No sign of a rest for me.' Thus it happened that he was in sole charge when the news of the armistice was confirmed.

'*November 11th. So! It's over! I can scarce realise the stupendous event. Cease hostilities! Good Lord is it really true!*'

He wrote this diary entry at noon, having paraded the squadron. 'Everyone has taken it very quietly, just as a Britisher would!' There were about a hundred officers and men present. 'I think I must have felt the "history" of the occasion, standing out there addressing all these men, the majority much older than I, and quietly asking them to behave "properly" when celebrating. I was 21 years old.'

Nearer the fighting, and more distant from it, in Paris, in London and almost everywhere, the scenes were irresponsible and even hysterical. 'Heard the news at nine o'clock,' wrote First-class Air Mechanic Alexander Paice. 'Shall never forget the sight from all the aerodromes around, and ours too, of Very lights being fired. We marched round Menin with a Scotch regiment. They had a bagpipe band.'

Within a few weeks the RAF had shed huge numbers of personnel, and room in a greatly truncated peacetime service could be found for very few. Most of those selected were glad to stay, and many eventually reached high rank, but one who refused a permanent commission was Garland. He never piloted an aeroplane again. 'Strangely enough I lost interest completely the moment the war was over.' For some, like Gordon Taylor, flying had become a vocation; but civil aviation as yet had barely been born. Some became barnstormers, touring the country giving flying displays, others entered the precarious world of long-distance first-timing and record-breaking. Most of the 'intrepid flyers' of the twenties and thirties had begun their careers in the flying services. But the vast majority, like Garland, resumed or reactivated their peacetime careers.

Figures of aircraft deliveries confirm the massive expansion of the Royal Air Force in 1918. The total for 1916 was 6,633; this more than doubled in 1917 to 14,832; and in 1918 it more than doubled again, to 30,782. The figures were reflected in the swarms of machines which fought the aerial battles that year, also in the war-time aggregate of casualties, more than a third being sustained in the last seven and a half months of the war.

Was Trenchard's policy of the offensive, with all its tragic losses, justified by results? Was his basic aim of easing the burden of the men on the ground achieved?

Much depends on whether the work of the corps two-seaters really made a decisive contribution to the ground battles; and if they did, whether the information they gleaned, and the fire-power they enhanced, could have been accomplished without the elbow room provided by the scout squadrons. Could it all have been achieved by some other means? Was there an alternative?

The tasks allotted to the RFC were dictated by the ground situation and by military strategy. Apart from the work of the 41st Wing and the Independent Force, a tiny proportion of the whole, and then only in the last year of the war, the RFC, and then the RAF, functioned

[251]

as an integral part of the army. Only the armies involved, British and German especially, can make a true assessment.

Whether the squadrons could or should have been better equipped, better trained and better handled remains open to study; but the leaders of the armies on both sides agreed, time and time again, and certainly from 1916 on, that air support had become indispensable to all ground operations. More than that, in periods of crisis, air superiority had become decisive.

PUBLISHED SOURCES

A. G. D. ALDERSON, *The First War in the Air* (Published privately 1990)

HAROLD BALFOUR, *An Airman Marches* (Hutchinson 1973)

MAURICE BARING, *Flying Corps Headquarters – 1914–1918* (G. Bell and Sons 1920)

RICHARD TOWNSHEND BICKERS, *The First Great Air War* (Hodder 1988)

W. A. BISHOP, *Winged Warfare* (Blackwood, 1968)

EZRA BOWEN, *Knights of the Air* (Time-Life 1980)

CHAZ BOWYER, *The Air VCs* (Kimber, 1978, and Grub Street, 1993)

— *History of the RAF* (Hamlyn 1977)

— *The Flying Elephants* (Macdonald 1972)

ANDREW BOYLE, *Trenchard, Man of Vision* (Collins 1962)

ANTHONY BRUCE, *An Illustrated Companion to the First World War* (M. Joseph 1989)

J. A. CHAMIER, *The Birth of the Royal Air Force* (Pitman 1943)

LIONEL CHARLTON, *Charlton, an autobiography* (Faber 1931)

ALAN CLARK, *Aces High* (Fontana/Collins 1973)

CHRISTOPHER COLE, *McCudden VC* (Kimber 1967)

— *RFC Communiqués 1915–1916* (Kimber 1969)

— *RFC Communiqués, 1918* (Kimber 1988)

BRYAN COOPER, *The Story of the Bombers 1914–1945* (Octopus, 1974)

V. P. CRONYN, *Other Days* (Published privately, 1976)

LORD DOUGLAS OF KIRTLESIDE, *Years of Combat* (Collins 1963)

MARTIN GILBERT, *First World War Atlas* (Weidenfeld and Nicolson, 1970)

[253]

JOHN HAMMERTON (EDITOR), *War in the Air, Aerial Wonders of Our Time* (Amalgated Press, c. 1936)

W. J. F. HARVEY, *Pie in the Sky* (Colin Huston, 1971)

PETER HEARN, *The Sky People – A History of Parachuting* (Airlife 1990)

— *Flying Rebel, A Biography of Louis Strange* (HMSO 1994)

DAVID HENDERSON, *The Art of Reconnaissance* (Murray 1914)

PRUDENCE HILL, *To Know the Sky* (Kimber 1962)

ROBERT JACKSON, *Fighter Pilots of World War I* (Barker 1977)

J. E. JOHNSON, *Full Circle* (Chatto 1964)

IRA JONES, *King of the Air Fighters* (Ivor Nicholson and Watson, 1938)

ARTHUR GOULD LEE, *No Parachute* (Kimber 1968)

— *Open Cockpit* (Jarrolds 1969)

CECIL LEWIS, *Sagittarius Rising* (Peter Davies 1936 and Greenhill 1993)

GWILYM H. LEWIS, *Wings Over the Somme* (Kimber 1976 and – a new edition – Bridge Books 1994)

PETER LIDDLE, *The Airman's War* (Blandford Press, 1989)

WINIFRED LORAINE, *Robert Loraine* (Collins 1938)

JAMES MCCUDDEN, *Five Years in the RFC* (Aeroplane and General 1918)

ALEXANDER MCKEE, *The Friendless Sky* (Souvenir Press 1962)

WILLIAM MACLANACHAN, *McScotch* (Routledge, 1936)

NORMAN MACMILLAN, *Into the Blue* (Jarrolds 1929)

T. B. MARSON, *Scarlet and Khaki* (Jonathan Cape 1930)

L. MILLER, *The Chronicles of 55 Squadron RAF and RFC* (Unwin Bros 1919)

ALAN MORRIS, *Bloody April* (Jarrolds 1967)

JOHN H. MORROW JR, *The Great War in the Air* (Airlife 1993)

GEOFFREY NORRIS, *The Royal Flying Corps, A History* (Muller 1965)

VINCENT ORANGE, *Coningham* (Methuen 1990)

WALTER RALEIGH AND H. A. JONES, *The War in the Air, Vols I to VI, with Maps and Appendices* (Clarendon Press Oxford 1923–1937)

LINDA RHODES-MOORHOUSE, *Kaleidoscope* (Barker 1960)

MANFRED VON RICHTHOFEN, *The Red Air Fighter* (Aeroplane and General 1918)

R. L. RIMELL, *The Airship VC* (Aston Publications, 1989)

D. H. ROBINSON, *The Dangerous Sky: A History of Aviation Medicine* (Foulis 1973)

ROBERT SAUNDBY, *Air Bombardment: The Story of Its Development* (Chatto 1961)

HILARY ST G. SAUNDERS, *Per Ardua* (OUP 1944)

A. J. L. SCOTT, *Sixty Squadron* (Heinemann 1920)

MICHAEL SHAW, *Twice Vertical, the History of No. 1 Squadron* (Macdonald 1971 and Ian Allen 1986)

GORDON S. SHEPHARD, *Memoirs* (Published privately 1924)

CHRISTOPHER SHORES, NORMAN FRANKS, AND RUSSELL GUEST, *Above The Trenches* (Grub Street 1990)

JOHN SLESSOR, *The Central Blue* (Cassell 1968)

LOUIS STRANGE, *Recollections of an Airman* (John Hamilton 1933)

A. J. P. TAYLOR, *The First World War* (Hamish Hamilton 1963)

FRANK D. TREDREY, *Pioneer Pilot – The Great Smith-Barry* (Peter Davies 1976)

S. F. VINCENT, *Flying Fever* (Jarrolds 1972)

H. J. WILLIAMSON, *The Roll of Honour RFC and RAF for the Great War 1914–1918* (Naval and Military Press 1972)

DENIS WINTER, *The First of the Few* (Allen Lane 1982)

FRED WINTERBOTHAM, *The Ultra Spy* (Macmillan 1989)

Encyclopaedias: *Encyclopaedia of Air Warfare* (Spring Books 1975)

Magazines: Aeronautics, Aeroplane, Aerospace, Aviation News, Flight, Cross and Cockade (GB) Society Journal, Journal of the RAF Historical Society, Air Mail (Journal of the RAF Association).

INDEX

[257]